YIANNIS DESYPRIS

777 wonderful Greek ISLANDS

**a complete travellers guide
with 81 maps of the islands and
360 colour illustrations**

EDITIONS
TOUBI'S ®
ΕΚΔΟΣΕΙΣ

Texts: YIANNIS DESYPRIS
Translation: PHILIP RAMP
Photographs: A. CHARAMOGLIS, Y. DESYPRIS, S. FILAKOURIS, G. GEORGANTAS, G. GIANNELOS,
 T. GIGANTES, E. GRIGORIOU, N. IMELOS, N. KONTOS, J. KOUROUPIS, CH. KOURTARAS,
 E. PAPAPANAGOPOULOS, CH. PANOPOULOS, K. SKOUFALOU, A. SOLARIS, P. SPYROPOULOS,
 M. TOUMBIS, A. VLAVIANOS, P. VOUTSAS, J. CAPEROUN, R. MIELMANN, I. MINDLIN, C. PAVARY, A. SAILLET
All the underwater photographs are by G. CHANOUMIDIS

Artistic supervision: NORA DRAMITINOU - ANASTASOGLOU
All the processing and printing was done at:
GRAPHIC ARTS M. TOUMBIS S.A., Athens - Tel. (01) 9923874

ISBN 960 - 7504 - 08 - 9

The paintings in this guide are by the famous Greek painter and engraver K. GRAMMATOPOULOS (pages 3, 74-75 and 200-201) who has painted the Aegean with passionate love.

The cover photograph is from the Santorini calender. The island in the background is the last to appear in the Mediterranean in 1573 ("Mikri Kameni"). During the period 1707-1926 various areas of land appeared which gradually joined together, making up "Nea Kameni" seen today.

Sun-drenched isles of Greece
savouring the cool of the sea.
Bare islands with snow- white villages clinging
to the lips of cliffs gazing at the blue sea.
Islands dense with groves of olive, pine or ilex.
Your dazzling white beaches and fishing harbours.
Your castles, monasteries and wealth of churches.

The breeze bears the message. Yes. We're coming to you.
We who know you, so closely bound have we become
we are in need of you.
And those of us who do not know you but whose one dream
is meeting you, a dream of yearning coming true.

Contents

Forward 5
Map
of Greece,
islands divided
into
seven units 6

1 ARGOSARONIC GULF

Aegina 12
Moni 14
Angistri 14
Salamina 15
Poros 16
Hydra 18
Dokos 19
Spetses 21
Spetsopoula 22
The islands
and islets of the
Argosaronic Gulf 23

2 CYCLADES

Map of Cyclades 26
Kea 28
Makronisos 29
Kythnos 30
Piperi 31
Serifos 32
Serfopoula 33
Voos 33
Sifnos 34
Kitriani 35
Milos 36
Kimolos 39
Glaronisia 39
Antimilos 39
Arkoudia 39
Polyaigos 39
Andros 40
Tinos 44
Mykonos 48
Dragonisi 50
Delos 53
Rheneia 53
Megalos
Revmataris 53
Syros 56
Yaros 56
Didimi 56
Strongylo 56
Paros 60
Pantieronisi 63
Tigani 63
Glaropounta 63
Revmatonisi 63
Gaidouronisi 64
Vriokastro 64
Antiparos 65
Saliangos 65
Diplo 65
Kavouras 65
Despotiko 65
Strongyli 65

Naxos 66
Ios 72
Lesser
Cyclades 76
Irakleia 76
Schinousa 76
Koufonisia 76
Keros 76
Donousa 76
Amorgos 78
Nikouria 79
Gramvousa 79
Anydro 79
Sikinos 80
Kardiotissa 80
Kaloyeri 80
Folegandros 81
Santorini 82
Nea Kameni 84
Palaia Kameni 84
Aspronisi 84
Thirasia 89
Anafi 90
The islands
and islets
of the Cyclades 91

3 DODECANESE

Rhodes 94
Prasonisi 103
Symi 106
Ayia Marina 107
Seskli 107
Nimos 107
Halki 108
Alimia 108
Tilos 109
Kos 110
Kastri 115
Nisyros 116
Yali 116
Astypalaia 118
Hondronisi 119
Ligno 119
Ayia Kyriaki 119
Koutsomyti 119
Kounoupi 119
Kalymnos 122
Telendos 125
Pserimos 125
Leros 126
Leipsi 129
Arki 129
Marathi 129
Agathonisi 129
Patmos 130
Tragonisi 132
Karpathos 134
Saria 136
Kasos 138
Kastelorizo 139
Rho 140
Strongyli 140
The islands
and islets
of the Dodecanese 141

4 EUBOEA-SPORADES

Euboea 144
Styra 150
Petalioi 151
Sporades 152
Skiathos 154
Tsougrias 156
Skopelos 158
Desa 159
Alonissos 161
Gioura 162
Dyo Adelfia 162
Kyra Panayia 162
Peristera 162
Piperi 162
Pappous 162
Prasso 162
Skantzoura 162
Psathoura 162
Psathouropoula 162
Skyros 163
Valaxa 164
Skyropoula 164
Sarakiniko 164
Islets around Euboea
and Sporades 165

5 NORTH & EAST AEGEAN

Thasos 168
Koinyra 171
Samothraki 172
Limnos 174
Ayios Efstratios 176
Lesbos 177
Nisiopi 181
Chios 186
Oinousses 191
Pasas 191
Psara 191
Antipsara 191
Daskaleio 191
Kato Nisi 191
Ayios Nikolaos 191
Samos 192
Samiopoula 196
Icaria 202
Diapori 203
Fourni 204
Thymena 204
Ayios Minas 204
The islands and islets of the
North & East Aegean 205

6 THE IONIAN ISLETS

Corfu 208
Vlacherna 211
Pontikonisi 211
Diapontia Islands 215
Ereikousa 215
Mathraki 215

Othoni 215
Paxi 218
Panayia 218
Ayios Nikolaos 218
Mongonisi 219
Kaltsionisi 219
Antipaxi 219
Lefkada 220
Madouri 222
Sparti 222
Chelonaki 222
Skorpios 222
Meganisi 223
Kalamos 223
Kastos 223
Arkoudi 223
Atokos 223
Drakonera 223
Provati 223
Petalas 223
Makri 223
Oxeia 223
Sesoula 223
Ithaca 224
Lazaretto 225
Cephalonia 226
Zakynthos 234
Pelouzo 236
Marathonisi 237
Megali Myzithra 237
Mikri Myzithra 237
Ayios Nikolaos 238
Strofades 239
Kythera 240
Antikythera 242
Elafonissos 242
Proti 242
Sfaktiria 242
Sapientza 242
Schiza 242
Ayia Margiani 242
Venetiko 242
The Ionian islands
and islets 242

7 CRETE

Chania 248
Elafonisi 251
Ayioi Theodoroi 252
Souda 252
Rethymno 253
Herakleion 256
Dia 256
Paximadia 261
Lasithi 262
Spinalonga 266
Pseira 268
Ayios Nikolaos 268
Islets around
Crete 271
Agria Gramvousa 271
Pontikonisi 271
Gavdos 271
Gavdopoula 271
Gramvousa 271
Chrysi 271

The Mediterranean is renowned for its ancient history, its civilisation, its light and its beauty. The Greek archipelago is its crowning jewel. These islands crowd the northeast part of the Mediterranean, sparkling in the sun. There are over 3000 of them and if rocky outcroppings are included the number reaches 9500, 140 of which are inhabited.

Most of them are in the Aegean, the sea that lies between Greece and Asia Minor. Delos is at the center of this sea, the home of Apollo, the god of light according to mythology. What islands could have more light than those in the Aegean?

But these islands are not only unique for their sun and light. There is also their natural beauty, their lacy coastline with its dazzling white beaches and the blue sea ruffled in summer by the cooling meltemi wind. There are the villages, gazing at the sea from on high, the castles, churches and monasteries. History and civilization stretch back four to five thousand years here. One must not forget the simple, good-hearted residents who welcome you in their melodious voices.

All the islands are beautiful but each one has its own charm and history. In the space at our disposal we will supply as much information as we can, at the very least giving the distinctive "mark" of 777 of these islands, be they large or small.

You of course will find other beauties we have not described.

We have divided the islands into seven geographical units which are not simply geographical in most cases as the islands in each group share many common characteristics. Starting with the islands of the **Argosaronic** Gulf, which are close to Athens, we proceed to the **Cyclades**, the so-called "white islands", from their dazzling white villages perched on bare rock, creating a strong contrast to the blue sea. Cosmopolitan Mykonos and stunning Santorini are a part of these islands.

East of the Cyclades are the **Dodecanese** with fabulous Rhodes, an international tourist center and Kos with its "International Hippocratic Foundation".

The second largest island in Greece, **Euboea**, is another entity, along with the **Sporades**, verdant islands with their own special flavor. Opposite are the islands of the **North** and **East Aegean**. Among them are the large islands of Lesbos, Chios and Samos.

These are the Aegean islands. There are also the **Ionian Islands**, a separate entity lying along the coast of western Greece. These include lovely Corfu and Ithaca, the home of Odysseus. All are green and have a different look and culture than the Aegean islands.

Crete, the largest island in Greece, has to be treated on its own. Volumes have been written about its Minoan civilisation founded 4,000 years ago, not to mention its natural beauty, its renowned ravines and gorgeous sand beaches.

Cyprus is not included. Though Greek in character it is a separate state.

The book refers to a total of 777 Greek island, 212 of which are described, while the remainder have their position defined (in tables at the end of each chapter).

The ship and airline schedules to and from the islands are subject to change.

THE IONIAN ISLETS

1 ARGOSARONIC GULF

2 CYCLADES

3 DODECANESE

4 EUBOEA - SPORADES

5 NORTH & EAST AEGEAN

6 THE IONIAN ISLETS

7 CRETE

KAVALA

THESSALONIKI

ALEXANDROUPOLI

THASSOS

SAMOTHRAKI

LIMNOS

VOLOS

SPORADES

AGIOS
EFSTRATIOS

5

ALONISSOS

SKIATHOS

SKOPELOS

4

SKYROS

LESVOS

NORTH & EAST AEGEAN

EUBOEA

PSARA

CHIOS

ATHINA

ANDROS

CORINTH

SALAMINA

TINOS

SAMOS

EGINA

KEA

MYKONOS

IKARIA

POROS

SYROS

FOURNI

1

KYTHNOS

YDRA

ARGOSARONIC

SPETSES

SERIFOS

2

PAROS

NAXOS

PATMOS

LIPSI

SIFNOS

LEROS

KIMOLOS

ANTIPAROS

KALYMNOS

MILOS

SIKINOS

KOS

IOS

AMORGOS

FOLEGANDROS

NISIROS

THE IONIAN
ISLETS

CYCLADES

THIRA

ANAFI

ASTYPALEA

SYMI

6

KYTHIRA

TILOS

RODOS

3

CHALKI

ANTIKYTHIRA

CHANIA

7

KASTELLORIZO

RETHYMNO

KARPATHOS

HERAKLIO

AGIOS
NIKOLAOS

KASSOS

DODECANESE

CRETE

Submerged in endless blue you cannot help but admire this incredible world, the delicate, fragile life of the Greek seas. A world for from noise in a ceaseless struggle far a life full of colour, motion, creation, ready to share all its secrets with anyone, asking only love. Nothing more, nothing less.

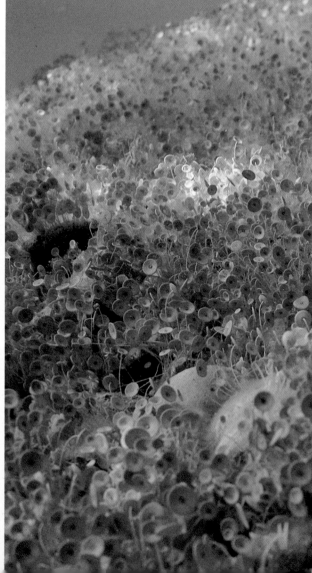

The islands of the Argosaronic Gulf are like priceless gems decorating this gulf with lavish beauty. Fortunate are the inhabitants of Athens and Piraeus who can escape the tumult of the city in so little time. The nearest of them, the historic **Salamina**, is also the most densely populated. From Perama in Attica you can get to Paloukia opposite in a quarter of an hour and from there go wherever you want on the island by car. Further south is lovely Aegina with its pine trees, sand beaches and the famous Temple of Aphaia all only an hour by boat from Piraeus. It is also densely populated, but less so than Salamina. Even further south is alluring **Poros**, opposite the Peloponnese, and beyond that the celebrated Hydra with its traditional architecture. At the entrance to the Gulf of Argolis is **Spetses**, picturesque and verdant. Possessing a great naval tradition, it like Hydra played an important role with its fleet and its worthy sailors when the Greek nation rose up in arms against the Turks.

Spetses, the most distant of the islands, is only four hours from Piraeus. But if you make the journey on the speedy hydrofoils ("Flying Dolphins"), which have schedules to all the islands (except Salamina), then it will take only half as long. Not to mention that in summer the trip may be extended beyond Spetses to Monemvasia Kythera and Nafplio, the capital of the Argolid. Besides these four main islands there are also smaller islands which

PIREAS

SALAMINA

SARONIKOS

AGISTRI

AEGINA

POROS

Galatas

ARGOLIKOS

YDRA

SPETSES   SPETSOPOULA

number more than 100, when you count the rocky islets. We describe (or simply fix the location of) a total of 88, only 11 of which are inhabited. A visit to the uninhabited ones, on your own boat, can hold surprises in store.

So the islands of the Saronic and the Argolis Gulf, which for the sake of brevity is called the Argosaronic Gulf, make for memorable excursions, be they for just a day or several days.

The temple of Aphaia on Aegina

Aegina

When we think about Aegina, what springs to mind is a pine-covered island with a hill on which the fine ancient temple of Aphaia stands dominant. If one draws imaginary straight lines linking this temple with the Parthenon and the temple of Poseidon on Cape Sunion, the result is an almost equilateral triangle whose vertices gaze at each other and constitute the most beautiful items that Attica has had to show since ancient times.

Below the temple of Aphaia are attractive bays and sandy beaches, and although much of Aegina is built on, this is certainly less the case than it is with Salamina.

Aegina - the second largest of the islands of the Argosaronic Gulf - the largest is Salamina - lies in the centre of the Gulf and has an area of of 85 square kilometres and a shoreline of 57 km. The chief occupation of its permanent residents, who number more than 11,000, is the growing of pistachio nuts. The 'Aegina pistachio' is famous and is the island's most important product. However, apart from the permanent residents, there are others, the Athenians who have a second home or a luxury villa on Aegina and come here for weekends almost all the year round. Aegina lies only 16 nautical miles from Piraeus and the crossing by the ships or ferries which provide a daily service takes only an hour. There are also the 'flying dolphin' hydrofoils, which cut this time down to half an hour. In addition, for those who are not content with Aegina alone and want to explore other shores, the same services make it possible to visit, from there, the other islands of the Argosaronic Gulf (Poros, Hydra and Spetses) or to go to Methana, Ermioni or Porto Heli - or at a greater distance, to Tolo and Nafplio. It has to be noted that some of these services are less frequent - or completely non-existent - in the winter.

The above applies to the main port of Aegina, because there are also boat services from Piraeus direct to Souvala on Aegina and, in summer, direct to Ayia Marina with its fine sandy beach.

From the port of Aegina, the local buses provide a regular and easy means for the visitor's sightseeing on the island.

HISTORY

Mythology tells us that the first king of the island was the hero Aeacus, son of Zeus and the nymph Aegina, who renamed the island, which had been called Oenone, in honour of his mother.

Aegina was inhabited in the Neolithic period, as can be seen from the finds at Kolona, near the town of Aegina, which date from around 3000 BC. Later, the Minoans came to the island, to be followed by the Achaeans and Dorians.

From the middle of the second millenium BC, Aegina began to develop its trade and at the same time emerged as a strong naval power. Its vessels took its products, chiefly ceramics, to the Cyclades, Crete and mainland Greece. It reached the zenith of its development in the 6th century BC, when, as an independent power, it was the first city in Greece to mint coins.

In spite of the fact that Aegina was a rival of Athens and Piraeus, it helped the Athenians at the Battle of Salamis, but the Athenians, who had never trusted it, finally seized it in the mid 5th century.

The subsequent history of the island follows roughly the same course as that of the rest of Greece. It made an important contribution to the struggle against the Turks in 1821, and Aegina was the seat of the first Greek government, under Kapodistria, before being succeeded in this role by Nafplio.

Getting to know the island

The picturesque **port of Aegina** immediately gives the visitor the feeling of being on an island. The breakwater with its chapel, the old houses, many of which are surprisingly well-preserved, the little boats, the caïques, the busy waterside - all make up a cheerful picture calculated to put the visitor in a mood to enjoy the island.

The town of Aegina has much for the visitor to see: the **Archaeological Museum**, Kolona, the remains of the ancient temple of Apollo near the harbour, the cathedral, in which the first Greek government after the War of Independence was sworn in, and the first Greek Governor's residence. One and a half kilometres outside the town is the Church of Sts Theodore, or the 'Beautiful Church', dating from the 13th century and with fine wall-paintings.

There are a number of sights to visit outside the town. First and foremost among these is the **temple of Aphaia** (11 km. east of Aegina town), dedicated to an ancient goddess who was the protectress of the island. The temple is in the Doric style and was built after the Battle of Salamis (480 BC) on an idyllic site with a view out over the sea, with the shores of Attica in the distance. You can end up at the fine sandy beach of **Ayia Marina**, 3.5 km. away, which has full tourist facilities.

The enticing harbour of Aegina.

There are also bathing beaches on the island's northern coast, as, for instance, at **Souvala** and **Vaïa** (13 km.), as well as on the west coast, as at **Faros** and **Marathonas** (4 km.). The road which passes through Faros and Marathonas ends at the picturesque fishing village of **Perdika** (9 km.), which looks out on the pine-covered islet of **Moni**, with sandy beaches and a camping site.

In the interior of the island, about half way along the road to the temple of Aphaia, on the left, is **Palaiochora**, a ruined medieval village, built as a refuge from pirates for the people of the island, and the **Nunnery of St Nektarios**, in which the Saint to which it is dedicated lived for the last years of his life and which houses his relics. The feast day of the Nunnery is 9 November and attracts large crowds of pilgrims. Another religious house, that of **Our Lady Chrysoskalitissa** stands near the village of Tzikides (6 km.). If you continue along the road to the south-east from this village, you come to Pacheia Rachi, a village on the foothills of the conical Oros (531 m.), Aegina's highest mountain, which has near its summit the remains of a sanctuary to Zeus Hellanius.

The church of Ayios Nektarios.

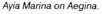
Ayia Marina on Aegina.

Angistri

Three nautical miles to the west of Aegina lies the charming and verdant islet of Angistri with its 400 permanent residents and sparklingly clean sea. It can be reached by regular daily services from Piraeus, and from Aegina itself. The island is well-supplied with hotels and is a popular resort in summer.

The are dense groves of pine and picturesque coves. Its small harbour is on the West side. Most of its settlements are also there while the east side is still far from tourist activity. There one can enjoy his swim in peace.

Salamina

This is the island closest to Athens, an island whose name in its ancient form of 'Salamis' is so bound up with Greek history. Salamina is an attractive island with an area of 95 sq. km. and a shoreline of 104 km., tucked into the top of the Saronic Gulf. At one time it was covered with pine trees; now a large part of its area is built up and it has a population of more than 28,000.

It spite of this, it still has remote sandy beaches with picturesque fish tavernas, particularly on its western side.

Salamina is reached by small vessels which sail from Piraeus to Paloukia, Kamatero, Selinia and Peristeria (in the case of the last two, only in summer) and by a ferry from Perama to Paloukia and from Perama (Megara) to Faneromeni.

HISTORY

Salamis was the island of Ajax, Homer's hero who led his people in the war against Troy. It is, however, best known for the famous sea battle which took place in its straits between the Athenian fleet and the Persians in 480 BC. Xerxes, king of the Persians, set up his throne on Mt Aegaleo, on the mainland looking down on the island, in order to watch the battle, sure that the Athenians would give way before his vastly superior forces. But the Athenians were the victors and it was this battle which finally freed Athens from the dreadful threat which had hung over it, allowing it to move into the most glorious years of the life of the city - the Golden Age - which was to play

so important a role in the shaping of the history of Europe.

Earlier (7th century BC), Megara and Athens had vied with each other for the island. In the end, Athens prevailed.

Getting to know the island

The main port for the ferries is **Paloukia**, which lies on Salamina's east coast. At this point the island is at its narrowest, so that only three kilometres away, to the west, we come to the sea again, this time at the Bay of Salamina, on which lies **Salamina** (Koulouri), the island's capital. The town has a small archaeological museum, in which finds - chiefly pottery - from the Mycenaean period can be seen.

West of Salamina, at a distance of 7 km., stands the **Nunnery of Faneromeni**, whose katholikon (principal church) dates from the 11th century. Further west (1.5

km.) is the point where ferries leave for Perama (Megara).

Six kilometres to the south of Salamina is **Aianteio** (Moulki). This is believed to have been the site of the city of Ajax in ancient times. Today it is an extensive seaside settlement with small villas, most of which are weekend homes belonging to Athenians. From Moukli, two earth roads lead, respectively, to **Kanakia** and **Peristeria**, which have good, relatively uncrowded, sandy beaches. A third road leads to the bay of **Kaki Vigla**, with a village of the same name.

South of Paloukia (4 km.) is another busy port, that of **Kamatero**, with the village of **Ambelakia** close to it. The latter is the site of ancient Salamis. There are still traces of the ruins of its acropolis. Three kilometres further to the south we reach **Selinia**, a fishing port, which in summer is quite busy and has small vessels providing a direct service to Piraeus.

Poros

Poros means 'crossing', and it is from this that the whole island takes its name. It lies in the south-west of the Saronic Gulf, opposite the Argolid in the Peloponnese. On the edge of this crossing, built in amphitheatre form on the slopes of a hill, is the cheerful island town which is the port of Poros and the island's most important settlement. Opposite, ten minutes away by boat, are the green shores of the Peloponnese with the famous lemon forest, from which in May the scent of the lemon blossom wafts across to Poros. This dense forest of lemon trees is probably unrivalled in Greece.

Poros is a green island with an area of 33 sq. km. and a shoreline of 42 km. Its permanent population numbers 3,500. There is a daily service, provided by both ferries, which do the trip in two and a half hours, and by hydrofoil (1 hour), from Piraeus, which is 31 nautical miles away. Aegina, Methana, Hydra, Spetses and Ermioni can be reached by the same means, while the 'flying dolphins' (hydrofoils) also go to Porto Heli, Leonidi, Kyparissi, Monemvasia and Kythira, and in summer to Tolo and Nafplio. Galatas, which is opposite on the shore of the Peloponnese, is reached by ferries and small craft.

HISTORY

Poros, called Calaureia in ancient times, was the island of Poseidon, god of the sea. This is evident from various literary references and from the traces of the temple of Poseidon, which are to be found in the middle of the island. This fact may account for why Poros was chosen to be the headquarters of an amphictyony (alliance) set up in the 7th century BC whose members were seven cities, some close by but others from the broader region, including Athens and Aegina. Subsequently, the fortunes of Poros followed those of the other islands of the Saronic Gulf. In the War of Independence against the Turks in 1821, Poros fought alongside the other islands, and in 1830 became Greece's first naval base.

Getting to know the island

We have already described the port of Poros - the island's capital - in the introduction. It should be added here that it is worth visiting the **Archaeological Museum** and taking a walk as far as the clock-tower, the town's highest point and the island's 'trademark'. The port is our starting-point for visits to the rest of the island's sights.

A road which heads north-west brings us to what is perhaps the island's finest beach, **Neorio** (3 km.). It has dense pine trees and is a popular resort in summer. The road which goes east from the port brings us to **Askeli** (3 km.), a village also with pine trees on the crystal-clear water's edge. High on its hill, with a magnificent view towards the lemon forest is the **Nunnery of Zoödochos Pighi**. These beaches can also be reached by caïque from the port of Poros.

The traces of the temple of Poseidon lie in the centre of the island, on a hill with a panoramic view over the Poros straits and the green shores of the Peloponnese opposite.

It would be a grave omission to visit Poros without going to the famous **lemon forest** which stands opposite on the coast of the Peloponnese. The boat takes no more than ten minutes, and after landing, an uphill climb amid the dense grove of lemon trees provides a unique experience. Water flows to left and right and branches of the lemon trees above shade us from the sun. Vistors who are lucky enough to be there in May will undoubtedly find the scent of the small white lemon blossoms positively intoxicating.

Poros built amphitheatrically on a hill.

Aerial view of Poros.

Hydra

Whatever description the visitor may have had of Hydra will certainly prove to have been inadequate when one sees this unique island town for the first time. It

stands around and above its circular harbour with its yachts, with its large two and three-storeyed houses piled one on top of the other on the rocks, starting from the quay and reaching up to the tops of the hills. These tiled houses, faithful to the traditional architectural style, make a lasting impression from the very first moment.

Shaped like cubes, these houses are severely simple, with a roof terrace or possibly a court-yard. The courtyards always have flowers growing in them, though these are difficult for the visitor to see, since the outer wall is high. The walls are usually grey in colour. Severity of line predominates everywhere, but a white window frame is sufficient to break the monotony and to give the houses a cheerful appearance.

This picturequeness has helped to make Hydra a 'cosmopolitan' island in the summer and a haven of peace in winter. First and foremost among its admirers are the artists, and for this reason the School of Fine Arts of the Athens Technical University has a branch here. Moreover, the island is comparatively near the capital, the distance from Piraeus being 37 nautical miles, which are covered by ship in 3 hours and by hydrofoil in approximately half that time. These services are daily all the year round. Aegina, Methana, Poros, Spetses and Ermioni can be reached by the same means, while the 'flying dolphins' also go to Porto Heli, Leonidi, Kyparissi and Monemvasia, and in summer to Tolo and Nafplio.

Lying beteen the Saronic and the Argolis Gulf, Hydra has an area of 50 sq. km. and a shoreline of 55 km. It is a mountainous island, the highest peak being Erotas (593 m.). Its population is fewer than 3,000 inhabitants. Unlike the other islands of the Argosaronic Gulf, most of it is bare and pines are to be found only in its south-western part.

HISTORY

The oldest settlement to have been found on the island is Mycenaean. At a later period Hydra was seized by Hermione, which subsequently sold it to Samos. We know of no major historical events here down to the 17th century AD, when the island began gradually to acquire a powerful merchant fleet, which was later, at the time of the Napoleonic Wars, to monopolise sea transport throughout the Mediterranean. When the uprising against the Turks broke out in 1821, Hydra had a population of 30,000 (most of whom had sought refuge on the island) and 150 vessels. The island's wealthy sea-captains - the Kountouriotis brothers, Miaoulis, Sachtouris and Tombazis among them - fitted out their vessels as warships and spent whole fortunes in order to help in the Struggle. The Hydra fleet joined those of Spetses and Psara to inflict serious damage on that of the Turks. Their feats and the heroism of their crews became a byword throughout Europe. Besides their vessels, the island seamen made use of fire-ships - small boats loaded with explosives which they brought by night alongside the Turkish vessels and then blew them up. The superiority of the Hydriots and their companions in arms at sea was the determining factor in the success of the Greek Revolution.

Aerial photograph of the harbour.

Corner of Hydra.

Getting to know the island

The old mansions of the captains of 1821 (built by Genoese or Venetian architects) dominate the **port of Hydra** These include those of Kountouriotis, Tombazis (which houses the branch of the School of Fine Arts), Voulgaris, Miaoulis, Kriezis and Tsamados (now occupied by the Merchant Marine School). Some of these are open to visitors and thus provide an opportunity to admire their interior decoration, with the marble floors, wooden ceilings and old furniture.

The old cannons used for the town's defence are still in place at the entrance to the harbour. In the middle of the breakwater, close to the sea, is the Monastery of the Dormition of the Virgin, now Hydra's cathedral. In its courtyard stands a statue of the freedom-fighter Miaoulis. A climb through the narrow alleys of the town to the top of its hills should not be missed. From the top the visitor can admire the view of the harbour or the view of a memorable sunset. A fine view can also be obtained by climbing to the **Monastery of the Prophet Elijah**, in the centre of the island, at a height of 500 m. From the Monastery, hikers can make the ascent of the island's highest peak, Erotas (593 m.).

Those who are more drawn to the sea can swim in the deep waters of **Spilia**, near the port, at the organised beach of **Mandraki**, at **Kaminia** with its large pebbles, and at **Vlychos**. The last three are fairly close to the port and can be reached either by boat or on foot. Further off are the beaches of **Molos** and **Bisti**. South of Molos, in that part of the island which has some greenery, is **Episkopi**, where finds from the Byzantine period have been made.

Vehicles are prohibited on Hydra and so the island's beaches can be reached only by caïque.

West of Hydra is the bare and rocky islet of **Dokos**.

Hydra.

Spetses

Mention of Spetses always brings to mind the image of its high harbour wall, the cafés in front and the old picturesque houses behind. This is Dapia, as it is called, from which the visitor goes down to the pier where the boats tie up. The road down makes a turn and continues to the east. You have the sea and a brisk northerly breeze on your left and the lofty old mansions with their little windows and their salt-encrusted walls on your right. This road brings you out finally at the picturesque ancient harbour, which even today is full of various craft and is the place to find quaint fish tavernas.

Spetses is an island with a great seafaring tradition, like Hydra. Its symbol is the figure of Bouboulina, the legendary woman sea-captain, the heroine who made a major contribution to the uprising against the Turks in 1821. With Spetses as her base, she set out with her vessels to besiege Nafplio and Monemvasia and later, mounted on a white horse, was one of the first to enter Tripolitsa when it was freed from the Turkish yoke.

Spetses is an island green with pine trees and lies at the entrance to the Argolic Gulf, 1.7 miles from Kosta in the Peloponnese. It has an area of 22 sq. km. and a population of approximately 4,000. It has a sound tourist infrastructure and thus in summer has many visitors, mostly Athenians, who come in search of its peaceful beaches by day and its vivid night life.

Spetses can be reached every day from Piraeus, a distance of 52 nautical miles, both by ferry and by 'flying dolphin'. It is possible to drive as far as Kosta in the Peloponnese, opposite the island, but cars must be left there as they are not permitted on the island.

From Spetses you can visit by ship or "flying dolphin" Hydra, Poros, Aegina and all the other stops made along the coast of the Peloponnese.

HISTORY

Spetses, whose name in antiquity was Pityousa, was inhabited around 2,500 BC, as demonstrated by finds made in the Ayia Marina area. Between then and the 17th century, when Spetses, like Hydra, began to develop into a major seafaring power, its recorded history contains little of interest. In the uprising of 1821 its ships fought against the Turks and its contribution to final victory was amongst the most important.

Harbour of Spetses with Dapia.

Spetses, the capital of the island, is on the north-eastern coast, opposite Kosta in the Peloponnese. The square of Dapia, above the harbour, has great charm. Cannons used in the War of Independence of 1821 still stand next to the café tables. Behind the square is Bouboulina's house. It is worth visiting the museum and some of the old mansions which have now been refurbished and are reminiscent of the past glory and wealth of the island. The cathedral (St Nicholas) and the churches of All Saints and Our Lady are also worth a visit. Among the attractive beaches which can be reached by caïque are **Vrellos** and **Zonkeria**, on the north coast of the island, where the pines grow on the very water's edge, and the idyllic bays of **Ayia Paraskevi** and **Ayioi Anargyri**, both with fine sandy beaches, on the south-western

coast. Close to the town are the beaches of Kounoupitsa and Ayia Marina.

South of Spetses is the green islet of **Spetsopoula**, which is, however, privately-owned.

The harbour of Spetses with the Peloponnese opposite.

THE ISLANDS AND ISLETS OF THE ARGOSARONIC GULF

AEGINA

Moni.................................. *W Perdika.*
Angistri............................. *W Aegina.*
Metopi............................*NW Angistri.*
Nisida...................*250 m. NE Aegina.*

SALAMINA

Megali Kyra................. *NE Salamis.*
Mikri Kyra. .... *NE Salamis.*
Leros............................. *NE Salamis.*
Arpedon. .... *NE Salamis.*
Atalanti. ....*E Seleni.*
Pera.......................... *S Kaki Vigla.*
Peristeria. .... *S Peristeria.*
Kanaki.............................*W Kanakia.*

POROS

Plateia................................*N Poros.*
Bitsi....................................*N Poros.*
Daskaleio........................ *W Poros.*
Bourtzi.............................. *S Poros.*
Modi....................................*E Poros.*

HYDRA

Dokos............................... *NE Hydra.*
Petasi............................. *W Hydra.*
Trikeri...............................*SW Hydra.*
Drapi.................................*SW Hydra.*
Asteri...............................*SW Hydra.*
Strongylo........................*SW Hydra.*
Karteli..............................*SW Hydra.*
Disakia............................*SW Hydra.*
Ventza. ....*SW Hydra.*

Alexandros....................... *SW Hydra.*
Tsingri. .... *SW Hydra.*
Stavronisi. ....*S Hydra.*
Vlychos. .... *W harbour.*
Palamida...........................*NW Hydra.*
Kivotos.............................*NW Hydra.*
Erimonisi. ....*NW Hydra.*
Pontikonisi...................... *W Hydra.*

SPETSES

Spetsopoula..................*SE Spetses.*
Mikro......................... *E Spetsopoula.*
Ayios Ioannis. .... *E Spetsopoula.*
Petrokaravo................ *NW Spetses.*

OTHER ISLETS

Ayios Georgios............*N Kamatero.*
Psyttaleia.........................*W Pireaus.*
Katramoniso.....................*W Voula.*
Fleves. ....*S Vouliagmeni.*
Arsida. ....*SW Anavyso.*
Patroklou.........................*W Sounion.*
Plateia................. *S Ayioi Theodoroi.*
Ovrios................. *S Ayioi Theodoroi.*
Pachi. .... *S Pachi Megara.*
Pachaki. .... *S Pachi Megara.*
Revithousa...........*SE Pachi Megara.*
Makronisos Meg.. *E Pachi Megara.*
Diaporioi Nisoi............. *NW Aegina.*
  Ayios Thomas......... *NW Aegina.*
  Ayios Ioannis.......... *NW Aegina.*
  Tragonisi. .... *NW Aegina.*

Ledon. .... *NW Aegina.*
Psarou. .... *NW Aegina.*
Molathi..................... *NW Aegina.*
Ypsili................................ *NW Aegina.*
Stachtorrogi..................... *NW Aegina.*
Plateia. .... *NW Aegina.*
Laouses Nisoi................ *N Aegina.*
  Kordeliaris................ *N Aegina.*
  Makronisos. .... *N Aegina.*
  Panayitsa. .... *N Aegina.*
  Eleousa........................*N Aegina.*
Ayios Petros....... *E Korfos Corinthia.*
Kyra................................ *W Angistri.*
Spalathronisi.................. *W Angistri.*
Dorousa.......................... *W Angistri.*
Petrokaravo......................*S Aegina.*
Tselevinia Nisia.................*S Poros.*
  Skyli..................................*S Poros.*
  Spathi...............................*S Poros.*
  Soupia...............................*S Poros.*
Ktapodi. ....*SE Ermioni.*
Kounoupi.......................*NE Spetses.*
Chinitsa........................*N Porto Heli.*
Korakia.......................*NW Porto Heli.*
Koronida.................... *N Gulf Argolis.*
Efyra...........................*S Iria Argolis.*
Plateia. ....*SE Tolos Argolis.*
Romvi. ....*S Tolos Argolis.*
Daskaleio. ....*S Tolos Argolis.*
Koronida.................*S Tolos Argolis.*
Bourtzi.......................... *W Navplion.*
Ay. Georgios...*11 n.m. SW Sounion.*

This is the most picturesque island complex in Greece, lying right in the middle of the Aegean Sea. The Cycladic archipelago, which seems to be an extension of Euboea and Attica to the southeast, consists of around 2,200 islands, islets and various rocky outcroppings. We describe (or simply fix the location of) 148 of them which are, in our opinion, the most important. Only 33 of those are inhabited.

All of these together form an imaginary circle around sacred Delos, the island which, according to mythology, appeared from amid the waves to become the land of Apollo. And truly where could a place with more sunlight than the Cyclades have been found for the god of light?

These islands were inhabited very early, by the Neolithic period. Their high point began in the 3rd millenium B.C., when the famous Cycladic civilization developed, a civilization older than the Minoan but which later grew in tandem with it and produced exquisite works of art such as the marvelous Cycladic figurines (small statues of people). The Minoan Cretans became the rulers of the Cyclades in the 2nd millenium B.C. and founded colonies in Milos and Santorini. They were followed by the Myceneans in 1450 B.C. and then the Dorians in 1100 B.C. The Ionians came in the 10th century and in the 7th century B.C. created the religious center at Delos. The Persian tempest shook the Cyclades in 490 B.C. and they were later conquered by the Macedonians, the Rhodians and the Romans. The Byzantine period was a very long one. It began in 395 A.D. and lasted for approximately 800 years. During that period the Byzantine churches were built on the island. The rule of Byzantium was so lax that under its sovereignty the island was occupied by Goths, Slavs and Normans and for many years was used as a pirate base.

A highly important period began in 1204 with Venetian rule which lasted for over 300 years and left its stamp on the islands. The castles and towers one sees today are Venetian works. The Turks captured the islands in 1537 under Barbarossa. Later, most of them took part in the Greek struggle for independence and were united with Greece in 1832.

Paraportiani church on Mykonos
The culmination of traditional Cycladic architecture

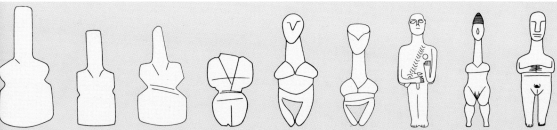

Today the Cyclades are called the "white islands" because the villages built with the renowned Cycladic traditional architecture look pure white on the usually barren earth, creating a superb contrast to the deep blue colour of the sea.

With their dry climate cool summers abundant sunshine and fabulous sand beaches the Cyclades guarantee you an unforgettable holiday.

The trip to the Cyclades can be made by ferry from Piraeus, Rafina, and Lavrion as well as by plane from Athens to Mykonos, Paros, Milos, Santorini, Naxos and Syros.

ANDROS

Gavrio
Batsi
Apikla
ANDROS

MAKRONISI

KEA

KEA
(Ioulis)

JAROS

KYTHNOS

KYTHNOS

Merihas

SYROS

Ano Syros
ERMOUPOLI

Finikas

SERIFOS

SERIFOS

APOLONIA

Kamares

PAR
(Par

SIFNOS

ANTIPAR

KIMOLOS

POLYAGOS

MHLOS *Apollonia*
(Plaka)

Adamantas

FOLEGANDROS

SIKINOS

FOLEGANDROS

SIKINO

MILOS

Castle

Airport

Monastery

Cave

Archaeological site

Anchorage

CYCLADES

Distances between harbours in miles

Column headers (left → right): TINOS, Chora · SYROS, Ermoupoli · SIKINOS, Alopronia · SIFNOS, Kamares · SERIFOS, Livadi · SANTORINI, Fira · RAFINA · PIREAS · PAROS, Parikia · PAROS, Naoussa · NAXOS · MYKONOS · MILOS, Adamas · LAVRIO · KITHNOS, Merichas · KIMOLOS · KEA, Korissia · KARYSTOS · IOS · IKARIA, Ag. Kyrikos · FOLEGANDROS · DILOS · KRITI, Iraklio · ASTYPALEA · ANDROS, Gavrio · ANDROS, Chora · ANAFI · AMORGOS, Vathi

Distance matrix (each row lists the distances to the columns above, ending with the named harbour):

- TINOS, Panormos: 22, 23, 55, 49, 92, 83, 45, 42, 45, 23, 76, 54, 45, 66, 41, 45, 72, 63, 30, 149, 109, 15, 69
- TINOS, Chora: 12, 44, 42, 74, 62, 86, 30, 26, 30, 12, 67, 58, 45, 54, 43, 46, 55, 60, 15, 136, 101, 31, 28, 59
- SYROS, Ermoupoli: 41, 37, 73, 83, 26, 25, 30, 19, 63, 55, 40, 41, 45, 55, 68, 17, 132, 102, 31, 30, 61
- SIKINOS, Alopronia: 21, 27, 7, 10, 53
- SIFNOS, Kamares: 13, 57, 79, 32, 40, 47, 49, 27, 54, 34, 14, 52, 50, 94, 43, 104, 99, 61, 67
- SERIFOS, Livadi: 65, 73, 33, 39, 45, 46, 38, 28, 22, 45, 59, 45, 92, 41, 112, 105, 61, 70
- SANTORINI, Fira: 130, 57, 54, 47, 68, 7t, 105, 84, 99, 110, 22, 88, 26, 63, 19, 61, 98, 30, 40
- RAFINA: 72, 26, 36, 119
- PIREAS: 95, 97, 103, 94, 87, 32, 86, 45, 62, 111, 143, 93, 174, 189, 89, 146, 136
- PAROS, Parikia: 13, 19, 29, 52, 68, 49, 34, 58, 68, 38, 66, 31, 21, 114, 95, 52, 53
- PAROS, Naoussa: 11, 23, 60, 71, 54, 42, 61, 67, 36, 60, 16, 114, 87, 50, 44
- NAXOS: 25, 63, 77, 60, 45, 57, 72, 28, 57, 19, 107, 80, 54, 42
- MYKONOS: 70, 67, 53, 56, 53, 57, 49, 55, 12, 128, 95, 39, 32, 52
- MILOS, Adamas: 65, 46, 26, 62, 83, 54, 115, 40, 64, 105, 115, 83, 83
- LAVRIO: 26, 63, 17, 27, 86, 116, 46, 63, 154, 144, 59, 111
- KITHNOS, Merichas: 42, 21, 40, 65, 104, 53, 132, 123, 51, 90
- KIMOLOS: 60, 75, 34, 95, 48, 91, 96, 71, 61
- KEA, Korissia: 21, 81, 104, 52, 100, 26, 48, 100
- KARYSTOS: 91, 103, 59, 164, 144, 20, 39, 102
- IOS: 78, 18, 44, 82, 62, 78, 35, 36
- IKARIA, Agios Kyrikos: 59, 147, 75, 72, 54
- FOLEGANDROS: 58
- DILOS: 124, 91, 41, 49
- KRITI, Iraklio: 96, 157, 103
- ASTYPALEA: 118, 36, 53
- ANDROS, Gavrio: 86
- ANDROS, Chora: 78
- ANAFI: 46

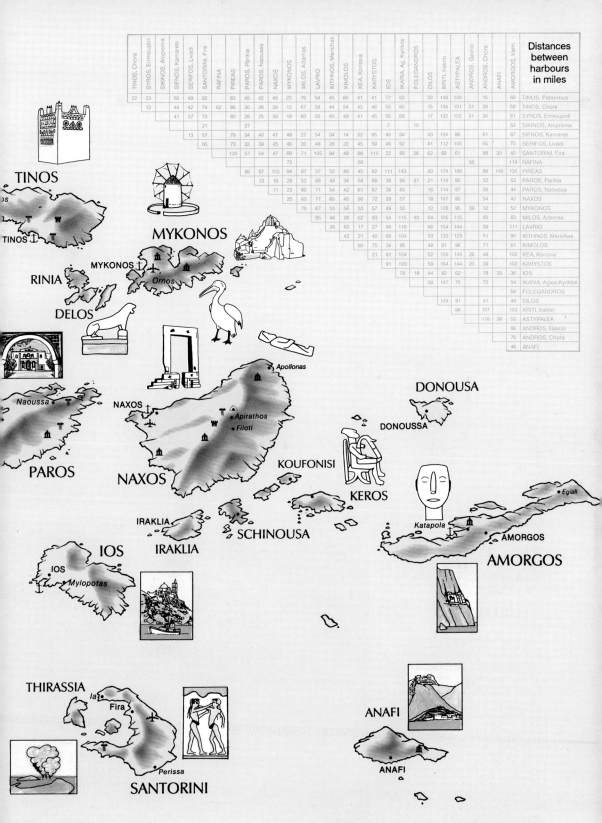

Map labels: TINOS · MYKONOS · RINIA · DELOS · PAROS · NAXOS · IOS · THIRASSIA · SANTORINI · ANAFI · DONOUSA · DONOUSSA · KOUFONISI · KEROS · SCHINOUSA · IRAKLIA · AMORGOS · Naoussa · Ornos · Apollonas · Apirathos · Filoti · Katapola · Egiali · Mylopotas · Ia · Fira · Perissa

Kea

Kea is the Cycladic island which lies closest to Attica - 16 miles from Lavrio. It thus provides an opportunity for a taste of the Cyclades on Tzia, as it is called by the locals, three hours from Athens.

From the port, Korissia, we climb to Chora and stroll among the pictureque alleys with their arches and the old houses in the Cycladic style. Chora, the chief settlement, is built on high ground, as is the case in most of the Cyclades. It differs, however, from the general rule in the Cyclades in that the houses have tiled roofs. The visitor can then go on to the Kastro to admire the view, which includes the remarkable torrent bed which runs down to the sea - a sea which glitters in the rays of the sun. If you have time, you can then go down to the beach with its attractive coves in order to enjoy a swim in the cleanest of water. One can visit Otzias and Panayia Kastriani; one can go to Pisses, Koundouros and, further off, to Poles, a sandy beach next to the ancient Carthaea. And on a summer's evening you can settle down in a little taverna next to the sea at Korissia or Vourkari. If you have escaped from Athens to come here, as the *meltemi* wind cools you, you will find that you have imperceptibly put every care out of your mind. You will have completely forgotten the noisy city from which you set out in the morning - and this in spite of the fact that you are only three hours away from the capital.

Kea is a mountainous island, its highest peak being Profitis Ilias (568 m.). It has an area of 121 sq. km., a shoreline of 81 km. and a population of 1,800. The interior of the island is an exception to its generally bare landscape with its scattered olive trees and streambeds, full of bushes and oleanders, running down to picturesque coves.

Kea can be reached by ferry from Lavrio (16 nautical miles) and from Piraeus. On the islands, buses go from Chora to Korissia, Yaliskari, Vourkari and Otzias. As far as accommodation is concerned, although the tourist infrastructure has not yet been developed, hotels and rented rooms can easily be found.

HISTORY

Kea was already inhabited at the end of the Neolithic period (before 3000 BC), as can be seen from finds which have come to light at Kefala. The Ionians came to the island around 1000 BC and built four cities: Ioulis, Coresia, Poiessa and Carthaea.

The lion of Kea.

The island played its part in the struggle against the Persians, sending ships to the Battle of Salamis. It was later a member of the Athenian League (478 BC).

The Venetians conquered Kea at the beginning of the 13th century. Subsequently, the island fell victim to repeated pirate raids. The Turks made their appearance here in 1537, but their rule was not firmly established and Kea frequently changed masters. Between 1789 and 1790, the heroic freedom-fighter Lambros Katsonis used Kea as a base for his attacks on the Turkish fleet.

The Agia Marina monastery.

Korissia. This is the island's port and it is situated in a bay with a fine sandy beach.

Kea (Chora). Also sometimes called 'Ioulis', since it stands on the site of the ancient city of that name. It is 6 km. from Korissia on a hill (320 m.), on the highest point of which is **Kastro**, with scanty remains of the ancient walls and of a temple of Apollo. It has narrow alleyways and old Cycladic houses - as well as a certain number of more modern ones. There is a marvellous view over the streambed with its lush vegetation. A walk of 15 minutes brings us to the **Lion of Kea**, carved on a rock in the 6th century BC. Tradition says that this was the lion which drove out of the island the nymphs who had been killing its womenfolk. Kea also has an archaeological museum.

Monastery of St Marina. This is 5 km. to the south-west of Chora and is built round an ancient three-storey tower.

Pisses. A cove with a sandy beach on the site of the ancient Poiessa. Ten kilometres from Chora, it is on the west coast.

Koundouros. A small tourist centre with a bay with crystal-clear water, 15 km. from Chora.

Poles. A bay with a sandy beach on the site of the ancient Carthaea, of which some ruins remain. In the south-east of the island.

Vourkari. The next cove north of Korissia. The first calling-place for yachts, with good shops and considerable tourist and artistic traffic created by the well- know gallery "Voulkariani".

On the promontory of **Ayia Irini** opposite an important prehistoric Bronze Age settlement has been found.

Further to the north, at **Kefala**, other excavations have revealed an even older settlement.

Otzias. A picturesque enclosed cove with a village, 6 km. north of Korissia.

Monastery of Kastriani. Seven kilometres after Otzias on the north coast of the island in a wild and rocky landscape with a fine view. It has a guesthouse.

Chora, or Ioulis, the capital of Kea.

The archaeological site of Ay.Eirene and in the background the pictaresque Vourkari.

Makronisos

In antiquity, Makronisos was known as Eleni because of a legend in which Helen stopped off there on her way to (or from) Troy. It lies between Kea and Lavrio (Attica) of which it is an administrative part. It has an area of 15 sq. km. and a shoreline of 28 km. There were settlements here in ancient times, as can be seen from occasional traces of ruins. After World War Two, it served as a place of internal exile for many Greeks.

Kythnos

Kythnos lies between Kea and Serifos and is 52 nautical miles from Piraeus. it has an area of 99 sq. m. and a coastline of 97 km. The population numbers 1,500. It is a mountainous and generally bare island with a wealth of beautiful and enclosed coves.

It lies outside the mainstream of tourism and so is ideal for those who wish to enjoy the sea in peace and quiet.

Kythnos can be reached from Piraeus both by ferry, which then goes on to Serifos, Sifnos, Milos and Kimolos, and by the 'flying dolphin' which plies between Piraeus (Zea) and Kea-Kythnos.

HISTORY

The first inhabitants of the islands are said to have been the Dryopes and the island took the name of their king, who was called Cythnus. It was, however, known by other names, such as Thermia - the locals still use this name - a name derived from the hot springs of spa water which can be found at Loutra. In historical times the island was a member of the Delian Confederacy. It was conquered in 1207 by the Venetians and in 1537 by the Turks. It was one of the first of the islands to join the 1821 uprising and was united to Greece in 1832, together with the rest of the Cyclades.

View of Chora. *Below: The seaside at Ayia Eirene, near Loutra.*

Kythnos is the first island that the ships on their way to the western Cyclades call at. The four hours from Piraeus are sufficient to transport us into a different world, the world of the Cyclades: the harbour at Merichas with its sand and fishing boats, the crystal clear sea sparkling in the sunlight, the cool *meltemi* breeze which gives limpidity to the atmosphere, and on the bare mountain the two villages in the Cycladic style, Chora and Dryopida, with their gleaming white houses, their paved alleys and their old windmills.

Perhaps you will hear music coming from one of the cafés - cheerful island music played on the violin and lute. And the fast dance performed in the cafés is the Cycladic 'balos'.

On the eastern side of the island is a second port, Loutra, which attracts large numbers of summer visitors. To the southeast is Panayia Kanala, built on a rock and looking out to sea, which every year on 15 August and 8 September welcomes its pilgrims, who after the church service dance in its paved courtyard.

This is the world of the Cyclades - a world of peace and good cheer, full of life and light. It is so near to noisy Athens and a weekend is all that is needed to get to know it.

Merichas. This is the harbour at which the ferries put in and the port of Chora and Dryopida. The good sandy beach is busy in summer, particularly at weekends. North of Merichas are the sandy beaches of **Episkopi** and **Apo-krousa**, and to the south, that of **Flambouria**. Two bus services start from Merichas: for Episkopi - Chora - Loutra, and for Dryopida - Panayia Kanala.

Kythnos (Chora). Eight kilometres from Merichas, this village preserves the traditional architecture of the Cyclades, in spite of the addition of new houses.

Here there are two churches of note: that of the Transfiguration, with its carved wooden sanctuary screen, and that of St Sabbas, of the 17th century. Near Chora is the Monastery of Our Lady 'tou Nikous´, which under Turkish rule kept a secret school.

In recent years, stations for the production of electricity from the wind (wind park) and the sun have been set up at Chora.

Loutra. Five kilometres from Chora. It has two medicinal springs, one extremely hot and one hot, which are recommended for the treatment of rheumatic, arthritic and gynaecological problems. The Xenia Hotel operates a spa. Thanks to its fine sandy beach, Loutra has been developed as a tourist centre.

Dryopida. A large village, five kilometres from Merichas. Near the village is a large cave with stalactites called **Katafyki**. The beaches of **Kalo Livadi** and **Lefkes**, as well as the cove of **Ayios Stefanos** can be reached on foot from Dryopida.

Panayia Kanala. A monastery on the south-eastern coast of the island, 7 km. from Dryopida. Its feast days are on 15 August and 8 September. Below the monastery are a sandy beach, fish tavernas and a few rooms to rent.

Opposite Panayia Kanala lies the unihabited islet of **Piperi**.

The small island of Ayios Loukas, north of Mericha. Connected to Kolona by a strip of sand.

Serifos

From a distance, Serifos looks like a large rock sticking out of the water - a rock which mythology says is the petrified form of the tyrannical king of the island Polydectes. However, as you come closer to this bare island, you begin to realise how beautiful it really is. It has its chief village - Chora again - clinging to the top of a steep hill overlooking the port. Chora has with every justification been made subject to a preservation order as a traditional settlement. The island has meadows, coves and, above all, sandy beaches. In having so much excellent sand so close to its port it is unique among the Cyclades. In addition, it has a wealth of other sandy beaches no more than half an hour's walk away. Livadakia, Karavi, Lia, the enclosed bay of Ayios Sostis, the famous Psili Ammos with its pictureque little taverna, and Ayios Yannis are ideal for those who like walking and swimming. If you wish to go a little further afield by caïque or car, then you can pay a visit to the old fortified monastery of the Archangels (Taxiarches), the attractive bay of Koutalas, Megalo Livadi, or Sykamia.

Though its bars and discos are full in summer, Serifos serves more for the enjoyment of peace and quiet and the simple island way of life.

The island lies between Kythnos and Sifnos and is 70 nautical miles from Piraeus. It has an area of 73 sq. km., a shoreline of 70 km. and a population of 1,200. It can be reached from Piraeus by a ferry service, which continues to Sifnos, Milos and Kimolos. There is also a ferry service linking Serifos with other islands of the Cyclades apart from those on the western route.

HISTORY

The island was inhabited by the Ionians. It was an ally of Athens and fought with it in the struggle against the Persians.

The Romans used Serifos as a place of exile. it was taken by the Franks in 1204 and by the Turks in 1537, gaining its liberty from the latter in 1821.

The harbour of Seritos with its dazzling white sand beach and Chora at the peak of the hill

Getting to know the island

Livadi. The port of Chora, this is where the ferries put in. It is a busy place in summer and round about 15 August finding accommodation can be a problem. Near the harbour a vast sandy beach stretches out in the shape of a horseshoe.

Chora. Buses cover the 5 km. from Livadi to Chora, which is built high up on a steep hill above the port. With its gleaming white houses, paved alleys and windmills, it is one of the finest villages in the Cyclades and has remained unaffected by modern tourist traffic. Spread out in the shape of an amphitheatre on the hillside, it is divided into two districts: **Kato Chora** and **Epano Chora**. In the latter, the square with the Town Hall, the village's only neo-classical building, the church of St John and the church of St Athanasius is most attractive. Chora also has a small **Archaeological Museum** and the ruins of a Venetian fortress. The view from the top of the hill towards the bay and the nearby Cycladic islands is unique.

Panayia. Five kilometres northwest of Chora, with a church of the 10th century dedicated to Our Lady (Panayia), form which the village takes its name.

Monastery of the Archangels. The island's most important building, 4 km. from Panayia. Its thick high walls give it the appearance of a fortress. It dates from the 17th century.

Koutalas. A small settlement on a beautiful bay with a sandy beach, 17 km. south-west of Chora.

Megalo Livadi (13 km. west of Chora) and **Sykamia** (9 km. north-west of Chora) are small fishing ports with sandy beaches.

North-east of Serifos, at some distance, is the uninhabited islet of **Serfopoula** and east of this is the imposing rock of **Voos**.

Above: Going down from Chora to Livadi.

Below: View of Livadi from Chora.

Sifnos

When you enter the port of Sifnos - Kamares - you are ringed by mountains - high, bare mountains, topped by a white chapel or a monastery. On one side of the bay are the houses, the hotels and the shops, and, at the far end, a beach. The bay is most attractive and its beach sheer temptation, but the real beauty of the island lies on a plateau which is reached by bus, six kilometres from the the port. There you will encounter a unique spectacle: the whole of the plateau with its olive trees is covered with sparkling white villages which virtually blend into one another: where one ends, another begins. This sight is unique in the Cyclades. Next, one can go on to Kastro, a medieval village, before descending to the beaches - Faros and Platys Yalos, one of the finest in the whole of the Aegean. Whether you stay on the coast or in the interior of the island, memorable holidays in Sifnos are guaranteed.

Sifnos lies in between Serifos, Kimolos and Antiparos and is 78 nautical miles from Piraeus. It has an area of 74 sq. km. and a shoreline of 70 km, with a population of approximately 2,000. The island is reached on the ferries which run on the Piraeus - Kythnos - Serifos - Sifnos - Milos - Kimolos line, and there are also sailings to other islands in the Cyclades.

Girls in the traditional costume.

HISTORY

Sifnos was first inhabited by the Carians and the Phoenicians. They were followed by the Ionians. The island was very wealthy in antiquity, thanks to its gold and silver mines. Proof of this is the treasury which the Siphnians built at Delphi in the 6th century BC to house their offerings. However, it appears that something went wrong with the mines; either they were worked out or flooded by the sea - we do not know which - and their production ceased. The Siphnians suddenly found themselves poor.

In 1207, the Venetian Marco Sanudo conquered Sifnos and it was incorporated into the Duchy of Naxos. In 1537 it was conquered by the Turks. It played its part in the struggle for liberty in 1821 and was united with Greece in 1832.

Getting to know the island

Kamares. This is the port at which the ferries tie up. It has a good beach, but it is exposed to the north wind. There is a bus from Kamares to the main villages and beaches of the island. Most of the road is asphalt.

Apollonia. The capital of the island, 6 km. from Kamares, with gleaming white houses. The name comes from the god Apollo, who was worshipped on the island. It has a folk museum, tavernas, a pizza parlour and cafés which serve the island's traditional confections.

Artemonas. A most attractive village, 2 km. north of Apollonia. Here too the white houses are a fine example of Cycladic architecture.

Kastro. The former capital of the island. This is a medieval village, 3 km. east of Apollonia, built on a hill, with very old houses, narrow alleyways covered by arches and a small archaeological museum.

Chrysopighi. A monastery popular with the locals and with visitors, with a picturesque 17th century church, built on a rock which forms a small promontory. Next to it is a beach with crystal-clear water. It lies between Faros and Platys Yalos.

Platys Yalos. The island's finest beach and one of the best in the Cyclades, which accounts for its popularity. It is 10 km. from Apollonia and is on a bay which is sheltered from the *meltemi* wind.

South of the bay is the islet of **Kitriani**.

Faros. A seaside village on a sheltered beach, 7 km. south-east of Apollonia.

Vathi. A small village on a very attractive enclosed bay with shallow water. It can be reached by caïque from Kamares and by road from Apollonia.

Monasteries of Sifnos: Sifnos has a number of old monasteries, such as those of the Prophet Elijah and of St Symeon (both on mountain tops with magnificent views), that of the Archangels at Vathi, of Our Lady 'tis Vrisis', and Chrysopighi. In addition, there are many picturesque churches and half-ruined towers scattered throughout the island.

Sifnos has a tradition in pottery-making, and in the production of certain kinds of sweetmeats.

Above: Pottery is an age-old tradition of Sifnos.

Below: The picturesque Vathy.

Milos - Kimolos

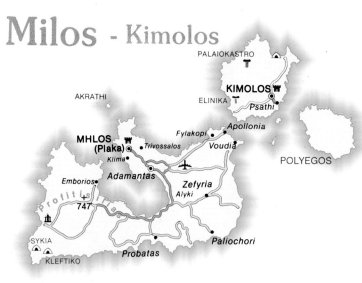

The island lies to the north-west of Santorini and south of Sifnos and Serifos. It is of volcanic origin, explaining the wonderful shapes and colours of the rocks along all the island's beaches. Here nature has created art-works of sculpture in the cliffs, and paintings in the coloured rock formations and fairytale caves, quiet beaches and superb stretches of sand.

Milos has great mineral wealth, and its mines are among the oldest in the Mediterranean.

Milos is at the south-western extremity of the Cyclades, 87 nautical miles from Piraeus. It has an area of 151 sq. km., a coastline of 125 km. and a population of 5,000.

It is reached from Piraeus by the ferry service on the Piraeus - Kythnos - Serifos - Sifnos - Milos - Kimolos route. Many other islands can be reached from Milos by ferry, particularly in summer.

There is also an air service to Athens.

The name of Milos is known throughout the world because of the famous statue of Aphrodite (Venus) which was discovered here and which has long been an adornment to the Louvre.

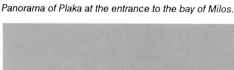

Panorama of Plaka at the entrance to the bay of Milos.

HISTORY

Milos was one of the first of the Cycladic islands to be inhabited. This is evidenced by the Neolithic remains at Fylakopi and the fragments of obsidian, a black mineral found only on Milos. This mineral, which resembles glass and which was used to make tools (knives and spearheads) played an important role in the island's development. Milos was an important centre of Cycladic civilisation, which began to develop earlier than the Minoan civilisation of Crete and then kept pace with it. The domination of the Minoans over Milos and the Cyclades began about 2000 BC and continued to c. 1450 BC. The Minoans were followed by the Myceneans and, in 1100 BC, by the Dorians. Later, after the Peloponnesian War, Athens, in revenge for the island's pro-Spartan sympathies, laid Milos waste, killing all the men and selling the women and children into slavery. However, the island flourished once more in the Hellenistic period, when among the works of art of Milos was the famous Aphrodite (Venus).

Milos was converted to Christianity at an early date. Its famous catacombs are unique in Greece and are the resting place of more than 2,000 early Christians. The island was conquered in 1207 by the Venetians and in 1580 by the Turks. Before the Turkish conquest, Milos had been seized by pirates and one of these, Ioannis Kapsis, had proclaimed himself king of the island. Milos was liberated and incorporated into Greece in 1832.

Adamantas. The picturesque port of Milos, at the head of the large bay, with the old church of the Holy Trinity and a beach with tamarisks.

There is a bus service from Adamantas to the villages of Trypiti, Plaka, Triovasali, Fylakopi (antiquities), Pollonia (Apollonia), Voudia, Zefyria (Chora), Palochori, Hivadolimni and Provatas. A trip round the island by caïque is recommended, as this enables one to enjoy the sight of its unique white cliffs with the emerald waters to be found at the south-western extremity of the island, at Kleftiko.

Milos (Plaka). The present capital of the island and one of the most attractive villages in the Cyclades. It stands at the entrance to the bay at a height of 200 m. The view from **Marmara** and the paved courtyard of **Panayia Korfiatissa** is magnificent and the sunsets seen from there are among the finest in the Aegean. Also worth visiting is the Frankish castle above **Panayia Thalassitra**, a church whose architecture is noteworthy. The **Archaeological Museum** is at Plaka and contains a cast of the famous **Aphrodite** (Venus) which was found at Milos. It also has a **Folk Museum**.

South of Plaka, between the settlement of **Trypiti** and the seaside village of **Klima** is the site of the **ancient city of Milos**. Of this, there are remains of the walls, foundations and the ruins of a Roman theatre. It was near the theatre that in 1820 the statue of Venus was found by a farmer. At that time, a French warship was stationed at Milos. The French, following negotiations of their ambassador at Constantinople, took the statue to France.

South-east of ancient Milos, 15 minutes from the road to Trypiti, are the famous catacombs, an Early Christian burial place of the 3rd century AD, unique in Greece. They consist of an underground central corridor and four other smaller corridors, of a total length of 185 m., which join it and on the

37

left and right of which are tombs carved out with arches above. It is believed that in the catacombs, which were used not only as a burial place, but also as a place of worship, more than 2,000 Christians were buried.

Fylakopi. Called ´Flakopi´ locally, this is on the road from Plaka to Apollonia. It is one of the most important archaeological sites in the Cyclades, since all the periods of Cycladic civilisation, which coincides with the entire Bronze Age, are represented there.

There are three prehistoric cities which succeeded one another, each on the ruins of the preceding one. The first city was built in the Early Cycladic period (3rd millenium BC).

The second in the Middle Cycladic (2nd millenium) - this is believed to have been a Minoan colony - and the third in the Late Cycladic (after 1450 BC), under Mycenean influence.

Papafranga Cave. This is a sea cave with a sandy beach near Fylakopi, formed by vast white rocks.

Apollonia (or Pollonia). A settlement at the north-eastern end of the island with a fine beach. It lies opposite the island of Kimolos. In summer there are regular trips from here by caïque to the Glaronisia islands (30 minutes). These are volcanic islets whose rocks are made up of mineral crystals in the form of rods of a height of up to 30 metres. Kimolos (30 minutes) can also be visted by caïque.

Sykia Cave. The finest sea cave on Milos - in the south-west of the island on the west coast. Its colours are striking and it can be reached from the Monastery of St John (22 km. from Adamantas and then one hour, 10 minutes on foot) or - better - by caïque from Adamantas.

Kleftiko. The most imposing sight on the island with high white rocks, white islets and a sea cave. It is near the Sykia cave, but on the island's south coast. Its name (from 'kleftis' = thief) comes from the fact that pirate caïques used to hide behind the rocks where they were invisible from the sea. Kleftiko is approached in the same way as the Sykia cave, that is, by caïque from Adamantas.

Emboreios. A small village on the western side of the bay with a beach. **Hivadolimni**, south-east of Emboreios, is one of the most attractive spots on the island.

Provatas and **Paliochori**. These are two attractive beaches on the south coast of the island. They can be reached by bus.

North-west of Milos, the unhabited islet of **Antimilos** is used as a breeding-ground for a rare species of chamois. At the entrance to the bay of Milos the rocky **Arkoudia** islets form striking patterns.

Kleftiko, Milos.

Kimolos

Kimolos is a small islet consisting of common chalk ('kimolia' = chalk). It is a mere half mile from its neighbour Milos and the caïque takes less than half an hour to come from Pollonia. It spite of this, it lies outside the mainstream of tourist trade and is ideal for the vistor who is not looking for luxury facilities, but is satified with a peaceful and carefree stay with the straighforward and hospitable islanders.

Kimolos, the small harbour of Psathi.

South-west of Sifnos and very close to Milos, Kimolos is 88 nautical miles from Piraeus.

It has an area of 36 sq. km., a coastline of 38 km. and a population of 780. It can be reached by ferries from Piraeus which follow the western Cyclades route.

HISTORY

The island, according to mythology, took its name from its first settler, Cimolus, the husband of Side, the daughter of Taurus. Its history, broadly speaking, has followed the same course as that of its neighbour Milos. The ancient city of the island lies under water off Kofto beach. Opposite the islet of Ayios Andreas there are remains from the Mycenean period.

From the quiet port of **Psathi** we climb on foot to **Chora** (20 minutes). This is a large Cycladic village with gleaming white houses with their pots of basil and geraniums. Chora has a small museum and a rural medical post. The churches of St John Chrysostom (17th century), of Christ (16th century) and of Our Lady of the Annunciation (17th century) are worth visiting.

At **Ellinika**, south-west of Chora, one hour approximately on foot or 20 minutes by caïque from Psathi, one can combine a visit to the island's chief archaeological site and a swim.

There, near **Kofto** beach, when the sea is calm, the remains of the ancient city of Kimolos can be seen under the water, while opposite the islet of **Ayios Andreas** or **Daskaleio** there are the remains of Mycenaean tombs.

Other interesting spots are **Vromolimni** on the north coast (one hour by caïque) with its cave, and medieval **Palaiokastro**, in the center of the island.

At **Aliki**, perhaps the best beach on the island, there are a few rooms to rent.

Opposite the harbour of Psathi is the island of **Polyaigos**, which is used as grazing ground.

Andros

According to mythology, Andros takes its name from Andros, grandson of Apollo. However, the island had other names in antiquity, including Gaurus, Lasia and Hydrousa. It seems that Andros was settled by the Carians, the Phoenicians and the Cretans. The Ionians came here around 1000 BC. From that point on, the island's prosperity increased. It became a major sea power, established colonies in Chalcidice, Thrace and Asia Minor and minted its own coins.

The god worshipped here was Dionysus. Tradition narrates that at the festivals in his honour - the Dionysia - wine flowed from a spring on the island. Andros quarrelled with Athens after the Persian Wars, but afterwards became

Andros is the most northerly island of the Cyclades and the second largest after Naxos. It is only 7 nautical miles from Euboea (from which it is separated by the Cavo Doro straits) and less than one nautical mile from Tinos. Like the other islands of the Cyclades it is washed by the Aegean and cooled in summer by the *meltemi* wind. It too has steep cliffs and beaches of white sand. It has, however, one advantage which the other islands lack: it is extremely verdant and irrigated with plentiful running water. There are large numbers of olive trees, pines and fruit trees on the island, while in its ravines, the site of villages such as Menites, Stenies and Apikia, the vegetation is lush. Andros also has Sariza with its famous spring water, which is bottled and available all over Greece, golden sands with crystal-clear water, and something else: an old-world nobility which is shared both by its houses and its inhabitants.

Andros can be reached from Rafina by ferry, and in summer by hydrofoil. However, it is advisable if you have a car to take it with you, since this is a big island with many places of interest, a good road network and, generally, a sound tourist infrastructure.

Andros is 89 nautical miles from Piraeus and 36 from Rafina. It has an area of 373 sq. km., a coastline of 177 km. and a population of 9,000. Of these many are seamen and quite a number are officers.

The neighbouring islands of the Cyclades can be visted by ferry from Andros. In summer the 'flying dolphins' supplement the ferry service.

The lovely Batsi. The largest summer resort on Andros.

a member of the First (476 BC) and Second (376 BC) Athenian league. After the Battle of Chaeroneia, the Macedonians became masters of Andros. In 200 BC, the Romans attacked the island, forcing all the inhabitants to flee and settle at Delius (now Dilesi) in Attica, and laid it waste, before handing it over to Attalus, king of Pergamum.

In Byzantine times, Andros was a flourishing cultural centre. Michael Psellus, teacher of Leo the Philosopher, taught at its famous academy of philosophy in the 9th century. It was also prosperous, thanks to the silk production which was developed in the 11th and 12th century.

The Venetians took Andros in 1207 and remained rulers of the island until 1556, when it was conquered by the Turks. In around 1789, the sea off Andros was the scene of the activities of the heroic freedom-fighter Lambros Katsonis. With Kea as his base, he became the terror of the Turkish fleet. His feats, however, came to an end in 1790, with the famous sea battle which took place in the straits between Andros and Euboea, at which most of his nine vessels were destroyed by 16 Turkish and 12 Algerian ships.

Andros made a major contribution to the uprising of 1821, while many Andriots were members of the 'Philiki Etaireia'-the secret society for promoting the Revolution.

The chapel of Ayia Thalassini in Chora.

Andros or Chora

Chora, standing on a headland between two beaches, is an attractive and sun-drenched town. At the tip of the headland there is a small rocky island with the remains of a **Venetian fortress**. Chora's architecture is a mixture of the Cycladic and the neo-Classical. The first style is to be encountered in the narrow alleyways with their white houses and the second in the squares with their fine mansions. As an island with a strong seafaring tradition, Andros has a **Maritime Museum** at Chora, with its statue of the Unknown Sailor, and its Yacht Club.

Chora also has an **Archaeological Museum** and a **Museum of Modern Art**. Of the Byzantine churches of note, the 13th century 'Palatiani', with a magnificent carved sanctuary screen, Our Lady Odeghetria and the 'Theoskepasti' stand out.

Near Chora are the beaches of Nimborio, Paraporti and Yalia.

Gavrio - Batsi - Chora - Korthi - Gavrio (97 km.)

Gavrio is the port at which the ferries stop. It lies in an enclosed bay with a beach. Three kilometres north-east of Gavrio, at **Ayios Petros**, there is a tall and well-preserved Hellenistic tower. From Gavrio we follow the asphalt road

along the coast in a south-easterly direction.

3 km. The beach of **Kato Ayios Petros**. This has good sand and tourist facilities.

3.5 km. Chrysi Ammos beach.

4.5 km. A road off to the left leads to the **Monastery of Zoodochos Pighi**, of the 14th century.

8 km. Batsi. The largest tourist centre on Andros, with a bay with an excellent beach. From Batsi, if we go off to the left, we come, after 14 km., to the verdant village of **Arnas**, which is on the foothills of the island's highest mountain, **Petalos** (1003 m.). From Arni (500 m.), the Gavalos peak can be reached in approximately an hour.

16 km. Palaiopoli. A village which stands on the site of the ancient city of Andros. Scanty remains of the walls and the ancient harbour have survived by the coast.

22 km. Road junction. The road continues to Korthi. You turn left for Andros (Chora).

25 km. On the left is the village of Melida, with the church of the

The statue of the "Unknown Sailor" on the harbour of Chora.

Archangels (Taxiarches) of the 11th century - one of the most important on Andros.

28 km. A road off to the left leads in 1 km. to Menites with its lush greenery. Its tavernas are under great plane trees with streams flowing past.

30 km. Mesaria. The village has a 12th century church, dedicated to the Archangels.

34 km. Andros (Chora).

From Chora, we recommend a deviation: you follow the asphalt road which climbs to the north. After 2 km., this road forks. The right fork leads to **Stenies**, a village of sea captains and shipowners, and the left - 4 km. on - to verdant **Apikia** with the famous **Sariza** spring. Its water, which is recommended chiefly for kidney troubles, is bottled in the village and distributed all over Greece. Its restaurants have balconies with a fine view of the green ravine.

In order to continue your tour of the island, you turn left towards Korthi a little further outside Chora.

46 km. Vouni. On the right, near the village of **Fallika**, is the oldest monastery on Andros, the **Panachrantou Monastery**, built in the 10th century by Nikephoros Focas.

56 km. Ormos Korthiou. A picturesque fishing port with a large pebble beach, exposed to the north wind. Most of the houses and shops are built on the western side of the bay, which is sheltered from the wind.

North of Korthi is the isolated **Pidima tis Grias** bay, with one of the finest landscapes on Andros, best approached by boat.

From Korthi you now follow the road which goes direct to Gavrio.

75 km. Road junction. On the right is the road you followed to go to Chora. You continue on the now familiar road for Batsi-Gavrio.

97 km. Gavrio. You have now completed our tour of Andros.

Above: The old Venetian bridge of Kastro, in Chora.

Center: Syneti, south of Chora.

Below: The harbour of Gavrio.

Tinos

Most of the visitors to Tinos are Greeks, since Tinos is the island of Our Lady, the greatest center of pilgrimage in Greece, rather like Lourdes in France.

Most of these people do not prolong their stay, and thus see little of the beauty of the island: the blindingly-white traditional villages have unadulterated Cycladic architecture and the famous dove-cotes which are constructed with great skill and imagination and are found almost exclusively in Tinos. These masterpieces of vernacular architecture should come as no surprise to us, since Tinos is the island of artists. Some of the most important Greek painters and sculptors of the 19th and 20th centuries, such as Halepas, Philippotis, Sochos, Ghyzis and Lytras, were from Tinos. In addition, Tinos has superb beaches with white sand, crystal-clear water and cool breezes in the summer.

The island has long spells of sunlight in the summer, which helps to make Tinos one of the most interesting places in the Cyclades.

Tinos lies between Syros, Andros and Mykonos and is 86 nautical miles from Piraeus and 62 from Rafina. It is a mountainous island with an area of 195 sq. km., a coastline of 106 km. and a population of approximately 8,000. It can be reached from Piraeus or Rafina by ferry or more rapid craft.

From the Tinos one can visit the other Cycladic islands.

HISTORY

According to mythology, Tinos was the home of Aeolus, god of the winds, a reference to the strong winds which often beat down on the island. The Ionians came here around 1000 BC. In the

Panayia, Tinos. Built in 1823 on the site where the miracle - working icon was found. Right the church forecourt.

6th century it was ruled by Eretria, while in 490 BC it was seized by the Persians, regaining its freedom after the battle of Marathon.

Poseidon was the god chiefly worshipped on Tinos, a fact evidenced by the remains of a temple dedicated to him and Amphitrite at Kionia.

In 1207, Tinos was conquered by the Venetians, the first Venetian rulers being the Ghizi family.

Venetian rule here lasted longer (approximately 500 years) than on any other island of the Cyclades. One result of this is that Tinos has the largest Roman Catholic community in the Cyclades. In 1715, Tinos was taken by the Turks, to be liberated by the Greeks in the War of Independence of 1821.

The year 1822 was an important one for Tinos, for it was then that the famous icon of the Blessed Virgin was discovered, after a nun in the Kechrovouni convent saw it in a dream.

She is honoured on the island today as St Pelagia of Tinos.

The island features in more modern history with the torpedoing of the Greek cruiser 'Elli' in Tinos harbour by an Italian submarine on 15 August 1940 - the Feast of the Dormition of the Virgin.

Getting to know the island

Tinos or Chora

The port of Tinos is full of life and movement in summer. Hotels, restaurants and shops are lined up on the quay, and from there a wide, straight, uphill road leads to the **Church of Our Lady**.

This is the road followed by thousands from all over Greece on 25 March and, even more so, on 15 August every year to venerate the wonder-working icon of the Virgin.

The church stands imposingly, high up at the end of the road. It is built of white marble and is ringed by a number of ancillary buildings. Its interior is dominated by the famous **icon of Our Lady**, one of those said to be the work of the Evangelist Luke.

It is studded with diamonds, sapphires and pearls, the offerings of emperors, kings and the faithful.

The church was built in 1823 on the spot where the miraculous icon was found. Among the buildings around the church are the **Gallery of Tinian Artists**, which contains works by Lytras, Iakovidis, Ghizis, Sochos and Philippotis, the sacristy, library, etc.

There is also an **Archaeological Museum** in Tinos.

The sheltered beach of **Ayios Fokas** is near Tinos town.

The harbour of Tinos, Megalochari avenue and the historic Xobourgo.

3. Kardiani - Isternia - Pyrgos - Ormos Panormou (36 km.)

You follow the new road which heads northwards and at 4 km. turn left for Isternia.

The road runs through the valley of Tarabados, with the greatest density of dovecotes anywhere on the island.

It continues high above the sea and the view is superb.

22 km. Kardiani. An attractive village with a ravine full of greenery, 260 m. above sea-level.

Kardiani Bay, which serves as the port for the village, is picturesque.

26 km. Isternia. Another beautiful village at an even greater altitude than **Kardiani** (330 m.) and with a magnificent view over the sea.

It is worth taking a walk among its picturesque alleyways and visiting the church of St Paraskeve with its marble sanctuary screen. At **Isternia Bay** you will find a sandy beach and clean sea. Next to the beach is **Ayios Nikitas**.

32 km. Pyrgos. The largest and perhaps the most attractive village on Tinos and one of the most picturesque in the Cyclades.Its gleaming white houses have marble lintels and steps, which give them a dignity entirely their own.

This is an artists' village. It is the birthplace of the painter Nikephoros Lytras, the composer Nikos Skalkotas and the sculptors Dimitris Philippotis and Yanoulis Halepas.

Painting and sculpture are a tradition throughout Tinos, but Pyrgos holds first place within this tradition. Among the sights to be seen in the village is the **house of Halepas**, which is also a museum.

36 km. Ormos Panormou. The end of the road. The pretty little harbour with its caïques and the houses above the beach give it a beauty of its own.

4. Porto (Ayios Ioannis)

This is a fine beach in the south-eastern part of the island, 6 km. east of Tinos.

Halfway there, a branch off to the right leads in 3 km. to the beach of **Ayios Sostis**.

EXCURSIONS

1. Kechrovouni Nunnery - Mesi - Komi - Kolymbithra (26 km.)

To follow this excursion, you leave the town and go into the interior of the island.

7 km. Kechrovouni Nunnery (Dormition of the Virgin). The most important religious house on Tinos, with some 50 nuns. It was built in the 11th century on a fine site. Among the cells of the Nunnery is that of the then Sister Pelagia, who in 1822 led the way to the spot where the icon of Our Lady was buried.

13 km. Xombourgo. You are now on your main route. On the left an earth road brings you close to the famous rock of Xombourgo, on which **ancient Tinos** was built in the 8th century BC.

It was there that the Venetians later built their famous Fortress **(Kastro)**, which was virtually impregnable and was the reason why the Turks took so long to conquer Tinos.

While they took almost all the Cyclades in 1538, Tinos did not fall into their hands until 1715.

19 km. Road junction near the village of Krokos. You go to the right towards Komi.

23 km. Komi. One of Tinos's largest villages, renowned for its traditional architecture.

From Komi you take the road which goes to the north coast of the island.

26 km. Kolymbithra. The name means 'swimming pool' and is appropriate to the fine bay with its marvellous beach, ideal for bathing. The area has started to be developed for tourist purposes.

2. Kionia

A visit to Kionia can be regarded as a walk rather than an 'outing'.

It is only 3 km. from Tinos town and can be reached by following the coast road in a westerly direction. It has a good beach and the sea water is clean, which attract many visitors. It is the site of the temple of Poseidon and Amphitrite.

Mykonos - Delos

Mykonos is now the most cosmopolitan island in the world, more famous than Capri, more fashionable than Hawaii. The question naturally arises: did this happen by chance, or does the island really deserve its fame?

To answer this, picture in your mind's eye a deep, blue sea, covered with little white waves, and set in it a bare island bathed in sunlight. Add to this a fishing harbour with caïques of every colour and an all-white town rising up the hillside from the sea shore. The domes and crosses of the innumerable churches stand out among the dazzlingly white houses, which are like cubes. And at the top of the hill, imagine that there are picturesque windmills with the breeze in their white sails.

All the alleyways of the town are paved and all the joints between the paving stones whitewashed. Every alley is a painting, every corner a revelation. On the right of the harbour the houses come down to the sea's edge. The foam of the waves beats against their walls, a little below their colourful window frames - green, red, blue, brown. Everything is in contrast: the white houses and the blue sea, the multi-coloured window frames - a contrast in an atmosphere which gleams with the freshness of the sea. This is the Venice of Greece, this is its Capri, this its exotic Honolulu.

We have tried here, in a few words, to give a picture of Mykonos, but any description, however hard we try to bring it life, lags far behind the reality. There is only one answer: to go there, to see it for yourself, to form your own opinion. The distance is not great: six hours by sea or half an hour by air.

The Alefkantra quarter, the Venice of Greece.

If you don't like crowds - the vastly varied crowds of Mykonos - don't go in summer. Choose a quieter time of the year - like early spring or late autumn. Then you will be able to decide for yourself whether it deserves the title of Greece's most picturesque island.

Mykonos lies between Tinos and Naxos. An island with very little vegetation, it has an area of 85 sq. km., a shoreline of 80 km. and a population of 5,500.

The island can be reached by air from Athens, Rhodes, Santorini and Herakleion (Crete) or by ferry from Piraeus (94 nautical miles), Rafina (71 nautical miles), the Dodecanese, Crete, and Thessaloniki.

In summer there is 'flying dolphin' service from Piraeus or Rafina. A local boat service takes visitors from Mykonos to nearby Delos.

The cosmopolitan harbour of Mykonos.

HISTORY

In the wealth of ancient Greek mythology there are two references to Mykonos. The first tells us that the island took its name from the hero Mykonos and the other that it was on Mykonos that Heracles slew the Giants and that the large rocks which lie scattered about the island are their petrified corpses.

In ancient times there were two cities on Mykonos, one of which was near the site of the present town. The Ionians came from Athens to Mykonos in the 9th century BC. From that point on, the history of Mykonos has been, broadly speaking, the same as that of the other islands of the Cyclades. Initially it was under the rule of the Athenians, but at that time it took second place to Delos, which was a major religious centre for many centuries.

Mykonos was conquered by the Venetians in 1207 and by the Turks in 1537. It played an important part in the 1821 uprising. The Mykonians gave their ships to Admiral Tombazis.

The famous beach of Platy Gialos.

Chora. The most picturesque port in the Cyclades. Here one can see the best expression of the traditional Cycladic architecture. In the white cuboid houses the straight line predominates, and is accompanied by French windows in a variety of colours, wooden balconies and stairs.

There is a large number of churches - in the island as a whole there are more than 350. These too are sparkling white, but with their domes painted blue or red. Of these, the famous church of **Our Lady Paraportiani** in the Kastro quarter at the end of the harbour is particularly worth a visit. It is perhaps the finest example of traditional architecture in the Cyclades. Near it is the **Folklore Museum** with a rich and varied collection, while the **Archaeological Museum** is in the north-eastern part of Chora and contains exhibits from the nearby island of Rheneia. One of the finest objects in the Museum is an amphora of the 7th century BC with depictions of the Trojan Horse and the Fall of Troy in relief.

Tourlos - Ayios Stefanos. This is a long sandy beach three kilometres north of Chora with tourist facilities. It can be reached by bus.

Ano Mera. A village in the Cycladic style in the interior of the island. There ia a bus service from Chora, whis is 9 km. away. Near the village is the Monastery of Our Lady Tourliani, of the 18th century, with a museum of ecclesiastical objects.

Ornos. A beautiful enclosed bay south of Mykonos. It has a good sandy beach and is a popular resort.

Psarou. A much-frequented, cosmopolitan beach.

Platys Yalos. Mykonos's most popular beach, with fine sand. There is a regular bus service from Chora. This is the starting-point for the caïques which go to the **Paradise** and **Super Paradise** beaches - the most attractive on Mykonos and favourites with nudists.

Elia. A large bay with a sandy beach, west of Super Paradise.

Kalafatis. A village with a famous beach, 12 km. from Chora.

Dragonisi. An uninhabited islet east of Mykonos.

Each corner its own picture.

*Pelican - mascot
on a street on Mykonos.*

Delos

This small barren island in the Cyclades was, mythology tells us, the birthplace of Apollo. And when you think about it, how could the god of the sun have chosen an island with more sunlight than Delos? The island is all light. There are no high mountains and no trees, and thus it is almost devoid of shade. In ancient times, tradition relates, there was a single palm tree on the island. It was against this that Leto supported herself to give birth to Apollo and Artemis.

It was this inhospitable island which they chose to make their religious centre. Thus the small island gradually became covered with temples, mansions, markets, stadiums and shops: a large city which was not only a religious, but also a cultural and commercial centre.

The centuries rolled by. The period of its greatest glory was followed by inevitable decline - wars, ruin and destruction. Today the island is a piece of land covered with ruins: fallen columns, sections of the famous mosaics which adorned the houses of the rich, a stadium, tiers of seats from a theatre, wrestling schools. Among this mass of ruins, five marble lions in a row still stand. These were the guardians of the sacred lake. They still gaze out to the east, waiting for the rising of the sun, the sun of Apollo its god.

Delos is south-west of Mykonos, six nautical miles away. Its area is only five sq. km. In summer small boats go every day from Mykonos, Tinos and Naxos to Delos. In winter the service is much more sporadic. It is not possible to spend the night on Delos.

HISTORY

Delos means 'that which appears', and according to mythology, the island appeared amid the waves to provide a place for Leto to give birth to Apollo and Artemis, thus escaping the wrath of Hera. In antiquity the island also had another name: Ortygis. It would seem that it was inhabited from the 3rd millennium BC.

The Ionians came to Delos at the beginning of the 10th century BC, and, later, round about the 7th century, made it their religious center and the headquarters of a large amphictyony, which included many of the islands of the Aegean. The Athenians, being Ionians themselves, took advantage of this fact, presented themselves as protectors of the island and, purifying it in 478 BC, formed the first Delian Confederacy. In this way they succeeded in bringing the majority of the islands under their influence and establishing their rule over the sea.

Among the measures taken by the Athenian 'protectors' was a decision to remove all the bones of the dead from Delos to the neighbouring island of Rheneia. It was forbidden for anyone to be born or to die on the sacred island. Women about to give birth were taken for that purpose to Rheneia, and it was on Rheneia

that the dead were buried. It was for this reason that on one of the islets between Delos and Rheneia - **Megalo Revmatari** - Hecate, the goddess of death, was worshipped. Another measure of the Athenians, which provoked the displeasure of their allies, was to transfer the treasury of the Confederacy from Delos to Athens in 454 BC. From ancient times, but particularly during the period of Athenian domination, the Delia - festivals held every five years in honour of Apollo, Artemis and Leto,- were renowned. Tradition relates that the Athenians sent to the Delia the ship of Theseus, which they had repaired and kept for many years. They would decorate it and load it with the animals destined for sacrifice and other offerings. When it arrived at Delos, it was received by the Delian maidens, who sang hymns and danced in honour of the three divinities.

The Macedonians put an end to Athenian rule in 315 BC. From that point on, the island acquired relative independence, which enabled it to develop its trade and to prosper. The coming of the Romans to the island not only did not put a stop to its commercial and cultural development, but actually promoted it. The city of Delos became a major commercial centre whose inhabitants were engaged in trade and came from many different parts of the ancient world. The majority of them were Egyptians, Syrians and Italians and these lost no time in building the temples of their own cults on the island.

The decline of Delos set in quite suddenly in 88BC with the Mithridatic War. The city was burnt down, its houses and temples demolished and its 20,000 inhabitants slaughtered. The final blow was delivered a few years later by pirates. From then on, the island remained virtually uninhabited, a prey to corsairs and antiquity-hunters, who visited it from time to time to carry off whatever they could. It was only at the end of the last century that French archaeologists began systematic excavations and brought to light and preserved what had remained of the island's ancient glory.

Visiting the ancient monuments

The boat from Mykonos normally ties up on the western shore of Delos, about 150 m. south of the site of the ancient sacred harbour.

Since there are a great many monuments spread over a wide area, to assist the visitor we shall divide them up into the following eight units.

The area of the ancient harbour. This area, behind the quay, contains the Agora of the Competialists, the Stoa of Philip V of Macedon and the Agora of the Delians.

The Hieron of Apollo. If you head north of the Processional Way, you come to the House of the Naxians and the Hieron (Sanctuary) of Apollo (6th century BC), which housed the statue of the god and the treasury of the Delian Confederacy. West of the Hieron is the Temple of Artemis, the Agora of Theophrastus (2nd century BC) and the hall of the High Columns (3rd century BC). The Stoa of Antigonus is to the north.

East of the Stoa of Antigonus is the Archaeological Museum.

The area of the avenue of the Lions. To the north of the Stoa of Antigonus you reach the Agora of the Italians, the largest monument on Delos. Immediately after the Agora of the Italians is the site of the Sacred Lake, now dried up, with the famous avenue of the Lions to the west of the Lake. Of the nine lions which were made in marble by the Naxians, who dedicated them in the 7th century BC to act as symbolic guardians of the Sacred Lake, five remain today - the most impressive and well-liked statues on the island. North-west of the avenue of the Lions is the large Institution of the Poseidoniasts and to the west of this, is the Hill House. To the north of the Sacred Lake is the Lake Palaestra (Wrestling school) (3rd century BC) and the Granite Palaestra (2nd century BC).

The area of the Stadium. The Stadium stands approximately one kilometre to the north-east of the avenue of the Lions. Half-way there is the Archegesion. In front of the Stadium is the Gymnasium.

The Theatre district. This extends south-eastwards from the quay and was the most densely inhabited and wealthiest quarter of the ancient city. Among the luxurious houses, the House of Dionysus, the House of the Trident, the House of the Dolphins and the House of the Masks might be mentioned: the names come from the subjects of their fine mosaic floors, which have survived. Also of interest is the House of Cleopatra, with statues of its owners, of Athenian Cleopatra and of Dioscurides.

The Theatre, which held an audience of 5,000, is in the centre of this district.

The Sanctuaries of the Foreign Gods. East of the Theatre district and below the sacred hill of Cynthus are the remains of the Sanctuaries of the Foreign Gods. Amongst these are the Sanctuary of the Egyptian Gods, with the temples of Serapion and Isis, the Sanctuary of the Syrian Gods and the Sanctuary of the Cabiri, gods of Samothrace.

To the east of the Sanctuary of the Egyptian Gods are the ruins of the Heraion, an ancient temple of Hera.

Sacred Mt Cynthus. The pathway with the steps which brings you from the temples of the foreign gods to the sacred mountain of Cynthus is that which was followed by the victors in the games of the Delia festivals, on their way to be crowned in front of the Sanctuary of Cynthian Zeus and Cynthian Athena. The remains of these sanctuaries are on the top of the sacred hill. Also on the hill is the prehistoric cave where Heracles was worshipped.

The Southern Area. The ancient Commercial Harbour was to the south of the present-day quay. In ancient times there were warehouses along the sea. At a distance of approximately one kilometre is the Bay of Phourne with the remains of the Temple of Asclepius.

The marble lions of Delos.

On the opposite page, view of antiquities and aerial photograph.

Syros

Those who wish to get to know the Cyclades could do much worse than begin with Syros, which lies at their centre and is their administrative capital. In any case, it is close to Piraeus (the trip takes only 4 hours) and there are frequent sailings.

From Syros, you can travel on to all the other islands of the Cyclades. For those in more of a hurry, Syros can also be reached by plane from Athens.

Between Kythnos and Tinos, Syros has an area of 86 sq. km., 87 km. of coastline and a population in excess of 20,000. It is a communications and transport junction and is visited by ferries from Piraeus, Rafina and to Tinos, Mykonos, Paros, Naxos, Ios, Santorini and other islands of the Cyclades.

Between Syros, Kea and Andros is the uninhabited island of **Yaros**.

Off the harbour of Ermoupoli are the islets of **Didimi** and **Strongylo**.

When those who know it think of Syros what springs to mind is a large harbour with a town which climbs high up on two hills - a town full of mansions, squares and grand churches. All the houses are old, of the last century, with their own colour and their own particular charm. Among these are the neo-Classical buildings with cornices at the windows, plaster decoration, heavy doors and the fine ironwork of their balconies.

This town is Ermoupoli and the large harbour, which even today continues to have a certain amount of movement, was for many decades of the last century Greece's most important commercial harbour.

And yet Syros is not only Ermoupoli, it is a whole island with fine beaches, attractive bays and antiquities. It is an island which has hotels, restaurants, tavernas, sports facilities and a hectic night life. In other words, it has everything the visitor might want for a short or longer stay.

Ermoupoli,
the beautiful capital
of the Cyclades.

HISTORY

The first inhabitants of Syros seem to have been Phoenicians. This is indicated chiefly by the name of the island, which would appear to be of Phoenician origin. There is also the fact that a part of the island is called 'Finikas' to this day. Syros played its part, like the other islands around it, in the development of the prehistoric Cycladic civilisation. Excavations at Halandriani and at Kastri have brought to light finds of impor-

tance which have been a great help in the study of this ancient civilisation. In dividing it up into periods, the term 'Keros - Syros' is applied to that from around 2700 BC to 2300 BC.

If we turn from prehistoric to historical times, we at once note the presence here too of the Ionians. In the 6th century BC, Syros was a flourishing island, the home of the philosopher Phere-cydes, the teacher of Pythagoras. After the Persian Wars, Syros was an ally of the Athenians. Then

followed the rule of the Macedonians, the Romans and the Byzantines.

An important date for Syros, as for all the Cyclades, was the year 1207 - the year when the Venetians came. The all-powerful Marco Sanudo took Syros and included it, together with most of the Cyclades, in his duchy, the Duchy of Naxos.

The island passed through the hands of many Venetian masters before finally falling to the Turks in 1537.

In the meantime, however, the island had begun to be colonised by large numbers of Roman Catholics, mostly engaged in commerce. Thus around 1700 there were more Catholics than Orthodox on Syros. This fact led a number of European countries, particularly France, to concern themselves with the fate of the Catholics of Syros and to undertake their protection. Thus, a Capuchin convent was founded here in the 17th century, while the Jesuits set up a house in Ano Syros - then the capital of the island (down by the sea there was only the harbour) - in the 18th. Syros, because of its large Roman Catholic population, maintained a neutral posture in the Greek Revolution of 1821. However, it took in large numbers of refugees from many parts of Greece to escape slaughter at the hands of the Turks. It was these refugees who, in the last century, built Ermoupoli.

Getting to know the island

Ermoupoli

The large harbour of Ermoupoli, with its many coffee shops and shops selling Turkish delight and 'halvadopittes' - the island's specialities - is an attractive sight. Near the harbour is the spacious Miaouli Square, dominated by its famous **Town Hall**, a neo-Classical building by the great architect Ziller. Next to the Town Hall is the 'Apollo' municipal theatre, a copy in miniature of the Scala of Milan. Not far away are the imposing church of St Nicholas and the monument to the Atafos Soldier. Higher up to the right, with a view over the sea, is the **Vaporia** quarter, with three-storey neo-Classical mansions which belonged to shipowners. There is a good Municipal Library, well stocked with old and modern volumes. The **Archaelogical Museum**, whose exhibits are mainly from the prehistoric period, is certainly worth a visit. The extensive Syros shipyards are in the southern part of the port.

Miaoulis square and Town - Hall.

Painted ceiling on neoclassical building in Ermoupolis.

Ano Syros. This is the medieval quarter of the town, built in the 13th century by the Venetians on the hill to the left; this accounts for the fact that the majority of the inhabitants are today Roman Catholics. The top of the hill is dominated by the Cathedral of St George. Still standing are the Capuchin convent with the church of St John (17th century) and the convent of the Jesuits with the church of Our Lady of Mount Carmel (18th century). The view from Ano Syros is magnificent.

TOUR OF THE ISLAND

To make a tour of the island you pass the following beaches (the kilometre distances given in brackets are the direct distances from Ermoupoli). These beaches are all served by a regular local bus service.

Vari (8 km.). A seaside village in a beautiful bay south of Ermoupoli.

Megas Yalos. (12 km.). On the southern side of the island, after Vari - a fine beach with full tourist facilities.

Angathopes, Poseidonia (Delagratsia), **Finikas**. (12 km.). Tourist resorts with very fine beaches in attractive bays with islets. Of these, the bay at Finikas is quite large.

Galissas. (8 km.). Another seaside village in a cove, with a fine beach, at present considered the island's top tourist attraction.

Kini. (9 km.). The most picturesque fishing port on Syros, with large numbers of boats and caïques, crystal-clear water and fish tavernas.

Ancient remains

Halandriani and **Kastri** (7 km. asphalt road, followed by an earth road, thereafter reached on foot). Here we find traces of the ruins of a prehistoric settlement of the Bronze Age.

Grammata. In the bay of the same name, which is on the island's north-west coast. There are ancient inscriptions on the surrounding rocks. It is reached by caïque.

*Above: Harbour of Ermoupoli
and Ano Syros.
Center: Megas Yalos and below
the gorgeous beach at Galissas.*

Paros
Antiparos

The gentle outlines of the island's mountains are in the background. A monastery stands out high up on the slopes and a chapel on the highest peak. Looking at these mountains, one would hardly think that they are the source of the best white marble in the world - that the Venus de Milo, the Hermes of Praxiteles and most of the master-pices of ancient Greece were carved from this marble.

Paros has long been a well-known tourist attraction, one of the favourite islands for visitors, together with Mykonos, Ios and Santorini. The beautiful capital of Parikia, the pretty village of Naoussa and the superb beaches are among its most popular features.

Paros is in the centre of the Cyclades. It has an area of 195 sq. km., a coastline of 119 km. and a population of 8,000. The island is famous for the quality of its wine, both red and white.

Parikia, the island's capital, on its large bay, which protects it from the *meltemi* wind, is an attractive sight. The white houses, in the Cycladic style are arrayed along the sea-front, in some cases on level ground and in others perched on rocks, a few metres above the sea. There is an old windmill, always freshly whitewashed, in front of the pier and in the background, in a small oasis of greenery, a large Byzantine church with a tiled roof: Our Lady Ekatontapyliani (or Katapoli-ani), whose feast day is 15 August, as is the case with Tinos.

The harbour of Parikia

Paros can be reached by air from Athens or by ferry from Piraeus (95 nautical miles), Rafina, the other Cyclades, Icaria, Fourni, Samos, Crete and Thessaloniki. In summer one can also go to Paros by hydrofoil from Rafina.

HISTORY

The island takes its name from Paros, the leader of the Arcadians, who went there in the 10th century BC. Before the Arcadians, the Minoan Cretans had settled on Paros, which they used as a naval base. Later came the Ionians, but the most glorious period in the history of Paros was the 8th century BC, when the island, thanks to the renown of its marble, acquired great wealth and became a major maritime power in the Aegean, establishing its own colonies. One of these colonies was Thasos, which was taken by Telesicles, father of the famous poet Archilochus. The

existence of Parian marble also meant that the island produced outstanding sculptors of its own at that period, including the famous Scopas.

However, this prosperity was disrupted by war with the Naxians and defeat at their hands. In the Persian Wars, Paros allied itself with the Persians, which provoked reprisals from the the Athenians.

In the 4th century BC, Paros was seized by the Macedonians, and later by the Romans. Thereafter it disappears from history for a long period - until 1207, when the Venetians included it in the Duchy of the Archipelago founded by Marco Sanudo. The Turks conquered the island in 1537 and laid it waste. In 1770, the Russians drove out the Turks and themselves stayed seven years, using it as a naval base. In the uprising of 1821, the Mykonian heroine Manto Mavroyenous, who was living on Paros, played an important part in the struggle, making available all her vessels. Paros was finally incorporated into Greece in 1830.

Parikia

The whole of Parikia, with its picturesque alleys, its white houses and their archways and its multitude of Cycladic churches, is a 'sight'. Of particular interest, however, is the large Byazantine **Ekatontapyliani Church**, one of the most important Early Christian monuments in Greece. It is the only church which is not white and the only church which is tiled in Parikia - the result of the careful restoration carried out by Prof. Orlandos. The name 'Ekatontapyliani' is derived from the legend that it had a hundred ('ekato') doors. However, its correct name is 'Katapoliani', meaning 'built on the site of Katapola', which in turn means 'hard by the city'. It is an Early Christian church of the 4th century, to which many alterations and additions were subsequently made. According to tradition, it was built by St Helen, the mother of the Emperor Constantine, to fulfil some vow which she had made to the Blessed Virgin when, on her way to the Holy Land to find the True Cross, she was caught in a great tempest which forced her to put in at Paros.

Some wall-paintings and a large number of old icons are preserved in the church.

The baptistry with its font in the shape of a large cross is striking.

Above Parikia, on the slopes of the mountain, is the Monastery of Sts Cosmas and Damian, which has a magnificent view over the sea and the town.

There are beaches to the right and the left of the port. However, the best beaches, protected from the *meltemi*, are at **Kaminia**, **Krio** and **Ayios Fokas**, to the north-west of Parikia.

Other places worth visiting in Parikia include the **Byzantine Museum**, which is within the precinct of the Ekatontapyliani, and, near it, the **Archaeological Museum**, which houses finds from the Neolithic to the Roman period. Among its most interesting exhibits are a 'Wingless Victory' of the school of Scopas, the Parian Chronicle, which records the history of the island from the 16th to the 3rd century BC, and an inscription and reliefs concerning the Parian poet Archilochus.

The area around the Venetian fortress, which is on a small hill to the right of the pier as we look at Paros from the sea, is also worth a visit. Here are the foundations of the ancient temple of Demeter and a large number of attractive old churches, of which the most important is that of Sts Constantine and Helen.

Another very beautiful church is that of the Presentation of the Virgin, behind the fortress.

In the quarter containing fine old mansions, near the Archaeological Museum, is the house of the heroine of 1821 Manto Mavroyenous. Parikia also contains the ruins of the Temple of Pythian Apollo and of the Asklepeion.

EXCURSIONS

1. Parikia - Lefkes - Dryos - Alyki - Parikia (50 km.)

This tour of the island does not include the Naousa area, which, because of its great interest, we shall deal with separately.

3 km. Elitas. A small village. You can take a road off to the right here to the Thapsana Nunnery, with a community of more than 20 nuns. The Nunnery occupies the place of an older foundation.

5 km. Marathi. To the right from this village are the ancient marble quarries. Scattered about the area are fragments of this marble - the material from which many masterpieces which adorn the museums and ancient temples of Greece were made.

7 km. Road junction. The road to

the left, which you do not take, leads, in one kilometre to the village of Kostos, the birthplace of the great teacher Athanasios of Paros. You take the road to the right.

11 km. Lefkes. The most beautiful village on Paros, built in the form of an amphitheatre on the surrounding hills, with gleaming white houses and and old churches and monasteries. The church of the **Holy Trinity**, built in white marble and with the whole of its interior in marble, and the Monastery of **St John Kaparos**, of the 16th century, should be visited.

The castle of Parikia with the church of Ayios Konstantinos.

14 km. A road branching to the left, which you do not follow, leads to Naousa. You take the road to the right.

15 km. Prodromos. The village owes its name to the church of St John the Baptist and Forerunner ('Prodromos'), of the 17th century. Here you turn left for Marmara.

16 km. Marpissa (Tsipidos). Another picturesque village with old churches in the Cycladic style and monasteries. Of interest are the church of the Transfiguration, which has a carved wooden screen and wall-paintings of the 17th century, and the Monasteries of St John the Baptist and of St Antony, with its fine katholiko (=main church). The latter is on a hill above the village. From Marpissa we do not turn right, but continue straight on towards the coast.

17.5 km. Piso Livadi. One of the largest resorts on Paros, with an extensive sandy beach. You continue along the sea to the south.

18.5. Logaras. A village less busy than Piso Livadi. You turn right and return to the main road.

19 km. Junction with the main road. You turn left.

20 km. A brief diversion to the left brings you to **Pounta** (not to be confused with the Pounta which is opposite the island of Antiparos).

23 km. Another brief diversion to the left leads to the fine and quiet beach of **Chrysi Akti**.

25 km. Dryos. A well-watered area with greenery - by way of contrast with most of the rest of Paros, where the water supply is derived from drillings. It has a fine beach, thanks to which it is developing as a tourist resort. Opposite is the small lislet of **Dryonisi**, ideal for fishing.

36 km. Angairia. This is the largest village in southern Paros. From here you can make a deviation to the left which leads in 2 km. to the good, large beach of Alyki.

Opposite Alyki are the uninhabited islands of **Pantieronisi, Tigani** and **Glaropounta**.

From Angairia you continue north-west, leaving behind the airport on you left.

44 km.A road off to the right leads (2 km.) to the village of **Psychopi-ana** or **Petaloudes**. The second name, which means 'butterflies', comes from the multitudes of these which can be seen here in the summer and which, on the least movement of a tree or bush, fly up in swarms, providing a beautiful and unusual spectacle. Not far from Petaloudes is the attractive Monastery of **Christ of the Wood**, which has interesting objects in its treasury.

45 km. Here you can turn off to go (3 km.) to **Pounta**, the nearest point for reaching Antiparos opposite. (In summer there is a caïque every half hour).

Opposite Pounta, between Paros and Antiparos, is the privately-owned green island of **Revmatonisi**.

50 km. Parikia. This completes this tour.

Lovely lane in Parikia.

2. Naousa - Ambelas (16 km.)

2 km. Treis Ekklisies. A fine basilica of the 6th century.

4 km. Monastery of the Archangels ('Taxiarches'). Near this monastery and on the asphalt road to Naousa, a brief deviation to the right brings you to the **Longovarda Monastery**, which dates from the 17th century and has fine wall-paintings in its katholikon, a library and an icon-painting studio. The community consists of some 25 monks.

8 km. Branch to the left with a road which leads to the finest beach on Paros, **Kolymbithres**, which has fine sand and huge rocks.

11 km. Naousa. One of the most picturesque little harbours in the Aegean. It is a real pleasure to stroll in its narrow streets with their old houses and attractive churches and to come to the **Venetian harbour**, where one can drink an ouzo, always accompanied by grilled octopus. Among the things worth seeing around here are the **Byzantine Museum**, the church of Our Lady Pantanassa, the church of St John the Divine and the many other churches, the remains of the Venetian fortress on the harbour, the Monastery of St Athanasios, where St Athanasios of Paros lived and taught, the Monastery of St George at Merovigli, one kilometre south of Naousa and the other monasteries in the area. Naousa is a place of great interest and is well supplied with tourist facilities.

From Naousa you can go as far of **Ambelas** (5 km.), a seaside village with tavernas which serve fish and where the traditional island music can be heard.

Near Naousa, at the north-western end of Paros there are many rocky islets, including **Gaïdouronisi** and **Vriokastro**.

Above: The picturesque harbour of Naousa.

Below: Renowned Kolymbithres and to the rear Naousa.

Antiparos

Antiparos is a small island to the south-west of Paros, to which it was once joined. It has low hills, a large number of good beaches and a charming litle harbour full of fishing boats. All around it are small islets forming narrow straits between them and Antiparos with shallow blue water.

Antiparos is renowned for its cave, which is of historical and natural interest.

The island has an area of 35 sq. km., a coastline of 56 km. and a population of 700. It is reached by caïque from Parikia (Paros) (3 nautical miles) or by ferry from Pounta opposite (0.5 naut. miles).

HISTORY

Between Paros and Antiparos lies a small islet, **Saliangos** where, in 1964, a Neolithic settlement dating from around 4000 BC was discovered. This fact lends support to the view that at that time the two islands were united and that man first made his appearance on Antiparos in the Neolithic age.

In the years of recorded history, Antiparos was once called Oliarus. When the Cyclades were taken by the Venetians, Antiparos, like Paros, became a part of the Duchy of Naxos. In the mid-16th century, the Venetians were succeeded by the Turks and for a brief interlude, by the Russians (in 1770). Antiparos played its part in the War of Independence of 1821 and later became part of the Greek state.

Getting to know the island

The harbour of Antiparos, with its tavernas, coffee shops and small hotels on the sea-front, is an attractive place. A central road flanked by shops leads back from the sea into a small and picturesque square. From this point you can go on to **Sifnaiïkos Yalos**, the remains of the 15th century Venetian fort, or to the camping site which is at the northern extremity of the island, on a beach opposite the islet of **Diplo**, which protects it from the *meltemi* wind.

Behind **Diplo** is another islet called **Kavouras**.

What, however, is of the greatest interest on Antiparos is its famous cave. This is in the south-western part of the island, on a hill. At its entrance is a small chapel dedicated to St John. From this point the countless steps begin. By these you descend into a great hole in the ground and see all round you vast stalactites and stalagmites in all kinds of fabulous shapes. Before the end of the steps, a branch off to the left brings you to the cave's finest stalactites and, in front of you, to a stalagmite which is called 'the altar'. An inscription records that here, on 24 December 1673, the Christmas liturgy was celebrated, in the presence of the French Ambassador to Constantinople.

The cave can be reached from Antiparos by caïque, which goes alongside the beautiful shoreline of the island, and then on foot (half an hour) or by donkey up to the cave. It can also be reached much more quickly by bus (every one or two hours) and from where the bus stops, again on foot (20 minutes) or by donkey.

Psaralyki, a beach with fine sand and swimming, is only 5 minutes from Antiparos town. Other beaches are **Sifnaiïkos Yalos**, those in the northern part of the island, opposite Diplo islet, and near the camping site - as well as in the south, at **Ai Yorgi**, opposite the islet of **Despotiko**, which itself has an excellent beach. South-west of Despotiko is the islet of **Strongyli**.

The cave of Antiparos.

Naxos

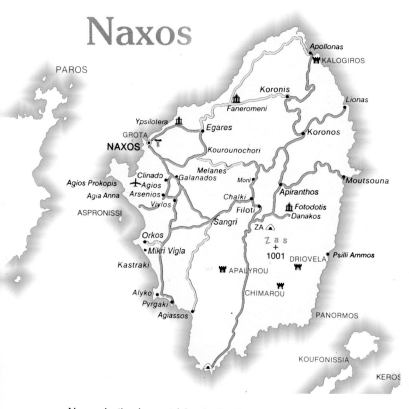

In mythology, Naxos is the island of Bacchus and Ariadne. Bacchus, the god of wine, was living here when Theseus, returning from Crete, abandoned Ariadne, the daughter of King Minos, who had helped him to slay the Minotaur, on the island. But Ariadne finally found consolation in the arms of Bacchus and became his wife.

Naxos was inhabited before the final years of the Early Cycladic period, that is, before 2000 BC, and played an important role in the development of Cycladic civilisation. However, the ´golden age´ for the island was the 7th and 6th centuries BC. At that period Naxos was master of virtually all the Cyclades and developed its trade and its art, particularly sculpture. Examples of this art can be encountered in many parts of Greece, as at Delphi with the marble sphinx of the Naxians and on Delos with the famous Lions and the House and

The gate of the temple of Apollo, "Portara".

Naxos is the largest island of the Cyclades, with their highest mountain - Za (Zeus), which in the distance looks like a large pyramid. Chora with its Frankish castle, a white medieval town built on a hill above the harbour, is an imposing sight. On the left of the castle, at the highest point of the small island which is now united with Chora, is the huge marble gate of the temple of Apollo - the ´Portara´ as it is called locally. There is another little island in the harbour which is just big enough to accommodate the Chapel of Our Lady Myrtidiotissa.

Naxos is a fertile island, with a rich variety of landscape: meadows alternate with long beaches, gorges full of oleanders with rugged mountains which contain the black emery.

It also has its pretty Cycladic villages and large numbers of Venetian towers scattered over it, old, very old, Byzantine churches, and the famous, more than life-size marble kouroi.

Until a few years ago, Naxos was outside the mainstream of tourism. Since then, things have changed.

The number of visitors has increased and so has the number of hotels and rented rooms to accommodate them. At the moment there is frenzy of building going on, particularly in Chora, so that the island can respond to the increasing influx of tourists.

Almost in the centre of the Cyclades and very close to Paros, Naxos is 103 nautical miles from Piraeus. It has an area of 428 sq. km., a shoreline of 148 km. and a population of 18,000.

Naxos can be reached by air from Athens and by ferry from Piraeus, Rafina, the other Cyclades, Icaria, Samos, the Dodecanese and Crete. In summer there is also a service provided by ´flying dolphins´ from Rafina.

The island is renowned for the quality of its cheeses, its honey and its meat. Citron, a fruit from which the island´s own liqueur is made, is considered a speciality of Naxos. Its other products are its marble and emery, a mineral used for the grind of metals.

The town of Naxos, the harbour and the Palatia.

Stoa of the Naxians. In 490 BC, Naxos was laid waste by the multitudes of the Persian army, which was then beginning its campaign against Greece.

In 479 BC, at Plataeae, the Naxians took part in the battle against the Persians, together with other Greeks. Thereafter, for many years the island was under the rule of the Athenians. In 338 BC, it was taken by the Macedonians and later (in 166 BC) by the Romans. This was followed by the lengthy Byzantine period, during which many fine churches were built on the island, some of which are the oldest to have survived anywhere in the Balkans. The Byzantine period was followed by Venetian rule. In 1210, the Venetian Marco Sanudo was made Duke of Naxos and built the famous castle of Chora. The Sanudo dynasty continued to rule the island for a long period and extended its rule far beyond it.

Venetian rule was succeeded in 1566 by Turkish occupation, during the course of which St Nicodemus

A Sphinx, a dedication of the Naxians at Delphi.

the Athonite was born and lived on Naxos which played its part in the War of Independence by sending an army to the mainland to fight with their compatriots.

Naxos or Chora

As we enter the harbour, on our left, on the islet of **Palatia**, are the remains of the **Temple of Apollo**, the building of which was begun at the end of the 6th century BC, when Ligdamis was the ruler of Naxos. Building stopped, however, when war broke out between Naxos and Samos. Today there are only the foundations and the imposing marble gate, the **Portara**, as it is known locally.

The **Venetian castle** is an imposing building standing on the hill above the harbour. The castle walls served as the outer walls of the mansions of the Venetian nobles, descendants of whom continue to live in them to this day. Above the doors we can still see the marble coats of arms of these families and their names: Barotsi, Dellarocca, Sommaripa. Also in the castle is the ruined tower of the Duke of Naxos Marco Sanudo. There is also the building of the school which the Cretan author Nikos Kazantzakis attended for a while, which today houses the **Archaeological Museum**, the building of the school of the Ursuline nuns and the Roman Catholic cathedral. On the northern sea-front of Chora, at **Grota**, remains have been found of a Mycenaean settlement.

Worth a visit are the Cathedral and **Monastery of St John Chrysostom**, 3 km. from Chora, with a fine view to sea.

Next to Chora are the beaches of Ayiou Georgiou and Palatia.

The chapel of Myrtidiotissa on the harbour of Naxos.

1. Naxos - Apeiranthos - Apollonas (48 km.)

You follow the main road which leads from Chora into the interior of the island.

5.5 km. Galanados.

6 km. The Tower of Belonia. On the right of the road. Belonia was a Venetian nobleman who for many years was lord of the whole of Livadi. Next to the tower is the two-aisled chapel of St John. One of the aisles was an Orthodox and the other a Roman Catholic church.

8 km. A path downhill to the left leads, in 15 minutes, to **Ai Mamas**, one of the oldest Byzantine churches on the island (built around the 9th century) with sculpture and traces of wall-paintings.

11 km. If you make a deviation to the right which takes you to the road for Chora, Glynados and Pyrgaki, you pass, after 500 m., close to **Ano Sangri**, a village on a hill with a fine view. In the village is the attractive **Monastery of St Eleutherios**, built in the Cycladic style. This is one of the oldest monasteries on Naxos and during the years of Turkish occupation was an important religious and cultural centre.

Half an hour on foot from Sangri are the ruins of an important ancient temple, the **Temple of Demeter** of the 6th century BC. A Christian basilica was built on top of it (St John Gyroulas) and its marble was used for building materials. Fortunately, most of the fragments of the ancient temple have been found and classified and restoration is planned.

Half an hour on foot from Sangri are the ruins of a 6th century Temple of Demeter.

Ten minutes away from Sangri is the Byzantine church of St Nicholas, with wall paintings from 1270.

12.5 km. If you leave the main route and go off to the right, you come, after 10 km., to the beach of **Ayiassos**, a little village with fine sand and a restaurant. On the road to Ayiassos, to the left, a path leads after half an hour's walk to **Kastro t´Apalirou.**

The square with the plane trees at Filoti.

16 km. Halki. A village of grandeur, in the middle of a vast olive grove and with a fine Byzantine church, **Our Lady Protothroni**, of the 12th century, and a three-storey **Venetian tower**, which was built in the early 17th century by Barotsi. Very close to Halki is the church of St George Diasoritis (11th century) with wall-paintings.

Also from Halki it is possible to go part of the way by car to **Epano Kastro** and then continue on foot (30 mins). In addition a road from Halki off to the left leads, after 4 km., to the village of **Moni**. A little before the village is the church of **Our Lady Drosiani** with interesting architecture and the oldest wall-paintings in the Balkans. From here a new road shertens the trip to Apollonas.

19 km. Filoti. The largest village on Naxos, built in the manner of an amphitheatre on the slopes of **Za** with tavernas and pizzerias. In the village is Our Lady Filotitissa, a fine church with a marble screen and old icons.

From Filoti, after the first bends in the road which goes uphill towards Apeiranthos, is the path which leads to the **Aria tou Za cave**, which is reached in 45 minutes. As the finds, which are in the Apeiranthos museum, show, this cave was a place of worship of Zeus. Later, according to tradition, it served as a church, dedicated to the Life-receiving Fount, and at the same time as a refuge for Christians during the Turkish occupation. From Filoti, following a poor earth road, you can go to **Pyrgos tou Cheimarrou**, a four-storey circular fortification built of vast blocks of marble, in the south-east of the island.

23 km. If you make a deviation to the right, you come, in 2 km., to the village of **Danako**. Above Danako is the **Fotodoti Monastery**, the oldest on Naxos, which looks like a castle in a fairy-story. According to tradition, it was built by the Empress Irene.

27 km. Apeiranthos or **Aperathou**. A famous mountain village, with marble mansions, Byzantine churches and points of interest for students of folklore. The local dialect with its drawl, the ease with which the local singers can improvise verses and the devotion of the residents to the folk tradition are reminiscent of Crete, from which they ultimately come.

At Apeiranthos, the church of our **Lady Apeirathitissa** with its marble screen, the small but interesting **Archaeological Museum**, the fine Zevgolis tower of the 17th century, which belonged to Venetian nobles and has been restored, and the Bardanis tower, with a coat of arms with lions, are worth a visit. In the Apeiranthos area there are many old churches, such as St Kyriake, of the 9th century, on the road to the emery mines, whose decoration is famous.

From Apeiranthos, a road off to the right leads, after 12 km., to **Moutsouna**, the port of the village.

33 km. You have now come from Apeiranthos and are on your main route. At this point, by turning off to the right, you can reach, after 2 km., the **church of Our Lady Argokiliotissa**. Thousands of pilgrims from all over the island gather here.

33.5 km. Another route off to the right leads, after 6km., to the beach of **Liona**.

34 km. Koronos. A pretty mountain village on the slopes of a steep ravine. Many of the inhabitants work in the emery mines.

39 km. Koronis. Also called **Komiaki** by the local people. This is the highest village on the island (700 m.) with a fine view out to sea.

47 km. There is a junction with the earth road which comes along the coast from Chora. A deviation a few metres to the left, on this earth road, brings us to the colossal marble **kouros of Apollonas**, of a length of 10.5 m. It lies in its original position, in a marble quarry. It was never finished, but we do not know why. According to one view, it is not intended to be a kouros, but the god Bacchus.

48 km. Apollonas. An attractive bay with a sandy beach and a village of the same name.

You come to the end of your tour. You can alternatively return to Chora along the north-west coast, via **Engares** (or via Moni - see 16th km Halki).

Worth a visit on this route are the monastery and the **tower of Ayia**, the bay of **Abrami** (a little off your route) with a beach and a taverna, the large **Monastery of the Faneromeni**, the village of **Engares**, with many orchards in which its famous apricots are grown and the **tower-monastery of Our Lady Ipsilotera**, built c. 1600.

Kouros and the harbour of Apollonas.

2. Naxos - Vivlos (Tripodes) - Pyrgaki (20 km.)

This excursion takes you to the fine spacious beaches of western Naxos. You follow the Apeiranthos road and at 5 km., before Galanados, turn right.

5.5 km. Glinado.

7 km. Ayios Arsenios. In this village, which is called locally **Ayersani**, is the Monastery of St John the Baptist, built in 1721.

A little before Ayios Arsenios, a road off to the right leads, after 4 km., to the beach of **Ayia Anna**, one of the biggest tourist centres on Naxos.

By the same road you can also reach the excellent beach of **Ayios Prokopios**, another tourist resort, but the quickest way to reach this beach is from Chora along the coast (6 km.).

8 km. Vivlos (Tripodes). A picturesque village with windmills and an old church, Our Lady Tripodiotissa, which has a fine wooden screen and icons.

10 km. Road junction with a road going off to the left to Sangri and there joining the main Chora - Apeiranthos road. You keep straight on.

14 km. If you go off to the right, you come, after 3 km., to a good beach at **Mikri Vigla** and Orkos, which are developing into summer resorts. The beach stretches south for 6 km.

15 km. Another deviation to the right leads, after 800 m., to the **Kastraki** beach.

18 km. Alyko. Here the asphalt road comes to an end next to a sandy headland covered with small cedars. Around this headland are bays with some of the best beaches on the island and with crystal-clear, emerald waters. The southern bays are best, as they are sheltered from the *meltemi*. However, the western side of the headland, with earth cliffs and virgin sands, is also excellent.

20 km. Pyrgaki. Three more sheltered bays with superb sand.

Above, the tower of Cheimarros, center, Ayia Anna Below, sand beach of Orkos.

3. Naxos - Melanes - Flerio (kouros) (11 km.)

You take the road to Apeiranthos and at 3 km. turn left for Melanes.

9 km. Kourounochori. Here the large Frangopoulos tower, at which King Othon was entertained in 1833, is a prominent feature.

11 km. Flerio. This is a picturesque site, with a spring of water nearby welling up from the foot of the mountain, with the island's finest **kouros** lying on its back in a garden. It dates from the 7th century BC, is 6.5 m. long and has one of the legs broken.

Ios

Many believe that Ios is the most beautiful island in the Cyclades. The pretty little chapel of St Irene at the entrance to the harbour, the town of Chora, white above the harbour, climbing up a hillside, with a chapel at the top - all this at once creates this impression. And then comes an exploration of Chora, with its narrow alleys, shops, bars, pubs and tavernas. Everything is on a charming small, doll's house, scale. This can be followed by a walk out of Chora to the level ground which has the old windmills standing in a line. After, there is a downhill walk to the beach, which is to the right of the town. A delightful bay with a wonderful beach lies before you. You see a mass of people on the sand, in the water, in the cafés, most of them young. They have come here from all over Greece, from all over Europe and from even further afield to enjoy the sun and the sea. This is the famous Mylopotas beach - one of the finest in Greece (length 1 km.).

This is Ios, the island where Homer is said to be buried. It lies between Naxos and Santorini and is 111 nautical miles from Piraeus. It has an area of 108 sq. km., a coastline of 80 km. and a population of 1,500.

The island can be reached from Piraeus by ferry all the year round.

From Ios, we can sail on to many of the other islands in the Cyclades, to Crete and to the Dodecanese.

HISTORY

Chora stands near the site of the ancient city of Ios. Tradition relates that Homer was buried on Ios. There is, in fact, a ruin at Plakoto, which is called the tomb of Homer.

As is the case with the other Cyclades, the Venetians were here and have left a fortress behind, in this case built in the 15th century.

Mylopot...

The port (Ormos, as it is called) has a good beach to the north, but most visitors go to **Mylopotas**.

There is an asphalt road - 2 km. - from the port to **Chora** and this continues to the Mylopotas beach. If you do not wish to climb along the uphill path, it is possible to take a bus. There is a regular service. A stroll about Chora, with its Cycladic churches and its marvellous view of the sea, is a pleasant experience.

Mylopotas bay is 3 km. from Chora, and can be reached by bus. It has a vast and excellent beach.

Manganari is a settlement in a large bay with an excellent beach, at the southern extremity of the island.

Ayia Theodoti has a beach, and a camping site. It is on the east coast of the island and can be reached by an earth road. It is also possible to go there by caïque if the weather is good.

Psathi is a small village on the east coast. It can be reached by car or caïque.

Above, Chora
and below the harbour of Ios.

"The Aegean", 1988
Oil on canvas (90 × 110)
Work by K. Grammatopoulos.

Lesser Cyclades

NAXOS

EPANO KOUFONISSI

KOUFONISSIA⊚

KATO KOUFONISSI

Messara•

⊚SCHINOUSSA

Agios Georgios•

IRAKLIA
⊚

Charavgı

•⊚ •*Mersini*

DONOUSSA •

⊚KEROS

A. ANTIKERI

K. ANTIKERI

Near Koufonisia is the uninhabited island of **Keros**. This was an important center of the very ancient Cycladic civilization. This explains why there are on Keros and the neighbouring islets remains of this civilisation, while various important finds are now in museums. Among them are the famous marble figurines of the harpist and the flautist of Keros, which are in the Archaeological Museum in Athens.

Schinousa

These are islands on what are termed in shipping 'unprofitable routes'. It is only a few years since their fine beaches, their unspoilt natural beauty, their plentiful fish and their simple and peaceful way of life were discovered.

Of these, **Irakleia, Schinousa** and the **Koufonisia** are approximately three miles south of Naxos. A little further off is **Keros**, now an uninhabited island, where many finds have been made by archaeologists.

Last is **Donousa**, east of Naxos and somewhat isolated. **Amorgos** is close to all of them and there is a regular service to and from there, as there is with Naxos.

All the islands can be reached by ferry from Piraeus. There is also a 'flying dolphin' service from Rafina to Irakleia, Schinousa and the Koufonisia.

The Lesser Eastern Cyclades are a starting-point for a visit to many of the islands of the Cyclades and in summer to the Dodecanese.

Although these islands have not yet developed their tourist facilities, the few small hotels and the rented rooms can cater to a number of visitors.

There are no motor cars on the Lesser Eastern Cyclades, apart from some agricultural vehicles. They thus provide an opportunity for walking, given that the distances are short, or for boat trips to their excellent beaches.

The large sand beach of Koufonisia.

Irakleia

This is perhaps the most primitive of the three islands (it has 120 inhabitants), with its port of **Ayios Georgios**, the ruins of the castle (15 minutes from the harbour) and **Irakleia** or **Chora**, which is one hour on foot from Ayios Georgios. From Chora it is possible to visit the **Cave of the Cyclops**, which is on the south-western side of the island (45 mins). A guide from the village and a torch will be needed.

irakleia

Donousa

On Irakleia there is the beach on the bay of Ayios Georgios - the island's port. There is also a good beach at **Livadi**, 15 mins from Ayios Georgios. Both are open to the north wind.

Schinousa

This is an island of low hills, with **Chora** roughly in the center, indented all round with bays with fine beaches. One of these serves as the little harbour of **Mersini**. Schinousa has another small village at **Mesaria**. There are 150 inhabitants.

On Schinousa there are six very beautiful coves with sandy beaches all round Chora. These are **Mersini**, 10 mins from Chora, **Tsingoura**, 15 mins, **Livadi**, 20 mins (all these three are protected from the *meltemi* wind), and, further off, **Almyros, Liouliou** and **Psili Ammos**.

Koufonisia

These consist of two islets, **Epano** and **Kato Koufonisi**. Kato Koufonisia is inhabited only seasonally and has a few deserted beaches. Interest thus centers on Epano Koufonisia (where the ferry puts in), which has some 300 inhabitants, large numbers of fishing boats and attractive beaches.

On **Epano Koufonisi** there are five excellent beaches in a row. The first is in the port. From that point, you continue to the northeast and encounter every five minutes a fine sheltered beach. After 25 mins you reach **Pori**, a circular bay, which looks as though it has been laid out using dividers.

This is the island's finest beach. On the north side of the arm which protects the bay there is a famous sea cave.

Donousa

This island has only 130 inhabitants, distributed among the villages of **Donousa** (the port, called Stavros by the local people), **Haravghi, Mersini** and **Kalotaritissa**.

There is a good beach in the bay where the ferry puts in, but there are also others, such as Kentros, perhaps the island's best.

Amorgos

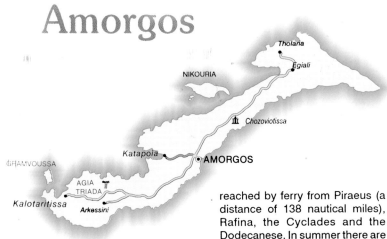

This is the most easterly island of the Cyclades and the nearest to Astypalaia and the rest of the Dodecanese. It has two ports: attractive Katapola and Ormos Aiyialis with its marvellous beach. The town of Chora stands high on the rugged mountains, while the renowned Hozoviotissa Monastery, gleaming white, is perched on the rock of a sheer cliff.

Amorgos has an area of 121 sq. km., a shoreline of 112 km. and a population of 1,800. It can be reached by ferry from Piraeus (a distance of 138 nautical miles), Rafina, the Cyclades and the Dodecanese. In summer there are also 'flying dolphins' from Rafina.

The local buses provide transport on the island. These go from Katapola to Chora, the Hozoviotissa Monastery and the Ayia Anna and Aiyiali beach. The island's attractive beaches - Ayios Pantaleimon, Faros, Paradeisia and Kalotaritissa - are reached by caïque.

In spite of the fact that the island's tourist facilities are still in their infancy, its hotels and rented rooms are capable of catering to large numbers of visitors.

HISTORY

Amorgos has been inhabited since prehistoric times, as is demonstrated by finds from the Early Cycladic Period. The presence on the island of Cretans of the Minoan period has also been established. At the top of a hill above the southern side of the harbour, at Katapola, the remains of ancient Minoa, said to have been the summer residence of Minos, have been found. There are the sites of two other ancient cities on the island: Arkesine and Aegiale.

The island later passed under the rule of the Athenians. It then belonged to the Ptolemies, and subsequently the Romans. It fell to other conquerors and finally, in 1209, to the Venetian Marco Sanudo, who incorporated it into the Duchy of Naxos. After three centuries, it was taken by the Turks, to be liberated in 1832 and united to Greece.

The attractive Aiyiali.

Getting to know the island

Katapola. This is the port of Chora, with an attractive harbour, consisting of three separate districts built on the slopes of the hills which overlook the sheltered bay. It is the most southerly of these hills, the highest and the most imposing, which has at its top the remains of the ancient Minoa.

Chora. This stands at a height of 320 m. and is linked with Katapola by a 5 km. asphalt road. A stroll in its picturesque streets with their gleaming white houses, typical examples of Cycladic architecture, is to be recommended.

Hozoviotissa Monastery. This is not only the most interesting monument on the island, but is one of the finest monasteries in Greece. It was built around 1017 and renovated in 1088 by the Emperor Alexius Comnenus. It has fine icons and important relics. What, however, makes it so impressive is the position in which it is built. It is perched on a vertical rock, 300 metres above the sea. It has a magnificent view out over the open sea.

Aiyiali. This is the second port of Amorgos, in the northern part of the island. It has a good beach. There is an earth road from Katapola, but it is of poor quality.

Out in the sea between Aiyiali and Katapola is the uninhabited islet of **Nikouria**, while to the south of Amorgos, before **Kalotaritissa** bay is the islet of **Gramvousa**. To the south-west, at a considerable distance, lies the islet of **Anydro**.

Above: Chora.

Below: The monastery of Hozoviotissa on a sheer cliff and crystal - clear water of Ayia Anna.

Sikinos

The north-western part of Sikinos is an almost vertical cliff. There, on its edge, at a height of 280 m., is Chora, primitive but at the same time attractive. The opposite side of the island, the south-east, is less dramatic and the ground rises gently up to Chora. The island's port, Alopronia or Ano Pronia, is on this side of the island, sheltered from the *meltemi* wind.

Sikinos has a large number of olive trees, producing a small-sized olive, said to be the source of the very best oil.

The island lies in the southern Cyclades, between Ios and Folegandros. It has an area of 41 sq. km., a coastline of 41 km. and a population of 300.

Sikinos has a poor tourist infrastructure, but with its beautifully clean sea and unspoiled natural features, it is ideal for peaceful holidays.

The island can be reached by ferry from Piraeus (a distance of 113 nautical miles), the Cyclades, Crete and the Dodecanese.

Between Sikinos and Folegandros are the uninhabited islands of **Kardiotissa** and **Kaloyeri**, of which the former is larger.

HISTORY

The island owes its name to Sicinus, son of King Thoas of Lemnos. It was also called Oenoe, a reference to its many vines. Its first inhabitants seem to have come there in the Mycenean era. They were followed by the Ionians.

In the 5th century BC it was under the domination of Athens. During the period of Venetian rule, it belonged to the Duchy of Naxos. In 1537 it was taken by the Turks, to be liberated in 1821 and later united with Greece.

Getting to know the island

Alopronia. The name is a corruption of Ano Pronia. This is the island's port and it has a small beach.

Chora. On the edge of a cliff above the sea, Chora is primitive, still untouched by the mainstream of tourism, and yet attractive to the visitor. The beautiful Church of the Pantanassa stands out, gleaming white, in the village. It has a carved wooden screen and old icons. At the north-east end of Chora a pathway climbs to the white-walled Chrysopigi Monastery (20 mins), which has a very fine view. It was here that the inhabitants used to take refuge from pirate raids. The katholikon (main church) of the monastery is dedicated to Our Lady 'the Life-receiving Fount'.

Episkopi. This is one hour, 15 mins on foot from Chora, to the south-west. Remains found here are very probably those of a temple to Pythian Apollo. A church dedicated to the Dormition of the Virgin stands on its site.

Other places worth visiting on Sikinos are Ayia Marina and Paliokastro.

Folegandros

The first inhabitants of the island were the Carians and the Phoenicians. They were followed by the Cretans, who, according to one version of the story, were led by one Pholegandrus, who thus gave his name to the island. Then came the Dorians and, later, the Athenians. The Venetians under Marco Sanudo were responsible for building the old part of Chora and the fortress at the beginning of the 13th century.

The Monastery of Our Lady.

This Cycladic island, which is now acquiring more and more admirers, was virtually unknown until a few years ago. Now they come to this island, which lies between Sikinos and Milos, prepared for whatever hardships they may encounter.

They disembark at the little port, Karavostasis, and from there they hasten, without losing any time, up to Chora, because it is up there that the interest lies. It is there that the Cycladic architecture, in its most genuine form, blends with the imposing landscape and becomes one with it. On one side are the picturesque alleyways, with their whitewashed paving stones, the white houses with their archways, staircases and wooden balconies, and, on the other, the sheer rock, 200 metres above the sea. Chora ends there, on the edge of this cliff, where there is a marvellous 'balcony' over the Aegean, which, if Santorini did not exist, would be unique in Greece. Folegandros also has to show, near Chora, the beautiful Church of Our Lady, with its unusual architecture, and the Monastery of Our Lady at the top of the hill. It is reached by a pretty paved pathway, always freshly whitewashed, which forms a zigzag on the side of the hill, next to the imposing cliff.

Folegandros also has to offer a paradise for scuba divers. The island has an area of 32 sq. km., a coastline of 40 km. and a population of 600. There are ferries from Piraeus, which is 105 nautical miles away, all the year round and a catamaran service in summer.

Picturesque lane in Folegandros

Getting to know the island

Karavostasis. A little port with fish tavernas, coffee shops, a very few hotels and rented rooms. It has a small beach with clean water and some rocky islets opposite.

Chora. Chora is 4 km. from the port. It is one of the most attractive and typical villages of the Cyclades. The houses of old Chora, within the **Venetian fortress**, are built on the edge of a sheer cliff and have a magnificent view out to sea. Chora has small hotels and rooms to rent.

Outside Chora, the white-walled and beautiful **church of Our Lady** and, on top of the hill, 20 mins away, the **Monastery of Our Lady** catch the eye.

Ano Mera. The third village of the island, 5 km. south-west of Chora, with a good folklore museum.

Angali. A small settlement with the best beach on the island, 20 mins on foot from the Chora - Ano Mera road.

Chryssospilia. A marvellous cave with stalactites and stalagmites near the sea on the north coast of the island. It can be reached only by caïque from Karavostasis.

Santorini

If one were to have to choose only two or three places which are worth seeing in Greece, Santorini would be without doubt among them. Such is the beauty of this island - a wild, other-wordly beauty created by an apocalyptic upheaval, by a volcano which lies in the middle of the island's bay like a black monster which is sleeping half immersed in the sea. And around the monster, like a half moon, is what remains of an island which has sunk: a vast multi-coloured rock, black, red, grey, brown. High up on the ridge of the rock, all round, is the evidence of the taming of, and the reconciliation with the wild and the weird: the white crown of houses, arches, terraces, churches with their domes. These are Fira, Firostefani and Imerovigli, with Oia further off and, opposite, on an islet, Thirasia, itself a remnant of the large island which has been lost.

Man, ignoring the monster and settling up there provocatively, boldly, has left his mark everywhere. Was it ignorance of the

View of Santorini with volcano. From the magazine "The Illustra

danger which brought him there to the cliff's edge? Was it the splendour of the superb landscape, the magnet of the marvellous spectacle?

This then is famous Santorini. Any visit to this, one of the best known of islands, will be unforgettable. You can enjoy a stroll in the charming alleyways of Fira, take a trip by car to Oia, on top of the red rocks, go by motor boat to the volcano and in the evening find whatever kind of entertainment appeals to you most.

ondon News", 31 March 1866.

You can visit ancient Thera and the Minoan city unearthed from the ash at Akrotiri. And if you still have time, you can go down to one of the beaches with their black pebbles, at Kamari or Perissa, to swim in their crystal-clear water.

Santorini or Thira is the southernmost island of the Cyclades. It has an area of 76 sq. km., a coastline of 70 km. and a population of approximately 8,000. The island is famous for the quality of its wines and for a dish made from chick-peas called 'fava'. Among its other products are tomato paste and minerals such as pumice and pozzolana.

Santorini can be reached by air from Athens, Mykonos, Rhodes and Herakleion (Crete) and by ferry from Piraeus (130 nautical miles), the Cyclades, Crete, the Dodecanese and Thessaloniki.

HISTORY

The first inhabitants of Santorini were the pro-Hellenes, who made their appearance there around 3000 BC. The influence of Minoan Crete on the island became obvious when excavations began at Akrotiri and revealed, beneath a thick layer of ash, a whole settlement with two and three-storey houses decorated with wall-paintings similar to those in the Minoan palaces of Crete.

When this settlement was built, the island was called Kalliste or Strongyle ('round') from its shape, since the volcano had not yet begun its destructive activity.

It was in around 1450 BC that an event took place which completely altered the history of the ancient world. This was the terrible eruption of the volcano, which was in the centre of the island, and the subsidence of the greater part of it into the sea. The tidal wave caused by the eruption, whose height has been calculated at about 100 m., struck the north coast of Crete and swept away the palace of Knossos. It was perhaps this which marked the end of Minoan civilization. The devastation was completed by major earthquakes

Fabulous wall paintings from Akrotiri.

and the ash which was propelled by the volcano over large distances. All that remained of the old Strongyle was the 'half moon' shape which we see today, with the sheer cliff, more than 300 m. high, on the western side and the level beach on the east. The half moon was itself subsequently covered with a layer of ash 30 to 40 metres thick. Eruptions, on a smaller scale, continued in the 3rd century BC, when Thirasia was separated from the main island, in the 2nd century BC, when the volcanic islets (Palaia Kameni) began to appear in the bay and down to 1928, while in 1956 a major earthquake demolished most of the houses of Santorini. Serious pieces of research have suggested that the island which was submerged was the controversial **Atlantis**.

In spite of the activity of the volcano, history, perhaps held back to some extent, continued its course on Santorini. In the 11th century BC, the Dorians came to the island, led by Theras, to whom the island owed its new name. The Dorians built the ancient city of Thera high up, on the south-eastern side of Santorini. (While on the subject of the island's name, it should be pointed out that Santorini is a later name for the island and is derived from 'Santa Irene', a very popular saint with the islanders.) In the Peloponnesian War, the island allied itself with Sparta and later passed under Athenian control. The Venetians came here in 1207 under Marco Sanudo, who incorporated the island into the Duchy of Naxos.

The Turks took the island a little later than the rest of the Cyclades (c. 1570). It was united to the new Greek state, together with the other islands of the Cyclades, in 1832.

Getting to know the island

Fira. Fira is the capital of the island and stands on the edge of a sheer cliff, 260 m. above the sea. The combination of magnificent landscape and volcano with the famous Cycladic architecture makes Fira one of the world's most beautiful places. The village can be reached by car from **Athinio** (10 km.), the port where the ferries put in, or one can climb on foot from the little harbour of Fira or go on a donkey, using the picturesque pathway which zigzags across the face of the rock. If, however, you want a more comfortable and up-to-date mode of ascent, you can use the cable car. It has to be admitted that rebuilding, the crowds and the noise have altered the face of Fira.

Nevertheless, a stroll through its streets is still a unique experience. The white houses with their arches, the terraces and balconies with their superb views, the domed churches, the tavernas, the bars and the shops with their bustle, have a charm of their own. You can visit the **Archaeological Museum**, which has important finds from Akrotiri (chiefly pottery) and ancient Thera, the old **Catholic Dominican Convent** and the Orthodox and Catholic cathedrals. What you should on no account miss is a visit to the **Nea** and **Palaia Kameni** islands, to see the volcano. On disembarking on Nea Kameni, you can take a 30 min. walk to see the crater.

Suitable shoes should be worn because the ground is warm. This trip can be made by caïque from **Skala ton Firon** (it takes only ten minutes). There is also a longer trip which takes you, apart from the volcano, to the islet of **Aspronisi**, the quaint island of **Thirasia** (both are parts of the old island of Santorini which sank) and to **Oia**.

The fabled Oia.

Another walk which is particularly worthwhile is to **Firostefani** (1 km.) and **Imerovigli** (3 km.), which are north of Fira and have the same magnificent view. At Imerovigli is the old Orthodox **Nunnery of St Nicholas**.

Finikia (10.5 km.). A little before Oia. A fine village with interesting churches.

Oia (11 km.). In the northern part of the island. Very picturesque and more primitive than Fira. The end of a bus route.

It has a Venetian fortress and old houses. The little road which goes downhill over strikingly red soil leads to the fishing harbour of Oia. North-east of Oia, out at sea and at a distance of approximately 7 km. from the shore is the second volcanic crater, Kaloumbos, whose eruption in 1650 caused great damage. The beaches of **Armenis** and **Ammoudi** are reached by more than 200 steps.

Mesaria (3.5 km.). A village in the middle of the island, surrounded by vineyards.

Monolithos (7 km.). The nearest beach south-east of Fira, from which there is a bus service.

Pyrgos Kallistis (6 km.). The highest village on the island, south of Fira, on the foothills of the Profitis Ilias mountain.

Monastery of the Prophet Elijah (10 km.). On the peak of the mountain (height 560 m.). An Orthodox monastery with old icons, relics and a folklore museum.

Episkopi or Mesa Gonia (8 km. south-east of Fira). A short distance from the village is its Byzantine church, of the 11th century.

Kamari (10 km.). A fine beach of black pebbles, 2 km. from Episkopi. It attracts large numbers of tourists.

Ancient Thera. 2.5 km. from Kamari and on the **Mesa mountain**. The remains, dug out from below the pumice, cover a large area and include temples, a market place, a theatre, baths and tombs. This ancient city was inhabited by the Dorians, the Romans and the Byzantines.

Ancient site of Akrotiri (16 km.). Two km. after the village of Akrotiri, on the south-western extremity of the island, is Santorini's most important archaeological site. It has been called a prehistoric Pompeii and it deserves the name. It was in 1967 that Prof. **Spyros Marinatos** discovered beneath a thick layer of pumice and pozzolana an entire Minoan city with two and

The famous Kamari beach.

three-storey houses decorated with wall-paintings resembling those in the Minoan palaces of Crete.

The most important of these wall-paintings are 'the naval expedition', the 'coming of spring' and 'boys boxing'. There were also large numbers of vessels, storage jars, bronze utensils and furniture which were found in the houses. The whole of this city was buried as a result of the fearful eruption of the volcano, around 1450 BC. Today the remains are protected by a vast roof which allows the daylight to pass through.

Emboreio (11 km.). A pretty village, with the second largest population, in the southern part of the island, with old narrow alleyways.

Perissa (14 km.). Another good beach, below ancient Thera, south-east of Fira.

Kokkini Beach near Akrotiri.

Untamed nature combined with Aegean architecture.

Below: Detail of its colourful debles of Kokkini Beach.

Santorini - Fira

Thirasia

Thirasia is the second-largest island in the group which makes up the caldera. Isolated from the main bulk of Santorini, it lies one mile to the south-west of Oia. The main village on the island is also called Thirasia, and it stands on the brow of a cliff with a view across to Fira and the whole of Santorini. To reach the village, you climb a flight of 145 steps from the little harbour.

At the southern extremity of the island is a cave near the sea, known as **Tripiti**, with two entrances. The north part of the island, where the chapel to St Irene stands, probably conceals valuable antiquities.

Fish tavernas and a few rented rooms are to be found at the little port.

Anafi

A small island with a disproportionately high mountain, which makes it look like a large cone rising out of the sea. It has a primitive harbour and its Chora, gleaming white, stands at a high altitude. These are one's first impressions of Anafi, a bare island once on an 'unprofitable' shipping route at the south-eastern extremity of the Cyclades, and known only as a place of exile.

Most of its inhabitants abandoned it in the reign of King Othon and went to settle on the northern slopes of the Acropolis in Athens, in a quarter known for that reason as 'Anafiotika'.

And yet these small islands of the Cyclades each have their own grace and charm. We go back to them wearied by the crowds and the noise of the city, choked by the exhaust fumes. And if we cannot stay for ever on these islands, we can go for a little while, in order to take a taste of peace and quiet, simplicity, a natural way of life. We can go for a swim in the crystal clear water, eat in some charming little taverna with the hospitable people of the island and stay in some simple room, far from noise and luxury.

'Anafi is the island which, in mythology, rose from the waves at the command of Apollo to save the Argonauts from the savage storm which overtook them on their voyage.

Why not benefit from this 'miracle' - as vistors, of course, not as castaways.

Anafi is 12 nautical miles east of Santorini. It has an area of 38 sq. km. and a population of approximately 300. Its distance from Piraeus, from which there is a ferry service, is 145 nautical miles.

HISTORY

Apart from the tradition which describes Anafi as the refuge of Jason and the Argonauts, there is another which relates that the first inhabitant of the island was Membliarus, who travelled with Cadmus in search of Europa. For this reason the island was also called Membliarus or Bliarus in antiquity.

On the hill occupied today by the Monastery of Our Lady Kalamiotissa, was the temple of Apollo Aegletus, which was associated with the ancient city. In the 5th century BC, Anafi was an ally of Athens. In 1207 it was taken by the Venetian Marco Sanudo. The island had other Venetian rulers and was frequently laid waste by pirates. It passed under the rule of the Turks in 1537. It took an active part in the uprising of 1821 and was united with Greece in 1832.

Getting to know the island

The ferry puts in at the little port of **Ayios Nikolaos**. The island's only road, of a length of 2 km., is that which goes from the port to Chora. This is a 30 min. walk. In **Chora**, the gleaming white houses with their genuine Cycladic architecture and the picturesque windmills stand out on the side of the bare mountain like a 'balcony' over the open sea.

East of Chora is **Kastelli** and a few remains of the ancient city. At the eastern end of the island is the Monastery of **Our Lady Kalamiotissa**. On this side too there are a very few remains of the temple of Apollo Aegletus, of the Classical period.

On the west coast, **Vayia**, with its spring water, of therapeutic value, but as yet unexploited, is about an hour away from Chora.

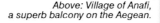

Above: Village of Anafi,
a superb balcony on the Aegean.

THE ISLANDS AND ISLETS OF THE CYCLADES

KEA
Makronisos.........................W Kea.
Grionisi. .... N Kea.
Spanopoula.........................N Kea.

KYTHNOS
Piperi. ....SE Kythnos.

SERIFOS
Serfopoula......................NE Serifos.
Vous.....................................E Serifos.
Mikronisi............................S Serifos.

SIFNOS
Kitriani................................S Sifnos.

MILOS
Akrathi................................N Milos.
Arkoudia.............................N Milos.
Antimilos. ....NW Milos.
Paximadi. .... SW Milos.
Glaronisia............................N Milos.

KIMOLOS
Polyaigos. ....SE Kimolos.
Ayios Evstathios.............S Kimolos.
Ayios Georgios. ....S Kimolos.
Ayios Andreas.............SW Kimolos.

ANDROS
Gavrionisia. ....S Gavrios.
   Gaidaros. ....S Gavrios.
   Tourlitis. ....S Gavrios.
   Akamatis.....................S Gavrios.
   Praso...........................S Gavrios.
   Megalo.........................S Gavrios.
Aginara. ....N Chora.
Theotokos..........................N Chora.

TINOS
Kalogeros. ....NW Tinos.
Dysvato...............................NW Tinos.
Panormos.............Bay of Panormos.
Drakonisi............ Bay of Kolymbithra.

MYKONOS
Ayios Georgios. ....W harbour.
Kavouras...........................W harbour.
Marmaronisi........Bay of Panormos.
Moles....................Bay of Panormos.
Dragonisi........................ E Mykonos.
Ktapodia. .... E Mykonos.
Praso. .... SW Mykonos.
Kromydi. .... SW Mykonos.

DELOS
Reneia. ....W Delos.
Megalos Revmataris. ......W Delos.

SYROS
Yaros. ....NW Syros.
Glaronisi.......................... SE Garos.
Didymi................................ E Syros.
Strongylo. .... E Syros.
Aspro.................................. E Vari.
Ambelos............................... S Vari.
Strongylo. ....SW Poseidonia.
Schinonisi. ....SW Poseidonia.
Varvarousa........................N Kinios.
Komeno.....................N Ermoupoli.
Nata. ....SE Syros.

PAROS
Portes..........................SW Parikia.
Ayios Spyridonas.........W Parikia.
Saliagonisi. .... W Paros.
Revmatonisi......................W Paros.
Tourlos. ....SW Paros.
Preza.................................SW Paros.
Glaropounta.....................SW Paros.
Tigani.................................SW Paros.
Pantieronisi......................SW Paros.
Dryonisi............................SW Dryos.
Krypsida. .... E Dryos.
Prasonisi............................ E Dryos.
Filizi...............................NE Ambelas.
Vriokastro. .... NE Paros.
Fonisses. .... NE Paros.
Tourlites. .... NE Paros.
Gaidouronisi..................... NE Paros.
Oikonomou.............. Bay of Naousa.

ANTIPAROS
Kavouras.......................N Antiparos.
Diplo..............................N Antiparos.
Petalides. ....SE Antiparos.
Despotiko. ....SW Antiparos.
Tsimintiri. ....SW Antiparos
Strongyli. ....SW Antiparos

NAXOS
Aspronisi...........................W Naxos.
Parthenos. ....W Orkos beach.

IOS
Petalidi.................................N Ios.
Diakofto..............................W Ios.
Psathi..................................NE Ios.

LESSER CYCLADES
Irakleia................................ S Naxos.
Megalos Avdelas..........SW Irakleia.
Mikros Avdelas.............SW Irakleia.
Venetiko......................NE Herakleia.
Schoinousa....................... S Naxos.

Argilos. ....S Schinousa.
Feidousa......................S Schinousa.
Aspronisi. .... SE Schinousa.
Kleidoura. .... NE Schinousa.
Kato Koufonisi. .... SE Naxos.
Glaronisi. ....NE K. Koufonisia.
Koufonisi. .... SE Naxos.
Prasoura. ....NE Koufonisia.
Keros................................ SE Naxos.
Megali Plaka......................S Keros.
Mikri Plaka. ....S Keros.
Tsouloufi............................S Keros.
Lazaros...............................S Keros.
Ayios Andreas. ....S Keros.
Plaki...................................S Keros.
Ano Antikeri. ....S Keros.
Kato Antikeri.....................S Keros.
Voulgaris............................E Keros.
Donousa............................E Naxos.
Makares. .... W Donousa.
Skylonisi. .... NE Donousa.

AMORGOS
Fokia....................................N Aiyiali.
Nikouria. .... W Amorgos.
Grambonisi. .... W Amorgos.
Petalidi. .... NW Amorgos.
Gramvousa...............N Kalotaritissa.
Psalida............................. W Amorgos.
Felouka. .... W Amorgos.
Paraskopos.................. W Amorgos.
Megalo Viokastro...........NE Chora.
Mikro Viokastro.................E Chora.

SIKINOS
Kaloyeroi. .... SW Sikinos.
Karavos............................ SW Sikinos.
Kardiotissa.................... SW Sikinos.

FOLEGANDROS
Ayios Ioannis.Opposite Karavostasi.
Pelagia....................SE Folegandros.

SANTORINI
Thirasia. ....W Santorini.
Nea Kameni. ....W Santorini.
Palaia Kameni..............W Santorini.
Aspronisi. ....W Santorini.
Christiana....................SW Santorini.
Eschati...........................SW Santorini.

ANAFI
Pacheia. ....S Anafi.
Makra.....................................S Anafi.
Anydros.....Between Anafi, Amorgos.

The Dodecanese lie to the east of the Cyclades. They are the final remains of the bridge between the Peloponnese and Asia Minor. Geologists say they are the peaks of the mountains of the Aegeis, the dry land that joined Greece to Asia and which sank into the Mediterranean sea four million years ago. The Dodecanese have been inhabited since the prehistoric period and were first ruled by the Minoans and then the Achaeans. But their economic and intellectual development slowly began with the arrival of the Dorians in 1100 B.C., reaching a great height in the 8th century. The three large towns of Lindus, Cameirus and Ialyssus which were built on Rhodes in the 6th century B.C. and constituted along with Kos, Cnidus and Halicarnassus in Asia Minor the Dorian Hexapolis, were the work of Dorians. This development was cut off prematurely by the Persian tempest which then shook all Greece.

After the defeat of the Persians, the Dodecanese became members of the Athenian Alliance in 408 B.C. and the three large towns of Rhodes united into one state. More particularly, Kos prospered in the 4th and the 3rd century B.C. because of the School of Medicine founded there by Hippocrates. The Romans occupied the islands in 146 B.C. to be followed by the long Byzantine period till the time of the Crusaders. In 1309 the Knights of the Order of Saint John became the rulers of Rhodes and

PATMOS LIPSI
LEROS
KALYMNOS
KOS
NISSYROS
ASTYPALEA SYMI
Rodos
TILOS
CHALKI
RODOS
KARPATHOS
KASSOS
KASTELLORIZO

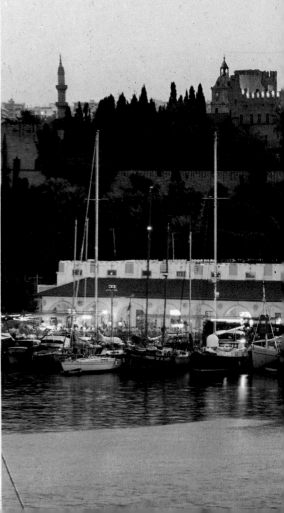

then extended their sovereignty to the other islands as well. In 1522 the islands were occupied by the Turks and in 1912 the Italians. The Dodecanese were united with Greece in 1948. At the crossroads of three continents the Dodecanese are a powerful pole of attraction for visitors who come to them in order to enjoy the healthy climate, the sun and the sparkling clean sea. To spend their holidays the way they want to, either in a cosmopolitan environment or on a quiet shore.

The Dodecanese are a complex of over 1,000 islands, islets and rocky outcroppings. We describe (or simply fix the location of) 163 of them, of which only 26 are inhabited.

Rhodes

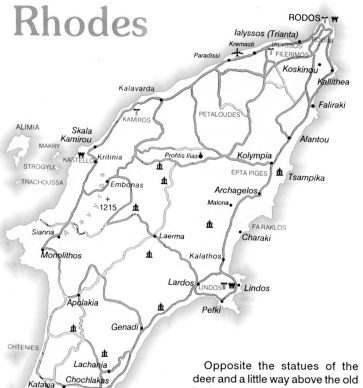

The ferries from Piraeus usually arrive at Rhodes at sunrise. At that time of day, the sun which gilds the sea also gilds the two statues - the deer and the fawn - which stand on columns at the entrance to the ancient harbour and which have become the symbol of the island. Tradition relates that their position was once occupied by the famous Colossus, one of the seven wonders of the world. This was an enormous bronze statue representing the god Helios (the sun) holding a burning torch. One foot stood on one side of the entrance to the harbour and the other foot on the other, so that ships passed beneath him. The search for this statue, which was thrown down by a major earthquake, continues, but the search is a vain one because, in fact, the Colossus was cut up into small pieces and sold as bronze to the Saracens.

Opposite the statues of the deer and a little way above the old harbour stands the Castello, the Palace of the Grand Master of the Knights of Rhodes. Next to it is the medieval town, scarcely affected by the passage of time. The new city with its modern buildings and large hotels extends mainly to the north-west, the point where the boundless beaches start and continue for kilometres.

Rhodes, the biggest of the Dodecanese and the fourth largest in Greece, lies in the south-east of the Aegean, very close to the coast of Asia Minor. The distance from Piraeus is 260 nautical miles. Its mountains are mostly pine-covered with well-watered, verdant and fertile valleys between them. The highest of these, Atavyros, is 1,215 m. high. The island has an area of 1,398 sq. km. and a shoreline of 220 km. Its population, a large percentage of which is employed in the tourist trade, is more than 90,000. The most important products of Rhodes are wine and olive oil, but it also produces folk artefacts such as ceramics, embroidery, textiles and carpets.

Rhodes, the pearl of the Mediterranean, as it has been called, is of the greatest interest both for its natural beauty and for its archaeological treasures. For this reason it was recently proclaimed by UNESCO a world cultural heritage monument.

With its marvellous climate and its well-organised tourist infrastructure, it is a place for holidays all the year round.

Rhodes can be reached direct by air from many of the capitals of Europe, as well as from Athens, Thessaloniki, Crete, Mykonos, Paros, Santorini, Kos, Karpathos, Kasos, Kastelorizo and Mytilene. There are ferries to Rhodes from Piraeus, Rafina, the Dodecanese, the Cyclades, the islands of the northern and eastern Aegean, Kavala and Cyprus.

HISTORY

Homer tells us in *The Iliad* that Rhodes took part in the Trojan War, sending 9 ships under the leadership of Tlepolemus.

Finds from excavations show that the island was inhabited in the Neolithic period. In the 16th century BC the Minoans came to Rhodes, to be followed in the 15th century by the Achaeans. It was, however, in the 11th century that the island started to flourish, with the coming of the Dorians. It was the Dorians who latter built the three important cities of Lindus, Ialysus and Cameirus, which together with Kos, Cnidus and Halicarnassus made up the so-called Dorian Hexapolis.

In the Persian Wars, Rhodes was forced to fight on the side of the Persians, but later, in 478 BC, joined the Athenian League.

A new era began for the island in 408 BC when its three major cities united and decided to build a new city at the north end of the island, on the site, that is, of the present-day city of Rhodes. This new city was one of the finest in antiquity and enjoyed great

The medieval town of Rhodes.

Dramatic depiction of the Colossus of Rhodes by the traveller Rottiers, 1826.

prosperity in the 4th, 3rd and part of the 2nd century BC. Its schools of philosophy, literature and rhetoric - at which a number of distinguished Romans studied - were famous. The city developed into a maritime, commercial and cultural center and its coins were in circulation almost everywhere in the Mediterranean.

At the time of the Peloponnesian War it wavered in its decisions; later it welcomed Alexander the Great. The struggle between Alexander's successors had its effect on Rhodes, which, because of its commercial ties with Egypt, allied itself with Ptolemy. This brought it into conflict with Antigonus, who attempted to seize the island, sending there Demetrius Poliorcetes with a large army. Demetrius, in spite of his famous siege engines, did not finally succeed in taking the city of Rhodes and after a year's siege signed an armistice.

In 164 BC, Rhodes signed a treaty with Rome, thus acquiring many privileges, which it later lost because of the complexities of Roman policies. It was finally laid waste by Cassius.

In the 1st century AD, the Apostle Paul brought Christianity to the island. In 297, the long Byzantine period began for Rhodes, in the course of which there were many attacks upon it by Arabs and Crusaders.

A new period of greatness opened up for the island when in 1309 the rule of the Knights of the Order of St John began. Drawn from eight states (France, Provence, Auvergne, Castille, Aragon, England, Germany and Italy), the Order's original purpose was the defence of the Holy Land and later the assistance of pilgrims. Under the rule of the Knights of Rhodes the medieval city with its famous monuments, including the Palace of the Grand Master, today the Castello, was built. The strong walls which the Knights had built withstood the attacks of the Sultan of Egypt (1444) and of Mohamet II (1480). Finally, however, Rhodes yielded before the large army of Suleyman the Magnificent (1522) and the very few remaining Knights capitulated and fled to Malta. In 1912, Rhodes was seized by the Italians, and in 1948, together with the other islands of the Dodecanese, was united with Greece.

The city of Rhodes

This, one of the finest cities not only in Greece but in the whole of the Mediterranean, is situated at the island's most northerly point. It is ringed by sea on the east and west and it has bright sunshine almost all the year round. It combines the cosmopolitan character of a super-modern city with the picturesqueness of the medieval town, which gives the impression of having been untouched by the passage of time.

The modern city

In the east of the modern city there is a significant portion of ancient Rhodes. This is the ancient harbour - its modern name is **Mandraki** - with the statues of the deer and the fawn at its entrance.

Tradition tells us that this was where the famous Colossus of Rhodes, one of the seven wonders of the ancient world, stood. A long mole which protects the harbour has in its middle three old windmills and at its northern end the Fortress of St Nicholas with the lighthouse. It is from Mandraki that the small vessels which go on daily cruises to Symi, Kalymnos, Pserimos, Patmos and Nisyros set out.

Very near to the entrance to the ancient harbour is the church of the Annunciation, the Orthodox cathedral, in the Gothic style, with wall-paintings by Fotis Kontoglou. In the whole of this area in front of Mandraki, as elsewhere, the Italians put up various buildings with large spaces between them. Among them is the Governor's Residence, a building with Gothic arches all round, which stands a little to the north of the Church of the Annunciation. Today it houses the headquarters of the Prefecture. The other buildings include the Town Hall, the National Theatre (opposite the Governor's Residence), and the law courts, south of the church of the Annunciation. Very close to the Governor's Residence, in an old Turkish cemetery with the graves of Turkish notables, is the Mosque

*Statue of Aphrodite
from the Museum of Rhodes.*

of Murat Reis. If you follow from here the main road which goes to the west coast, you pass the **casino**, which is housed in the Astir Pallas Hotel.

On the northern outskirts of the city is the famous aquarium. A sandy beach to the west of the **Yacht Club** is one of the most popular on Rhodes.

If you follow the Mandraki pier in the direction of the old town, you come to **Nea Agora** (New Market), a large, polygonal building with a series of arches on its facade and a large open space in the middle.

Near here in a beautiful garden and below the imposing walls and Palace of the Grand Master, are the installations for 'son et lumière' performances.

The medieval town

We enter the medieval town through the Gate of Freedom, which is near the New Market. In the first square we come upon, Symis Square, there are sparse

remains of the Temple of Aphrodite. On the left is the Municipal Art Gallery, which contains works by Greek artists. Very near this is the Museum of Decorative Arts and the Inn of Auvergne, the hostel, that is, where in the time of the Knights, those who spoke one of their eight 'tongues', in this case that of Auvergne, were accommodated. A little further on is the beginning of the famous Street of the Knights, which, in spite of the restoration of its buildings, you feel has remained untouched by the passage of the 500 years since it was first built (14th century). The Gothic order predominates. The Inns of the various 'Tongues' stand in a row, with impressive arched doorways, their emblems carved above these.

*Right: Deer and fawn
at the harbour entrance.*

Below: View of town of Rhodes.

You are now in the Collachium, the quarter of the Knights, and you climb the hill in the direction of the Palace of the Grand Master, the Castello, as it is now called. On your right, first is the Inn of Italy and then the Inn of France, the largest of them all. Still on the right, the next is the Inn of Provence, while on the left is the Inn of Spain.

In front of the Castello is the Loggia of St John.

The Palace of the Grand Master, the most imposing building of medieval Rhodes, is at the end of the Street of the Knights. It was built in the 14th century, but was demolished by the explosion of gunpowder which the Turks had stored in its basement in 1856. It was restored in 1939, during the Italian occupation. In this restoration, every effort was made to follow its original design faithfully. The Palace was intended as a residence for the Italian King Vittorio Emmanuele II or for Mussolini.

If you follow Orfeos St from the Castello in a southerly direction, you can visit the clock-tower and mosque of Suleyman, before coming to **Sokratous St**, the street with the most shops and commercial activity. At some points this street resembles an oriental bazaar.

If you go down Sokratous St to the end, you come to **Ippokratous Square**, one of the most attractive in Rhodes. It contains the Court of Commerce, a fine early 15th century building. From here, Aristotelous St, on one side of which is the city wall, brings you to the attractive Square of the **Jewish Martyrs**, which has three bronze sea-horses in its center. If you continue to follow the walls in an easterly direction, you come to the church of St Panteleimon (15th century) and the ruined church of Our Lady of Victory, which was built after the lifting of the Turkish siege in 1480. If you emerge from St Catherine's Gate, near St Pantaleimon, you are in front of the commercial harbour, where large vessels anchor.

You return to Ippokratous Square, still following the walls, and going along Ermou St, you come to Museum Square. This contains the Inn of England. The **Archaeological Museum** is housed in the restored building of the 15th century Hospital of the Knights.

Monte Smith

There is a frequent urban bus service to Monte Smith (starting from Averof St, New Market). This hill was the site of the ancient acropolis. Today you can see here the Stadium, of the 2nd century BC, and the Theatre, both of them restored, and a few remains of the temples of Zeus Polieus, Athena Polias and Pythian Apollo, of which four columns have been reconstructed. The view from the top of the hill over the city of Rhodes and the sea is magnificent. The distance of the hill from the center of the city is 2 kilometres.

Entrance to the Palace of the Grand Master.

Right, above: Sokratous str. and square of Jewish Martyrs. Below: Aerial photograph of old town.

EXCURSIONS

1. Rhodes - Ixia - Ialysos-Filerimos - Valley of the Butterflies - Kameiros - Monolithos - Kattavia (99km)

You leave the city on the road to **Ixia**.

On the left, you come to the small village of Kritika, and then the long beach of Ixia.

This is the area most developed for tourist purposes on Rhodes. Between the city and Ialysos, half the hotel accommodation of the island is to be found. One large hotel follows the other in a line behind the sun-drenched beach with its clean and calm waters.

8 km. Ialysos (Trianta). From here, you will make a 5 km deviation, to the left, to climb **Filerimos** hill, with its wonderful view of the city of Rhodes and to all points of the horizon.

Panayia church at Filerimo and below panoramic view of Ixia.

On top of this hill stood the acropolis of **ancient Ialysos**, one of the three major Dorian cities of Rhodes. Among the ruins, the foundations of the Temple of Zeus **Polieus**, of the 4th century BC, and of **Athena Polias**, of the 3rd century BC, and a Doric fountain of the 4th century can be made out. Together with the ancient remains are others of the Byzantine and medieval periods. Of particular note are the church of Our Lady of Filerimos, built by the Knights in the 15th century, and that of **St George**, which has wall-paintings of the 14th and 15th century. The Way of the Cross with its many steps and scenes from the Passion is very striking.

12 km. Kremasti. A large village with plenty of greenery, 800 m. from the sea.

15 km. Paradeisi. A village near the airport, also undergoing tourist development.

18 km. Road junction. The road to the left leads, after 6km, to the famous **Valley of the Butterflies**. This is a shady valley with a small river forming little lakes running down it. On the branches of the trees sit millions of golden-red butterflies. Touching a branch sends the butterflies into the air all at once, like a cloud. This unique spectacle can only be enjoyed in the summer, from June to September.

30 km. Kalavarda. From here a deviation to the left leads, after 8 km, to the village of Salako. If you continue the ascent of the fir-covered mountain in an encircling manner, after 12 km you reach Profitis Ilias, where there is a hotel at 800 m.

34 km. A brief deviation to the left brings you to the archaeological site of **Kameiros**, one of the three major Dorian cities of Rhodes. It differed from the other two in the curious fact that it was without fortifications. The remains, impressive in their extent, are on a hillside with a view towards the sea.

47 km. Skala Kameirou. A small port on the site of the ancient port of Cretinia, which was built by the Minoans of Crete. It is from here that caïques leave for Halki, which is very close.

52 km. Kritinia. Village with old houses. Nearby is a Venetian castle.

57 km. By turning off to the left, we can climb, after 5 km, to Embonas, one of the most attractive villages on Rhodes, and at the same time the highest (825 m.). Its beautiful houses have the local interior decoration and many of the residents still wear traditional costume. From here the ascent of the island's highest mountain, Atavyros (1,215 m.), begins.

65 km. The road to the left goes to **Ayios Isidoros**, Laerma and Lardos and meets up with the east coast road.

68 km. Sianna. Village with a fine view. Its stone houses are built in the traditional style.

73 km. Monolithos. A mountain village. Three kilometres away is the most imposing Venetian fortress on Rhodes, built in the 15th century on a towering rock (monolith - hence the name) and looking out over the sea.

83 km. Apolakkia. A village somewhat isolated because of its great distance from the city of Rhodes. For that reason, it retains more than any other the old manners and customs.

99 km. Kattavia (see page 103).

Section of archaeological site of Kameiros.

2. Rhodes - Kallithea - Lindos - Kattavia (93 km)

3 km. Rodini. Here there is a park with lots of greenery and small artificial lakes.

7 km. Reni Koskinou. A sandy beach belonging to the village, in the traditional style, of **Koskino**.

10.5 km. Kallithea. At one time famous for its medicinal springs, which no longer function. It stands on a bay with small rocks. The surrounding countryside is very green.

16 km. Faliraki. One of the most important tourist centres on Rhodes. It tourist development is due chiefly to its fine and extensive sandy beach, with water sports facilities.

23 km. Afantou. This village owes its name (meaning 'invisible') to the fact that in order to protect it from pirates, it was built in a hollow, so that it should not be seen from the sea. Its sandy beach is about 1 km away. Near the village is the **church of Our Lady at Katholiki**, built on the foundations of an early Christian basilica. To the north there is a golf course.

Pisturesque harbour of Kallithea.

27 km. Kolymbia. Another area which has been developed to meet the needs of tourism. The fine beach is 3 km from the main road. If you go off to the right, into the interior of the island, you come in 4 km to **Epta Pighes**, an extremely verdant spot with ample water which forms a lake. From here the road goes on to **Archipoli** and **Profitis Ilias** and then meets up with the west coast road.

30 km. Road junction. The road to the left leads to the fine beach of **Tsambika**. On the hill above the beach is the Monastery of Our Lady of **Tsambika**, with a fine view towards the sea.

The cosmopolitan Faliraki.

32 km. Archangelos. A large village in which traditional carpets and ceramic goods are produced.

36 km. Road junction. The road to the left leads after 4 km to **Haraki**, which has a small beach. Nearby is the fortress of **Faraklos**, one of the strongest on the island, built by the Knights, and to the north the marvellous beach of **Ayia Agathi**, on the bay of Malonas.

46 km. Kalathos. A village 6 km north of Lindos. To the south is the bay of **Vlycha**, which has a good beach.

LINDOS

52 km. Lindos. Perhaps the most attractive village on Rhodes. It has everything: its famous acropolis, the traditional architecture and decoration of the village houses, its beautiful beach and the picturesque little harbour of Ayios Pavlos.

The **Acropolis** can be reached on foot or, up to a point, on the charming little donkeys. At the beginning of the steps which lead to the acropolis, there is a trireme of the Hellenistic period carved on the rock on the left and on the right, steps dating back to ancient times. As soon as you go through the main entrance, you see the ruins of the **Castle of the Knights** and the Byzantine church of **St John**. On the acropolis you can visit the **Great Stoa**, which has been restored, and the Temple of **Athena Lindia**, of the 4th century BC, some columns of which have been restored. The ancient theatre and the few remains of the Temple of **Dionysus** can also be visited. The view from the rock of the acropolis, which rises sheer 115 m. above the sea, is unique.

The village is made attractive by its white houses, with traditional decoration inside - carved wooden ceilings and plates hung on the walls - and their courtyards paved with black and white pebbles. Many of these buildings, which date from the period of the Knights (15th and 16th centuries) have had a preservation order issued as ancient monuments.

The Acropolis, village and lovely shores of Lindos.

The **church of Our Lady**, with 15th century wall-paintings is worth visiting.

This village, with its 700 or so inhabitants, naturally makes its living almost exclusively from tourism. At the nearby beach there are restaurants and full facilities for all water sports.

The little bay with the chapel of St Paul, south of the Acropolis, is most attractive and good for swimming. Another beach is at Pefki, 5 km south-west of Lindos.

61 km. Lardos. A village with a sandy beach, about 2 km away. From here there is an asphalt road to Laerma (12 km) which links this east coast route, which you are now following, with that of the west coast.

74 km. Yennadi. A village which has not yet been affected by tourism, with a fine, quiet beach. If you turn off our main route at Yennadi, you can reach **Apolakkia**, on the west coast road by taking the road to the right.

83 km. Lahania. This village is about 2 km from the sea and extensive beaches.

85 km. Hochlakas. The road on the left leads to Plimmyri, another excellent beach, not much frequented.

91 km. Ayios Pavlos. From the village a road goes down to the southernmost point of the island, **Prasonisi**. This is a headland with sand and shallow water, which in winter is cut off by the sea from the mainland and becomes an island.

93 km. Kattavia. The last village on your route, with a tradition in textiles. At Kattavia the Excursion 1, covering the west coast, ends. If you want to return by Excursion 2, follow it in reverse order.

Lindos

Symi

Symi is one of the most picturesque of the islands of the Dodecanese, with mountains which descend steeply to the sea and form charming bays. In one of these, Ano Symi, or 'Chorio', as the local people call it, climbs up two hills to the left and right of the harbour, reaching the top of one of them, forming a whole town.

This picturesque village with its traditional architecture, its neo-Classical houses with their pediments, and the courtyards paved with pebbles - all creations of the 19th century - will make a wonderful impression on the visitor despite the fact that many of the buildings are abandoned and ruinous.

At the beginning of the present century, Symi had 30,000 inhabitants and was the capital of the Dodecanese and the world's largest sponge-fishing centre. Today, after a period of decline, it has no more than 2,500 inhabitants, mostly living in Chorio and the port. However, thanks to tourism, the population has started to grow again.

An asphalt road which starts out from Chorio and goes southwards passes through a small wood of wild cypresses and provides us with a marvellous view from a high vantage point. This is the road which leads to the famous Panormitis Monastery at the southernmost point of the island.

Symi is very close to the coast of Asia Minor, north-west of Rhodes, 21 nautical miles away. It has an area of 58 sq. km and a coastline of 85 km. It is 230 nautical miles from the port of Piraeus.

Here you can go by caïque to swim from a different beach every day. These can be enjoyed as early as May and as late as October; because of its mild climate and many hours of sunshine, Symi has a long summer.

Symi can be reached by ferry from Piraeus, the Cyclades, Crete, Rhodes and other islands of the Dodecanese (one service a week). Daily services are only via Rhodes. It is also possible to go by air as far as Rhodes and then take the local ferry on to Symi.

HISTORY

The myths tell us that the god Glaucus eloped with Syme, the daughter of the king of Ialysus on Rhodes and brought her to the island, to which she gave her name.

Symi was inhabited in prehistoric times. Homer relates that it took part in the Trojan War by sending three ships, under the leadership of its king, Nereus. The Carians were most probably its first inhabitants. Later came the Dorians, to be followed by the Rhodians and the Romans, the Byzantines and, in the 14th century, the Knights of St John of Rhodes. All the island's various conquerors seem to have concerned themselves with the fortification of the ancient acropolis, today's 'Kastro', on top of the hill of Ano Symi. Later Symi grew increasingly prosperous, thanks to the development of the art of shipbuilding, shipping and trade. The small, fast sailing ships built here by master craftsmen were renowned. In order to avail themselves of these craft, the Knights of Rhodes gave many privileges to the island. The same happened after the island fell to the Turks in 1522.

The Turks were also interested in its sponge-fishing and permitted it to practise this along all the coastline of Asia Minor. It spite of the part which the island played in the Revolution of 1821, which resulted in a reduction of its

privileges, it remained prosperous throughout the 19th century and money continued to flow into Symi. New luxury mansions were added to those already existing and at the beginning of the present century the population of Chorio reached 30,000. This was the period when Ano Symi was the capital of the Dodecanese.

Decline set in with the coming of steamships and the occupation of the island by the Italians in 1912. They cut off communications with Turkey opposite and made Rhodes the capital of the Dodecanese.

After the Second World War, during which it was bombed and burnt by Hitler's army, it was finally united with Greece in 1948.

Getting to know the island

Ano Symi or **Chorio**. Ano Symi, the capital of the island, makes an imposing sight when approached by sea. Its houses begin from **Kato Poli**, the safe harbour, and rise to the top of the hill with the **Kastro** and the **Megali Panayia**.

The top is reached from the 'Skala' square by following the **'Kali Strata'** with its 500 wide steps. On the left and right are the fine old houses with their neo-Classical features.

The attractive doorways, the ironwork balconies, the pediments below the roofs, the walls painted in ochre and other light colours and the bright colours of the door and window frames all create a marvellous picture. All this town, as well as Yialos, is quite rightly subject to a conservation order. Apart from the Kastro and the Megali Panayia, with its panoramic view, it is worth visiting some of the other churches with their carved wooden screens, Byzantine icons and courtyards paved with black and white pebbles. Also worth seeing are the **Museum**, which is housed in an old mansion, and the big square of Yialos, which was once the site of the shipyards where the fast ships were built by the experienced craftsmen of Symi.

Ano Symi can also be reached by bus from **Yialos** to **Chorio** and Pedi.

Pedi. A seaside village, 2 km east of Ano Symi, deep in a neighbouring bay with a sandy beach.

Emboreios. A little port, Symi's second, west of Chorio. It has a few residents.

Panormitis. This is the island's most important monastery and the second in the whole of the Dodecanese after that of St John on Patmos.

It is at the southernmost point of Symi within an enclosed bay with a sandy beach. The only indica-tion which we have of the date of its foundation is that additions were made to its buildings at the end of the 18th century. Dedicated to the **Archangel Michael**, it has in its main church an all-gold icon of the Saint, a wealth of ex voto offerings, wall-paintings and a wooden screen of first-class craftsmanship.

On its feast day (8 November) pilgrims flock here not only from Symi itself but from the whole of the Dodecanese. Its guesthouse can accommodate 500. There is also a restaurant.

Panormitis is reached by caïque from Yialos or by car (excursions are organised regularly).

Trips by caïque

In summer, caïques and small craft leave Yialos for the island's marvellous beaches, providing day trips.

On the east coast:

Ayia Marina. A charming rocky islet near Yialos with a chapel dedicated to St Marina and crystal-clear water.

Ayios Georgios Disalonas. Perhaps the most impressive of the beaches, because it has behind it a sheer cliff some 300 m. high.

Nanou. A large, pretty bay with scattered wild cypress trees and a small taverna.

Marathounta. To the south of Nanou, a smaller bay with clear water.

Faneromeni. A beautiful bay, 20 minutes on foot from Panormitis.

Panormitis. The site of the famous monastery. On the west coast, but it is much more quickly reached from the east.

Seskli. An islet at the southern most point of Symi with crystal-clear water. Good for fishing.

Nimos. A island at the northern tip of Symi with a beach and a small taverna.

On the west coast:

Ayios Aimilianos. A very pretty beach. An islet with a little chapel reached by a stone causeway.

Ayios Vasileios. One of the most attractive of the beaches on a large, deep bay surrounded by mountains with wild cypress trees.

Monasteries

Apart from Panormitis, of which an account has been given above, there is **Roukouniotis Monastery**, dedicated to the Archangel Michael, west of Chorio. Its main church has wall-paintings of the 14th century.

Kokkinidis Monastery, an old monastery which was restored in 1697.

The **Monastery of Sotiris tou Megalou** and the **Monastery of Stavrou tou Polemou** can be seen high up on the mountains, on the west coast, as we come from Tilos to Symi.

Traditional architecture is particularly characteristic of Symi.

Halki

Halki is beautiful, primitive and not much frequented, in spite of the fact that it is the nearest island to cosmopolitan Rhodes. It has fine beaches with clear water. In its picturesque port, which has the air of having been abandoned, you can pick out two churches by their high bell-towers. One of them is austere and simple and stands on the hillside, the other is a true work of art, next to the harbour. On top of the hill can be seen the white walls of the ancient acropolis and the Venetian fortress which succeeded it. There is no life, no movement among the grey ruins of the village. Only the undamaged and freshly-whitewashed church of Our Lady, somewhere in the middle of the village, is reminiscent of better times, when this was the capital of the island, with 4,000 inhabitants.

Halki lies to the west of Rhodes and is 35 nautical miles from its port and only 11 from Skala Kameirou. It is one of the smallest islands in the Dodecanese, with an area of 28 sq. km. and a coastline of 34 km. Its inhabitants all live in its single village, Nimborio, which is also the island's port. Halki is a rugged, mountainous island which has been gradually abandoned by its inhabitants and left with the visitors who come on day excursions from Rhodes.

In recent years the island has been proclaimed an international centre for meetings of young people and for this purpose a municipal hostel has been built.

HISTORY

The name Halki comes from the copper mines which the island once had. We have very little information about the prehistoric period, but excavations have shown that between the 10th and the 5th century BC it enjoyed a period of prosperity. The period between the end of the Classical period and the arrival of the Venetians in the 13th century is wrapped in obscurity. In 1522 it was taken by the Turks and in 1912 by the Italians. Halki was incorporated into Greece in 1948.

Getting to know the island

Nimborio. The capital of the island, on its east coast, on a bay protected by an islet at its entrance. It is built amphitheatrically on the surrounding hills. Its two-storey houses have tiled roofs and brightly painted door and window frames, but it looks like some ghost-town because most of the houses have been abandoned. The church of **St Nicholas**, down at the harbour, with it fine bell-tower, is worth a visit.

Not far from here is the fine sandy beach of **Pontamos**. **Ftenayia** and the islet of Alimia also have excellent beaches.

A concrete road, takes you after 2.5 km, to **Palio Chorio**. This is the former capital of the island, now in ruins, standing on the slopes of an imposing rocky hill. At the top of the hill can be seen the walls of the **Venetian fortress**, which was built on the site of the ancient acropolis. Within the walls stands the church of St Nicholas, with wall-paintings. The road, concrete for half its length, continues west and arrives, after about 3.5 km, at the Monastery of **St John**. Other monasteries on the island are that of the **Holy Cross** and of the **Archangel Michael**.

Tilos

In a cave some 3.5 km from the landing-place of Tilos were found the bones of 30 dwarf elephants. These show that Tilos was once united with the coast of Asia Minor opposite and, with the Cyclades, formed a part of Aegeis, the land which linked Greece with Asia Minor. When Tilos became an island, perhaps 6 million years ago, the elephants were forced to adapt themselves to their new - and poorer - environment and to evolve gradually into dwarves, with a height of between 1.20 and 1.60 m.

Lying between Nisyros and Halki, Tilos has an area of 63 sq. km and a coastline of 63 km. It is 220 nautical miles from Piraeus. Its terrain is stony, the only exception being a small fertile valley, roughly in the middle of the island, which runs down to the fine sandy beach of Erystos. Its permanent inhabitants, most of whom are farmers and stock-breeders, number only 300. This is due to emigration, which started shortly after the Italian occupation in 1912 and continued down to the 1950s.

Tilos is perhaps the most isolated of the islands of the Dodecanese, after Kastelorizo. But it is precisely this isolation which gives it its attraction and makes it ideal for holidays of peace and quiet.

Tilos can be reached by ferry from Piraeus, Rafina, the Cyclades, Crete, Rhodes and the other islands of the Dodecanese. You can also go by air as far as Rhodes and continue your journey by boat to Tilos.

HISTORY

Tilos was inhabited in the Neolithic period, as various archaeological finds have shown. It is also certain that the Minoans of Crete were here, as were the Myceneans later. The Dorians came to the island in around 1000 BC and, as Herodotus informs us, together with the Lindians of Rhodes colonised Gela in Sicily around 700 BC.

In the 5th century BC, the island became a member of the Athenian League, while in the next century it was independent and minted its own coins. It later became an ally of Kos and then of Rhodes. The Romans became masters of the island in 42 BC, and from then until 1310, when it was taken by the Knights of St John of Rhodes, its history is obscure. The Turks, after repeated attacks, seized the island in 1522 and held it until 1912, when they were replaced by the Italians. Tilos was incorporated into Greece in 1948.

Getting to know the island

Livadia. This is the port of Tilos and lies on a bay with pebbles and clear water. A village with few inhabitants, its architecture, with the exception of a large building put up by the Italians, displays features of the local tradition. The surrounding countryside is quite green. The things to see are an **Early Christian basilica** near the village, the few remains of the medieval **fortress of Agriosykia**, **Our Lady Politissa - Misoskali** (2.5 km) and the chapel of **St Nicholas**, with wall-paintings of the 13th century, to the south-east and further off, on the east coast of the island, the old village of **Yera** and the chapel of **Taxiarchis tou Lithou**, with wall paintings of 1580. North-west of Livadia is the abandoned village of **Mikro Chorio**, which has interesting churches dedicated to the Saviour and the Holy Girdle, with wall-paintings of the 18th and 15th centuries.

Megalo Chorio. The imposing capital of Tilos, standing at the bottom of a rocky hill with a fortress on its top. Until the early 18th century, the village was inside the **fortress**. There, the old **church of the Archangel** (Taxiarchis), of whose 16th century wall paintings some remain today, stood on the foundations of an ancient temple. Gradually the village started to move to the site which it occupies today and a new church of the Archangel was later (1827) built at the foot of the hill.

In the village's small museum you can see the dwarf elephant bones from the **Harkadi Cave**, which lies between Megalo Chorio and Livadia, on the side of a hill, not far from the road. Megalo Chorio is 7 km from Livadia.

The famous beach of **Erystos**, one kilometre long and with a restaurant, is 2.5 km to the south.

A municipal bus service links Megalo Chorio with Livadia, Ayios Antonios and Erystos. Two kilometres to the north-west, the tiny port of **Ayios Antonios** has a small sandy beach.

The fine beach of **Plaka** is 2 km from Ayios Antonios. The road goes on to the monastery of **St Pantaleimon** (2 km).

Monastery of St Pantaleimon. This monastery, dedicated to the island's patron saint, stands in a green gorge with a spring and a panoramic view to the sea. It is on the east coast, 13 km from Livadia, was founded in the late 15th century, and has wall paintings dating from 1776 and a beautiful pebble-paved courtyard. Its feast day is 27 July.

Kos

Kos is the island of Hippocrates, the third largest in the Dodecanese after Rhodes and Karpathos, with a fine port, vast beaches, clear seas and enormous historical interest.

It lies very close to the Asia Minor coast, between Kalymnos and Nisyros, and is 201 nautical miles from the port of Piraeus.

It is a mostly low-lying island, with a single mountain range on its eastern side, the highest peak of which is Dikaios at 846 m. It has an area of 290 sq. km and a coastline of 112 km. Its population is in excess of 20,000, most of whom are engaged in farming, the tourist trade, stockbreeding and fishing.

The climate is mild most of the year. This fact, taken together with the long hours of sunshine, the marvellous beaches and the attractiveness of the city of Kos have gradually raised the island to the level of an international tourist centre.

Kos can be reached by air from Athens and Rhodes or by ferry from Piraeus, Rafina, the Cyclades, the islands of the northern and eastern Aegean, Kavala, Crete, Rhodes and the other islands of the Dodecanese.

HISTORY

Kos was inhabited in prehistoric times by the Carians (from Asia Minor, opposite the island). These were followed by the Minoans of Crete and, around the 14th century BC, the Myceneans, who later took part in the Trojan War.

A few centuries later, the Dorians started to arrive. Around 700 BC they built the ancient city of Kos, which together with Lindus, Cameirus, Ialysus on Rhodes, Cnidus and Halicarnassus in Asia Minor formed the so-called Dorian Hexapolis.

In the 5th century BC, Kos was taken by the Persians, but after their defeat in Greece, the island became a member of the Athenian League (479 BC). In 460 BC, Hippocrates, the Father of Medicine, whose name is known throughout the world, since he was the founder of the first school of medicine, was born on Kos. After his death (357 BC), the people of Kos built the famous Asklepeion, in honour of the god Asklepios, which operated as a hospital, admitting thousands of patients from all over the Mediterranean and applying the methods of therapy taught by Hippocrates.

In 366 BC, the city of Kos was founded on its present site and the role of capital of the island was transferred to it from Astypalaia,

The statue of Hippocrates.

During the Byzantine period it was again prosperous, but was subject to constant raids by enemies, of whom the most dangerous were the Saracens.

In 1315, the Knights of St John of Rhodes became masters of the island and about a century later began to build the great fortress which today stands at the entrance to the harbour and other fortifications, using materials from the town which had been destroyed by the earthquake. The attacks of the Turks on the Knights were at first unsuccessful, but after their victory at Rhodes in 1522, they also took Kos, which they held for almost four centuries, that is, until 1912, when it was taken by the Italians. Kos was fated to be laid in ruins again by another earthquake - that of 1933. Kos was incorporated into Greece in 1948.

which was at its southern extremity. The new city, built in a position of advantage between East and West, was extremely prosperous and continued to be so until the 6th century AD, when it was destroyed by a major earthquake. At the period of its prosperity it was renowned for the manufacture of silk, which was used chiefly by the Romans.

Alexander the Great took Kos in 336 BC, and was succeeded on his death by the Ptolemies.

General view of harbour.

The city of Kos

Kos, the capital and chief port of the island, is on the north-east coast, very near to the shores of Turkey. It is a most attractive city, rebuilt after the 1933 earthquake, with an abundance of trees, flower gardens, avenues lined with palm trees and marvellous beaches which stretch for miles to the right and left of the harbour. Added to all this are the important ancient monuments in and near the city, such as the famous **Asklepeion**, which make it even more interesting.

Plane tree of Hippocrates and town castle.

The altar of Asklepeion and the temple of Apollo (second level).

The first thing which strikes one when approaching the city by sea is the large **Venetian castle of the Knights of St John**. It stands like a great dam in front of the harbour with only a narrow passageway to the north for small vessels. The castle, with a double wall and a moat, was built in the 15th century with materials - marble and stone - from the ancient city, which was destroyed by an earthquake.

South of the castle, a bridge, crossing over the beautiful Avenue of Palms, links the castle with the square where the famous **plane tree of Hippocrates** stands. It is said that this vast plane tree was planted by Hippocrates and that he taught medicine in its shade.

Opposite the plane tree is the attractive **Mosque of Gazi Hasan,** or of the **Loggia**, with its lofty minaret, built in 1786 - also with materials from the ancient city.

Further to the south is an archaeological site, the nearest to the harbour, which contains remains of the **ancient Agora**, with two columns which have been re-erected belonging to the **Temple of Aphrodite**, the **Stoa** of the 4th century BC (there are a few restored columns here too), a large basilica, a temple believed to have been dedicated to Heracles, sections of the ancient wall, etc.

The **Archaeological Museum**, in Eleftherias Square, the attractive main square of Kos, is worth visiting. By day a walk around the harbour with its coffee shops and confectioners, its yachts and

The arrival of Asklepeios on Kos. Hippocrates is part of the reception. Mosaic from the 2nd century A.D. (Arch. Museum, Kos).

small craft is an enjoyable experience, as is a stroll at night along the streets of the new city, north of the harbour, with its countless bars.

There are even bars which are specially designed for customers of a particular nationality, as indicated by the little flags which fly outside.

The Asklepeion

This stands at a distance of 4 km south-west of Kos town, in a very green area. It is the island's most important archaeological site. Because of the slope of the ground, the buildings were put up (beginning in the 4th century BC) on a number of levels, with steps between them. On the first level are the remains of a small temple and a fountain and on the three sides there are porticos, which obviously housed the medical school and were the place where the patients received treatment.

In the centre of the second level there are remains of the altar of Asklepios and, west of the altar, those of a temple to Asklepios in the Ionic order, built at the beginning of the 2nd century BC. To the east are the ruins of the temple of Apollo, of the 3rd century BC, also in the Ionic order. Its seven sparkling white marble columns, re-erected by the Italians, stand out among all the buildings of the Asklepeion.

On the highest level are the foundations and a few columns of a Doric temple to Asklepios. This temple, built in the 2nd century BC was the largest and the most sacred in the Asklepeion.

From here there is a fine view of the rest of the site and out to sea.

EXCURSIONS

1. Kos - Asfendiou - Tigaki - Antimacheia - Mastichari - Kardamaina

You follow the road to the Asklepeion and at the road junction for it go straight on.

9 km. Zipari. From here a deviation off to the left leads, after 4 km uphill, to the picturesque villages of **Asfendiou**, on the green mountain of Dikaios. These villages are **Evangelistria**, **Lagoudi, Zia, Asomatos** and **Ayios Dimitrios**. The houses are freshly whitewashed and their alleyways and courtyards full of flowers. They have a marvellous view of the sea and the coast of Asia Minor opposite.

Churches worth visiting are those of the Archangels at Asomatos (11th century) and the **Basilica of St Paul**.

10 km. Road junction. The road to the right leads, after some 2 km, to **Tigaki**, a tourist centre with a fine sandy beach.

13 km. Linopotis. From here a road off to the left leads, after 2 km, to the village of Pyli and, after a further 5 km, to the villages of **Asfendiou**.

13.5 km. Road junction. The road to the right leads, after 2 km, to **Marmari**, a seaside village.

23 km. Antimacheia. An area with four villages, almost in the center of the island. It is a junction and very close to the airport. Nearby is the **Venetian fortress**, which has been preserved in very good condition.

The road to the right leads, after 5km, to **Mastichari**, a little port with a sandy beach, very busy in summer. From Mastichari there is a regular boat service to Kalymnos opposite (45 minutes).

The road straight on goes on to **Kefalos**. You turn left for **Kardamaina**.

29 km. Kardamaina. A summer resort popular with tourists, the second after Kos itself, which has been developed in recent years, thanks to its vast and excellent beach, the best on the island. From here, in summer, there is a daily caïque service to **Nisyros**.

Above: Tigaki.
Below: Kardamaina.

2. Kos - Paradeisi - Ayios Fokas - Thermes (12 km)

You leave the city by the Avenue of Palms in an easterly direction.

2 km. Paradeisi. A seaside area with hotels, which has been developed in recent years.

3 km. Psalidi. There is a camping site here.

13 km. Thermes. Medicinal springs for the treatment of rheumatism and arthritis. The road ends here.

3. Kos - Antimacheia - Ayios Stefanos - Kefalos

23 km. Antimacheia.

40 km. Ayios Stefanos. a village close to one of the finest beaches on Kos. The Club Mediterranée premises are nearby, next to the Early Christian basilica of St Stephen, of which only some columns and a marvellous mosaic from the floor remain. Opposite the basilica is a picturesque rocky islet, **Kastri**, with a chapel dedicated to St Antonios.

43 km. Kefalos. The southernmost village on Kos, standing on a hill with houses which are well looked after and a windmill on the top of the hill. Its port is **Kamari**, 1 km away. South of the village are the remains of ancient Astypalaia, originally the capital of the island, founded in the late 5th century BC. From Kefalos an asphalt road of 8 km goes to the **Monastery of St John**, standing on a beautiful site at the southern extremity of the island.

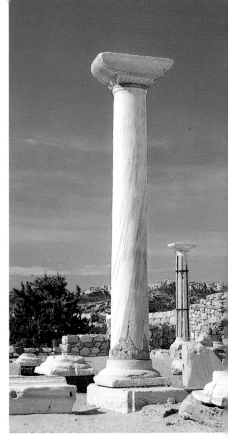

The lovely islet of Kastri (Ayios Stefanos).

The basilica of Ayios Stefanos.

Nisyros

Poseidon, god of the sea, we are told, one day snatched up a rock and flung it far away in order to kill the giant Polybotes. This rock, which fell into the sea, is Nisyros, the island with the volcano and the black rocks.

This is what mythology has to tell us. It adds that Polybotes was crushed under the rock - but he was not killed. He lives on and, trapped under the rock, gives a groan which makes the island shake every time there is an earthquake or the volcano erupts.

What strikes the visitor most about Nisyros is its wild beauty and its striking colours. There are few beaches. The rocks are black and the houses white, with their doors and windowframes painted in bright colours. In the middle of the island is a volcano with a huge crater. Also striking is the amount of greenery which there is on Nisyros.

Lying between Kos and Tilos, Nisyros has an area of 41 sq. km. and a coastline of 28 km. There are no more than 1,200 permanent residents, most of whom live in Mandraki. Nisyros welcomes mainly those who come on day trips from Kos and other islands. It also welcomes, however, those who have a love for it and come to spend their summers on this strange, peaceful island in the Dodecanese.

Nisyros can be reached by ferry from Piraeus (200 nautical miles), Rafina, Rhodes and other islands of the Dodecanese. The trip can be made from Piraeus more quickly via Kos. (Kos - Nisyros: 2 hours; Kardamaina (Kos) - Nisyros: 1 hour).

HISTORY

The first inhabitants of Nisyros seem to have been Carians. The island was taken by Artemesia, Queen of Halicarnassus. From the finds made on the acropolis, it has been concluded that the ancient city, which was walled, was inhabited continuously from the 5th century BC to the 5th century AD, while there was a still more ancient city of the Bronze Age near the port, as shown by the remains of an ancient jetty.

The Knights of St John, who later became the rulers of the island, built the Venetian fortress in 1315, and next to this, in 1600, the monastery of Our Lady Spiliani was built (its old icon was kept initially in the cave in the rock).

In 1522, the island was taken by the Turks and in 1912 by the Italians. Nisyros was united with Greece in 1948.

Getting to know the island

Mandraki

Mandraki, the capital and port of the island, stands below the imposing rock of the monastery of **Our Lady Spiliani** (1600) and behind the black rocks which are scattered about before it in the sea. It has pretty alleyways and a fine square shaded by the large deciduous trees which abound on the island.

A visit to the Monastery and to the **Venetian fortress**, from which there is a splendid view, is strongly to be recommended. The same is true of the **acropolis**, with its walls of the 4th century BC, and the ancient cemetery, which is near the church of St John and in which tombs and objects dating from the 7th and 6th centuries BC have been found.

Near Mandraki is **Hohlaki** beach with its striking black pebbles; the islet of Yali opposite has a fine sandy beach.

Above: Mandraki and the Panayia Spiliani.

Below: The volcano.

Mandraki - Pali - Emboreios - The volcano - Nikia

1 km. Paloi. Nice fishing village with a sand beach.

8 km. Emboreios. A village on a hill - almost deserted.

The main road does not go up to Emboreios but continues towards **Nikia**; after a short distance, it forks. The road to the right runs alongside one of the volcano's three craters. This has a diameter of 260 m. and a depth of 30 m. It is possible to make the descent into it from one of its sides. It is warm at the bottom and its vents emit steam and sulphur dioxide fumes, which produce a somewhat malodorous atmosphere. Nevertheless, it is worthwhile venturing down there. On the walls of the crater the strata of sulphur are clear to see and the whole landscape suggests the surface of the moon. If you return to our main route, you arrive in approximately 3.5 km at another crossroads. From this point, a road to the left leads in a little while to the monastery of **Our Lady Kyra**, at a height of 450 m. The monastery has a guesthouse and a marvellous view. You return to the main road and continue on your route.

14 km. Nikia. A picturesque village at a height of 400 m. with an exceptional view.

At a distance of 3 km. is **Avlaki**, on the coast, the southernmost point of the island.

Astypalaia

Astypalaia is the most westerly of the Dodecanese and the closest to the Cyclades. Because of this, as you approach it by sea and see its gleaming white 'chora' (main village) on the hillside and next to it a row of windmills, you think that you must still be in the Cyclades.

The earth of the island is brown and grey and there are little oases of greenery and beautiful bays with sandy beaches. Astypalaia is so narrow at one point in the middle that it seems as if it is divided into two. The south-western part, where Chora stands, is the home of the majority of its 1,000 or so inhabitants. It has an area of 97 sq. km. and the length of its coastline is 110 km.

An island once only irregularly served by steamer, Astypalaia, or 'Astropalia' as it is called locally, far away from tourist traffic, is ideal for a quiet holiday.

The island can be reached by air from Athens and by ferry from Piraeus, the Cyclades, Rhodes and other islands of the Dodecanese.

HISTORY

The ancient name of the island was 'Ichthyoessa', which indicates an abundance of fish going back to ancient times. The name 'Astypalaia' means 'ancient city', but mythology insists that the island was so named from Astypalaea, the sister of Europa, the mother of Minos.

The island was inhabited from prehistoric times and had a period of prosperity in the Mycenean period. Subsequently its fate has been, broadly speaking, that of the other Dodecanese and the neighbouring Cyclades islands.

The Romans used Astypalaia as a base for operations against pirates, and the Venetians who took it in 1207, after the temporary collapse of the Byzantine Empire, built under the Guerrinis the impressive fortress on top of the hill of Chora, on a site which had been occupied by the Byzantine, and most probably the ancient, acropolis. In 1540 the island was occupied by the Turks, and in 1912 by the Italians. Like the rest of the Dodecanese, it was united with Greece in 1948.

Courtyard with flowers beneath the imposing castle of Astypalaia.

On opposite page, overall view of Chora with windmills and castle.

Getting to know the island

Chora. Astypalaia, or Chora as it is called locally, the capital of the island, is a most attractive village. It spreads in amphitheatrical style over the sides of the hill on which stands an imposing fortress, and next to it is a row of windmills. The whole scene makes an instant appeal to the visitor. Its traditional architecture, so reminiscent of the neighbouring Cyclades, makes its own contributions to increasing the charm of the picture. These are the wooden balconies and outside staircases, all painted in vivid colours, the glassed-in balconies and the courtyards with their flower-pots.

The **fortress**, which was built by the Guerrinis when the Venetians became rulers of the island, is certainly worth a visit. Inside it, there are two churches of some note: **St George**, the island's oldest church, and the **Annunciation**.

The view from the fortress is incomparable. To the south, directly below the walls, the church of **Our Lady Portaïtissa**, one of the most beautiful churches in the Dodecanese, stands out gleaming white against the blue background of the sea. Its dome, with its relief garlands, and the lofty bell-tower, with its carved decoration, all make up a picture of rare beauty. Further off is the long beach of **Livadia**, with the village next to it. On the north-western side of the fortress is the harbour, **Pera Yalos**, as it is called.

It is at Pera Yalos that the very few hotels on the island are to be found. It also has restaurants which specialise in freshly-caught fish.

The **archaeological museum** is housed in the municipal library.

The bathing beaches of **Ayios Konstantinos** (to be reached by caïque) and **Marmaria** (on the road to Maltezana) are relatively close to Chora.

Twelve km. from Chora, to the west, is the monastery of **St John**, in an interesting setting. Other religious houses on the island are those of **Our Lady Fevariotissa** and **St Libya**, north-west of Chora, and of **Our Lady Poulariani**, at the eastern end of the island.

Livadia. A seaside village, 2 km. to the west of Chora, on a fine sandy bay.

Maltezana or **Analipsi**. The island's main road, which goes from Chora in a north-easterly direction, first passes over the narrow tongue of land linking the two parts of the island and then enters the eastern half, coming in a short distance to Maltezana, which is 8 km. from Chora and the lowest-lying and most verdant spot in the island. The houses are well-built and well-spaced.

Off Maltezana are the uninhabited islets of **Hondronisi, Ligno, Ayia Kyriaki, Koutsomyti** and **Kounoupi**.

Vathi. A small seaside village at the head of an enclosed bay with shallow water, resembling a lake. It lies 20 km. north-east of Chora and has a hostel and a fish taverna.

Kalymnos

Kalymnos is a small island, with an area of only 111 square km. Most of it is rocky, and the coastline is highly indented and has numerous caves. Among its bare mountains are little areas of fertile ground where citrus trees - especially mandarins - are grown.

The population is more than 14,000, most of them working in the fishing trade and as sponge-fishers. Today, of course, many people are employed in tourism.

Kalymnos lies between Kos and Leros, at a distance of 183 nautical miles from Piraeus.

You reach Kalymnos by ferry from Piraeus, Rafina, the Cyclades, Crete, the islands of the north and east Aegean, Kavala, Rhodes and the other islands of the Dodecanese.

The name of Kalymnos will always be associated with the world of sponge-fishing. The picture which springs to mind when we think of this island is of a pier with caiques moored against it: these are the craft which are used for sponge-fishing. There is a crowd of people on the pier: today is the day when the sponge-fishers set out on their long voyage to the coasts of Africa, where, risking their lives, the young men of the island will dive far down to the sea-bed to collect the sponges. This is a tradition which dates back many centuries. On the quay, the old people, the women and the children are waving goodbye to the fishermen, silently weeping. Months will pass before the menfolk return - the menfolk who return the farewells from their decorated boats. The caïques describe three circles inside the harbour and then disappear, sirens blowing.

This only happens once a year, though. The rest of the time, life flows quietly by in Kalymnos. Of course, in the summer there are quite a few visitors: tourism has been growing rapidly in recent years. This was only to be expected, since this island with its picturesque harbour, its beautiful beaches and its clear sea exerts an immediate attraction over the visitor.

Sponge - fishing,
a tradition on Kalymnos.

HISTORY

Kalymnos was inhabited in the Neolithic age. The first inhabitants seem to have been Carians, who colonised the island from Asia Minor. They were followed by the Minoans and later, around 1100 BC, by Dorians from Argos, who built a city on the island and named it after their homeland.

Homer tells us in *The Iliad* that ships from the "Kalydnian islands" took part in the Trojan War. The ΄Kalydnian islands΄ seem to have been the name given to a small group of islands including Kalymnos, and the Homeric epithet is the origin of the island΄s name today.

In the 5th century BC, Kalymnos was taken by Queen Artemisia of Halicarnassus, an ally of Persia.

After the Persian Wars, Kalymnos passed into the hands of the Athenian League. At about this time, its dependence on neighbouring Kos began. Later it was taken by the Romans, and in the late 13th century by the Genoese.

This was the time at which the castle of Chorio and the Pera Kastro (of Chrysochera) were built. The Knights of the Order of St John, who took the island in 1306, kept it until 1522, when in the face of the advancing Turkish hordes they were forced to abandon it in order to concentrate on the final battle menacing their capital, Rhodes. Turkish rule lasted until 1912, when Kalymnos was taken by the Italians. Under the Italians, the people of Kalymnos became famous for their resistance to the closing of the Greek schools. Many houses of Kalymnos were painted blue and white: the national colours of Greece. The blue paint can still be seen today, though of course it has faded somewhat.

Kalymnos was incorporated into Greece with the other islands of the Dodecanese, in 1948.

Overall view of Pothia.

Kalymnos (Pothia)

The capital of the island is a most attractive little town, and is also its main harbour. It is laid out like an amphitheater on the slopes of a rocky hill. Its brightly-painted houses give it a cheerful air, and it has a population of more than 10,000.

An evening walk along the seafront, with its row of shops, its caïques and yachts at anchor and its crowds of people, will be sufficient to show how lively a town this is.

Halfway along the seafront is the church of **Christ the Saviour**, with a marble sanctuary screen carved by the famous Tiniot sculptor and painter Yannoulis Halepas. The fine icons and wall-paintings are by important local artists.

Section of harbour.

Sponges from Kalymnos.

1. Kalymnos - Chorio - Myrties-Telendos -Emboreios (24 km.)

3 km. Chorio or **Chora**; this is the old capital of the island, with its church of Our Lady which was once the cathedral of Kalymnos. Some of the columns inside the church came from the ancient temple of Apollo. To the right of Chorio is the impressive Pera Kastro fortress.

3.5 km. A turning to the left leads in 3 km. to the village of **Argos**. The exact site of the ancient city by this name is not known. Near the turning to Myrties are the ruins of the church of **Christ of Jerusalem**, the most important church on the island. It was built in the 6th century by the Byzantine emperor Arcadius in thanksgiving for his survival of a great storm that broke out as he was sailing back from Jerusalem. Stones from the temple of Apollo were used as building materials. Parts of the ancient temple can be seen built into the ruins of the church.

4 km. Another crossroads. The road to the left leads to the pretty beaches of **Kantouni**, with a monastery of the Cross high up on a rock, and **Linaria**. All this area, together with the village through which we pass, is known as **Panormos**.

7.5 km. Myrties. This is perhaps the most attractive seaside village on the island, and it is developing into a tourist resort. The sea is clean, the beach is pebbly, and opposite is the attractive island of **Telendos**, separated from Kalymnos by a narrow channel.

8.5 km. Masouri. This village is also developing into a tourist resort, thanks to its outstanding sandy beach.

17 km. Arginontas. A little village at the head of a bay by the same name.

19 km. Skalia. An attractive coastal settlement near which is the **cave of Skalia**, one of the finest on the island.

Also of interest is the **Kefala cave**, on the north-west extremity of the island.

24 km. Emboreios. This is the last village along the coast, with a small population and vast beaches: an ideal spot for quiet holidays.

The **archaeological museum** is housed in a fine neo-Classical house to the north of the seafront, in the Ayia Triada district. Among the exhibits are a marble statue of Asklepios, Mycenean vases, and various other finds dating from between the Neolithic period and Roman times.

To the north-east, on the slopes of Mt Flaskias and close to Pothia, is the **Cave of the Seven Virgins** or **Cave of the Nymphs**. According to traditional accounts, the name comes from a story of seven maidens who, threatened with capture by pirates, took refuge in the cave and were never seen again.

In the same direction, but further to the south, is the **castle of Chrysochera**, built by the Knights of Rhodes on the ruins of an early Byzantine fortress. In the castle is a church of **Our Lady Chrysochera** ('of the golden hand').

2. Kalymnos - Vathy
(12.5 km.)

Vathy or **Vathys**, as the local people call it, is a village 12.5 km. to the east of Kalymnos in a verdant valley densely planted with citrus trees and above all with mandarins. Its little harbour, **Rina**, stands at the head of a superb fjord with steep cliffs to the left and right and quiet azure waters in between. This is one of the finest spots for swimming on the island, and perhaps among the greatest attractions of Kalymnos.

Rina, small harbour in narrow bay of Vathy.

Picturesque Myrties opposite the islet of Telendos.

Telendos

This islet, which looks simply like a large rock, was once joined to Kalymnos and was separated from it after a major earthquake which took place in the 6th century AD.

There is a regular service to it provided by small craft from Myr-

ties and a visit can be a pleasant surprise.

Its picturesque little tavernas and the few rooms to rent, but chiefly the marvellous beach with its black sand at the back of the island, tempt the visitor to extend his stay here to enjoy a peaceful and carefree holiday.

Pserimos

It has an excellent beach, a restaurant, fish tavernas and a few rooms for rent. It lies between Kos and Kalymnos, from which small craft provide a service daily in summer and twice a week in the winter. The trip takes 40 mins.

Leros

Lying between Patmos and Kalymnos, Leros is an island notable for the number and beauty of its bays. One of these, which forms the main port, Lakki, is the largest and safest in the Dodecanese.

Without high mountains, with plenty of greenery - particularly pines - it has an area of 53 sq. km. and a coastline of 71 km. Its population numbers more than 8,000, most of whom live in Lakki and in the three largest villages, which merge with one another: Platanos, the capital, Ayia Marina, the island's second harbour, and Panteli. These three villages, together with Lakki, also provide the chief interest on the island. An imposing fortress on the top of a hill above Platanos has a gorgeous view. It is from this point that the visitor can marvel at the lace-like beaches with their fine sand and blue sea, sparkling in the rays of the sun.

Leros is an attractive island with a good climate, so it is curious that it should have remained outside the mainstream of tourism to be found on the neighbouring islands. It will appeal most to those who favour quiet holidays.

Leros can be reached by air from Athens and by ferry from Piraeus, the islands of the Northern and Eastern Aegean, Kavala, Rhodes and other islands of the Dodecanese.

HISTORY

The island was inhabited in prehistoric times. It seems likely that its first inhabitants were the Pelasgians, the Leleges and the Carians. Next came the Dorians, who were in turn driven out by the Ionians. From that point on, Leros had close connections with the Ionian cities, particularly Miletus. Then came its capture by the Persians, who left after their defeat in Greece. During the Peloponnesian War, Leros was on the side of Sparta. In Byzantine times, it belonged to the Theme of Samos. In 1316, the Knights of the Order of St John became the rulers of the island, to be followed in 1522 by the Turks, who stayed until 1912, when they were succeeded by the Italians, who made Leros a naval base. This resulted in its being the scene of fighting during the Second World War and in Lakki being bombed mercilessly.

The union of Leros with Greece took place in 1948.

The Prophitis Ilias.

The Castle of Leros.

Lakki. This is the principal port of the island, on the enclosed bay of the same name. With its large buildings, wide streets and abundance of greenery, it produces a completely different picture from that of the villages which we shall see on a visit to the rest of the island. It is 3.5 km. from the capital, Platanos.

Platanos. The capital of the island, built in the manner of an amphitheater below an imposing fortress, with houses in the traditional style and picturesque alleyways. The small square with a plane tree in the middle, the town hall on one side and a cafeteria on the other, is an ideal place to sit back and plan your next moves. In the town hall there is a collection of antiquities and high up in the village, on the skirts of the fortress, the old church of **St Paraskeve**.

It is well worth visiting the fortress, which can be reached up steps.

It would seem that the castle occupies the site of an ancient acropolis (where a 7th century tomb has been found). Then a Byzantine castle was built on the hill, later being extended by the Knights of St John and taking the form we see today.

In the restored precinct is the church of **Our Lady or the Lady of the Castle**, dating from the early 14th century, with fine wall-paintings and a legendary icon of Our Lady.

Ayia Marina: From the square in Platanos, a road leads downhill in about 500 m. to the pretty village of Ayia Marina, to the north. This is the island's second harbour. There are a few traces of an ancient city. Ayia Marina and Platanos form, in effect, one village.

Panteli: To the south of Platanos is the third village on the island, Panteli, at the head of a bay by the same name which has a sandy beach.

Alinda: This is an attractive seaside village with a long beach and clear waters. It is 3 km. to the north-west of Platanos, at the head of the bay by the same name (also known as the bay of Ayia Marina).

To the west of the bay of Ayia Marina and close to it (across a neck of land) is the **bay of Gourna**, with two fine beaches, those of **Kokkali** and **Drymonas**.

In the vicinity is the picturesque chapel of St Isidore, which stands on a little island linked to the mainland by a cement causeway.

Partheni: This is a little village with an enclosed harbour on the north coast of the island, 9 km. from Platanos. Here there are caïque sailings for **Leipsi**, a nearby island. Also at Partheni is the island's airport.

Xirokampos. A coastal village at the southernmost extremity of the island, 8 km. from Platanos. It stands at the head of a narrow bay by the same name, with a sandy beach. On the hill of Palaiokastro, nearby, have been found the remains of a 4th century acropolis.

Leros

Leipsi

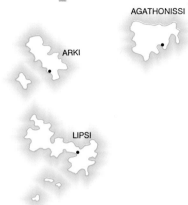

Leipsi is a quiet little island, 11 miles east of Patmos and eight miles north of Leros, still outside the mainstream of tourism. For this reason it is ideal for quiet holidays and the enjoyment of the sun and sea, with the hospitable islanders for company.

The island has an area of 16 sq. km. and there are no more than

The harbour of Leipsi

600 inhabitants, most of whom are farmers or fishermen. Its hills are gentle slopes, the highest, in the east of the island, being no higher than 300 m. Leipsi has coves all round its coast; one of these, the biggest and most sheltered, contains the harbour and village of Leipsi, which has a hotel and rooms to rent. In the pretty square are its white houses with blue door and window frames. Visitors should not leave without tasting the island's red wine, made from sun-dried grapes.

This was once plentiful: now very little is made. Those who are fond of walking can pay a visit to the Church of **Our Lady 'tou Charou'**, which was built in the early 17th century and is the most important on the island.

Leipsi can be reached by ship from Rhodes and the other Dodecanese. It is quicker, however, to go by caïque from Patmos or from Partheni and Ayia Marina on Leros. Apart from tractors, there are no motor vehicles on the island.

Arki

The biggest of a group of islands to the north of Leipsi, Arki lies 11 nautical miles from Patmos. Its port, with some 70 inhabitants, lies deep in a 'fjord', whose entrance is protected by other smaller islets. The houses of this unique village are built with dry-stone walling, without the use of mortar. .

On the islet of **Marathi** or **Marathonisi** opposite there is a fine sandy beach with a small guest-house and restaurant. In summer there is a daily boat service to and from Patmos.

Agathonisi

This is the northernmost island of the Dodecanese, 36 nautical miles from Patmos, with 130 inhabitants, most of them fishermen and farmers.

There is a boat service linking the island with Patmos twice a week.

Patmos

The island of Patmos is dominated by the imposing Monastery of St John, standing on the top of the hill above the harbour.

If you happen to arrive in the island's picturesque harbour in the evening, a large illuminated cross on the hill to the right will prepare you for the fact that you are about to visit a sacred island. Cruise ships bring their hasty visitors day after day. The buses are waiting to take them up to Chora, to see the famous monastery, to take a stroll in the attractive alleyways of the village, and then to be off again.

Patmos is a beautiful island, with many bays; it captivates the visitor from the first moment. You want to go everywhere - but the first and foremost objective is to visit the Monastery of St John the Divine and the Cave in which he wrote the Book of Revelation. In there, when you see the huge rock with the cleft in it which tradition tells us was made by an earthquake a little before the Apocalypse was started, few people fail to experience a sense of awe at what they see and are told.

Patmos lies at the north-western extremity of the Dodecanese, between Icaria and Leros. It has an area of 34 sq. km., a coastline of 63 km., and a population of 2,500. It is 163 nautical miles from Piraeus, and the first stop for the ferries going to Rhodes.

Patmos can be reached by ferry from Piraeus, the islands of the northern and eastern Aegean, Kavala, the Cyclades, Rhodes, and the other islands of the Dodecanese.

HISTORY

The ancient name of the island was 'Patnos', as can be seen from inscriptions of the 5th century BC. Finds from Kastelli hill, west of the harbour (of Skala), demonstrate the existence of an acropolis of the 4th century BC and a large city of the 6th - 4th centuries BC in the area around. The Romans used Patmos as a place of exile.

The Emperor Domitian exiled St John the Evangelist, called 'the

Divine' (= Theologian) to Patmos in the year 95 AD from Ephesus, where he had been preaching Christianity. It was on the island that St John, living the life of an ascetic in a cave, wrote the Apocalypse under the influence of visions, and some two years later left the island.

After that Patmos was a place of pilgrimage, but was left to the mercy of pirates. In 1088, the Blessed Christodoulos built, with the assistance of the Byzantine Emperor Alexius II Comnenus, the Monastery of St John, on the site of a temple to Artemis.

Some 50 years later, the Monastery, which owned the whole of the island, gave permission for houses

to be built around its walls, and so little by little Chora came into being.

In 1207 Patmos passed into the hands of the Venetians - more specifically, it became part of the Duchy of Naxos, which, however, gave almost complete independence to the Monastery and to the island as a whole. In 1537 began the long years of Turkish occupation. A glimmer of light in those dark days was provided by the setting up there in 1713 of the 'Patmian School'. During this period (16th - 19th century), however, the island's trade and shipping flourished. The Turkish occupation lasted (with a brief period of independence from 1821 to 1832) until 1912, when the island was taken by the Italians.

The incorporation of the island into the Greek state finally came in 1948.

St. John dictating Revelations to his disciple Prochoros. (Icon from the Monastery of Dionysios, Mt. Athos (p. 130).

Getting to know the island

The Cave of the Revelation. This lies halfway between Skala and Chora (4,5 km.). It takes the form of a 17th century monastery which was built around the cave where St John lived for some two years (95 - 97 AD) and wrote the Apocalypse, dictating it to his disciple Prochoros. Next to the Cave is the **church of St Anne**, built by the Blessed Christodoulos.

Above the Monastery of the Revelation are the buildings of the Patmian School, which today house a theological college.

Chora and the Monastery of St. John.

Chora. No ´Chora´ (= chief village of an island) in Greece is more impressive than this. The vast **Monastery of St John** dominates

it as a dark mass on the top of the hill, surrounded by gleaming white two and three-storey houses, most of them in the neo-Classical style.

Here we find narrow alleyways and, in the center of the village, a small but attractive square. At the entry to the village there are cafés and shops and, higher up, the entrance to the Monastery.

This has thick, high walls, crowned all round with battlements. it was built in 1088 by the Blessed Christodoulos. It is a Byzantine building and comes within the jurisdiction of the Patriarchate of Constantinople.

Its katholikon (main church) is cruciform with a dome, and has a beautiful sanctuary screen and wall paintings. Next to the katholikon is the treasury, which contains many relics of saints, priceless heirlooms, jewellery and votive offerings. The Monastery has eight chapels, one of which, that of the Blessed Christodoulos, contains his relics. Also of importance is the **Monastery library**. This contains some 3,000 books, many of which are extremely rare, 900 codices, and 1,300 documents, including a chrysobull of its donor, the Emperor Alexius I Comnenus.

To the south-east of Chora is the **Convent of the Annunciation,** built in 1937 around a religious house dating from 1613.

Skala. This is the island´s only harbour, more or less in its middle, lying in a narrow bay. At this point, the land forms a narrow neck, which seems to divide the island into two. Skala has seen a considerable development of its tourist facilities in recent years, so as to be able to serve its large number of visitors. It also has a camping-site at **Meloi.** West of Skala, on Kastelli hill, are the remains of the acropolis of the ancient city (4th cent. BC).

Grikos. This is an attractive seaside village 4 km. south-east of Skala. It lies in a corner of the bay of the same name, has a sandy beach and looks out on the islet of **Tragonisi**, which protects it from the wind. Near it is the fine sandy beach of **Kalikatzou**, which has a conical rock at the head of its promontory, and, further south, the beach of **Diakofti**, with its crystal-clear water. Further off is the famous **Psili Ammos**, with trees running down to the water, south-west of Diakofti. This is best reached by caïque from Skala.

Kambos. This lies in the north of the island, 6 km. from Skala, and is its most fertile and greenest part. Near it is the sandy beach of Kambos. East of Kambos, at a considerable distance, is the Monastery of **Our Lady ´tou Apollou´** and the church of **Our Lady ´tou Yeranou´**.

Scenes from the Monastery of St. John.

Spectacular village of Patmos with monastery. To the rear, Skala.

Karpathos

For many people the image which springs to mind when Karpathos is mentioned is that of a girl dressed in the multi-coloured traditional costume of the island and with her hair in a plait. This is probably because on Karpathos, and particularly in the village of Olympos, the women, defying the passage of time and the march of progress, insist on wearing this beautiful costume with its bright colours - and are proud of it.

Karpathos is the second largest island in the Dodecanese, with an area of 301 sq. km. and a coastline of 160 km. It lies between Rhodes and Crete and is 227 nautical miles from Piraeus.

This is a long, narrow, moutainous island, with picturesque villages perched on its green hillsides and attractive fishing harbours flanked with sandy beaches. Its highest mountain, Kali Limni, is more or less in the middle of the island and is 1,214 m. high. Its inhabitants, no more than 5,000 in number, are em-

ployed chiefly in farming, stock-breeding and fishing, while in the summer months a portion of the population is involved in the tourist trade. Karpathos is, however, most suitable for those who are looking for a quiet holiday, and particularly those who would also be interested in its rich folklore.

Karpathos can be reached by air from Athens (via Rhodes), Kasos, and Siteia in Crete or by ferry from Piraeus, the Cyclades, Crete, Rhodes and the other islands of the Dodecanese.

HISTORY

Karpathos is relatively near Crete, and it would seem that the island was first inhabited by the Minoans.

They were followed later by the Dorians, who enjoyed great prosperity in the 5th century BC. At this time the island had four cities of importance (Poseidion or Potidaion, Arkesia, Broukous, and Nisyros) and belonged to the Athenian League. This was followed by Roman domination, and, after the break-up of the Roman state, by the long Byzantine period, during which the island was repeatedly raided by pirates. In 1206 it passed into the hands of Leo Gavalas, and sub-

sequently into those of the Genoese, the Knights of Rhodes, and the Venetians. The Turks took Karpathos in 1538 and held it for almost four centuries. The island took part in the uprising against the Turks of 1821 and managed to gain its independence for seven years. In 1832 , however, by the Protocol of London, it again came into the hands of the Turks, until 1912, when it was taken by the Italians. The union of Karpathos with the Greek state finally came, together with the rest of the Dodecanese, in 1948.

Getting to know the island

Karpathos (Pigadia)

This is the island's capital and its chief port. It has an extensive sandy beach and stands on a hill on which the acropolis of the ancient city of Poseidion (Poseidonion was located.

The town is on the south-eastern coast, near the foothills of the tree-covered mountain of **Kali Limni.** Its houses are new, most of them built by Greek-Americans who come here for their summer holidays. An evening stroll along the road which runs above the harbour is to be recommended.

EXCURSIONS

1. Pigadia - Aperi - Othos - Arkasa - Menetes - Pigadia (39 km.)

This excursion is a tour of the main villages (with the exception of Olympos) by car. You set out in a northerly direction, parallel to the sea.

1.5 km. Basilica of St Photeini. On the right of the road, against the background of the sea, you can see the reconstructed pillars of this 5th - 6th century basilica, which was discovered in 1972.

8 km. Aperi. Once the capital of the island, this village with its fine mansions, most of which belong to Greek-Americans, is the seat of the Metropolitan of Karpathos. It stands in a verdant area at a height of 320 m. From Aperi, unsurfaced roads lead to the attractive spots of **Mertonas** and **Katodio** with their streams, and to the famous beaches of **Achata** and **Kyra-Panayia**.

10 km. Volada. This is a beautiful mountain village (at 440 m.) with a marvellous view out to sea and a large number of houses built in the traditional manner.

12 km. Othos. This is the highest village (510 m.) on the island, with the best view out to sea and over the whole of the south-eastern part of the island. It has a folklore museum in a typical Karpathian house which is well worth visiting, as is the church of **Our Lady**, dating from the 17th century.

At a distance of 3 km. from the village is a beauty-spot called **Stes**, which also has streams.

15 km. Pyles. This is a picturesque village, looking out on the west coast of the island. From here a branch of the road to the right leads, after 16 km., to **Mesochori**, one of the oldest and prettiest villages on Karpathos, and, after 4 more km., to the village of **Spoa**.

Both these villages have retained the traditional architecture, layout and decoration of the interiors of the houses, together with the old customs, in an unadulterated form. Spoa can also be reached from Aperi, which is nearer.

The road continues north towards Olympos. Between

Renowned sand beach of Kyra Panayia.

Pyles and **Mesochori**, a brief deviation towards the sea brings us to Lefko, a small village with a fine sandy beach. The whole of this area, like the islet of **Sokastro** opposite, is full of ancient remains, which, however, have not yet been excavated. From Pyles we continue to the left.

21 km. Finiki. This is a small seaside village with a sandy beach and a harbour with tavernas.

23 km. Arkasa. Another seaside village with a sandy beach, standing in a fertile area. Its name is derived from the ancient city of Arkesia, scanty remains of which can be found on the nearby **Palaiokastro** hill. In the same area are the remains of the church of **St Anastasia**, the marvellous mosaics from whose floor are now in Rhodes Museum. The distance here from Pigadia is 17 km.

31 km. Menetes. This is a village which is built like an amphitheater on the slopes of a 350 m.

mountain. Its old houses are perfectly preserved. The churches of **St Mamas** and of **Our Lady** are worth a visit.

34 km. At this point the road meets the one linking Pigadia with the airport, which is at the southernmost extremity of the island. From here a branch for 1 km. to the right and then 2.5 km. to the left leads to the fine sandy beach of **Abopi**, which can be reached in summer by bus from Pigadia.

39 km. Pigadia. This completes our tour.

2. Pigadia - Diafani - Olympos (16 nautical miles and 9 km.)

This excursion includes a trip to Diafani by caïque or boat, followed by a bus journey to Olympos.

Diafani. This is the island's second most important harbour, the port of Olympos. The boat puts in here.

Olympos. Called 'Elympos' locally, this village was until recently completely isolated, standing on the inaccesible mountains of the northern part of the island - a village where, as they say, time had stood still. Its history goes back at least five centuries, when the seaside city of Vroukounta (ancient Broukous) was destroyed by an earthquake. Olympos, safe from pirates in its lofty position, tries as much as possible to keep itself apart from the rest of the world. Indeed, to begin with it had walls built all round the houses for greater safety. Later, however, when the village grew in size and there was no longer room for the houses within the walls, it spread beyond them. As a result of this isolation, scarcely anything has changed at Olympos with the passage of time.

The traditional architecture of the houses has remained unaltered. The same can be said of the layout and decoration of the interiors. In other words, the whole village is a kind of museum. It is not, however, only in the buildings that tradition has been preserved. The manners and customs, the songs, the way of life have remained the same. Even the language which the villagers speak has changed very little, and for this reason the Doric dialect can still be heard in their speech - a rare phenomenon in present-day Greece.

We said above that Olympos was a village which had been isolated until recently - until recently because it has now been 'discovered' and there is an ever-increasing stream of visitors, a fact which to start with took the residents by surprise, and perhaps did not greatly please them. However, they have soon come to understand that their village must have something special about it which attracts visitors, and so they must not alter anything. The women must continue to wear their multi-coloured traditional costume, and now they respond to a shy request to photograph them by proudly striking a pose with the head held high and a restrained but confident smile on their lips.

Before leaving Olympos, the visitor should not miss a visit to the church of Our Lady, with its fine carved sanctuary screen and its atmosphere of late Byzantium. Also worth visiting are the churches of the Holy Trinity and St Onufrius. A stroll to the old windmills, which stand in a line, looking out to sea, is also recommended. If the miller's wife is there, she will, if asked, readily open out the sails of the mill and set it in motion, to demonstrate how it mills the corn - just as it has done for centuries.

Olympos is also a good place to try 'makarounes' - the speciality of Karpathos.

3. Trips by caïque

These trips are organised by travel agencies, with a view to making known the more inaccessible of the island's marvellous beaches.

Sailing north from Pigadia you encounter the following, in this order:

Achata. This is a little bay with an excellent sandy beach, surrounded by steep rocks.

Kyra-Panayia. Another fine sandy beach, with a chapel dedicated to Our Lady.

Apella. A picturesque bay with sand and crystal-clear water. It can be reached only from the sea. The surrounding area is very green. The half-ruined chapel of **St Luke** has traces of old wall-paintings.

Palatia. The ruins which can be seen here are in all probability those of the ancient city of **Nisyros** on the islet of **Saria** at the northernmost tip of Karpathos.

Tristomo. An enclosed harbour on the east coast of Karpathos, near the channel with the islet of Saria.

Vroukounta. This lies to the south-west of Tristomo. This is an area full of the remains of the ancient city of Broukous. It also has a **fortress** high on the hill, with the chapel of **St John** below.

Breathtaking village of Olympos with old windmills.

Kasos

MAKRONISSI
AMPATHIA
FRY
Emporios
Poli
Arvanitohori
PLATI
CHADIES
Agios Georgios

There is one day in the year, 7 June, when the visitor to the alleyways of the village of Kasos would meet a host of visitors, most of them Greek-Americans from New York. They would all have come to observe, together with the very few permanent residents, Kasos's most important anniversary, that of the 'Holocaust'.

Kasos is an island with a strong maritime traidition, but it is small and rocky and has been abandoned by a large part of its population, who went to seek their fortune abroad, particularly in America. Many of the island's people are still involved with the sea, as shipowners and captains, and are to be found on all the oceans of the world.

Kasos is the southernmost island of the Dodecanese and lies betwen Karpathos and Crete. It has an area of 66 sq. km. and its permanent residents, who are mostly farmers, stockbreeders and fishermen, are no more than 1,100 in number.

The folklore features which are present on Karpathos are equally marked on Kasos, though here the influence of neighbouring Crete is more apparent.

Kasos can be reached by air from Athens (via Rhodes), Karpathos, and Siteia in Crete, or by ferry from Piraeus, the Cyclades, Crete, Rhodes, and the other islands of the Doode-canese.

HISTORY

The Phoenicians were the first inhabitants of Kasos. Thereafter the island's history was similar to that of the rest of the Dodecanese and particularly of neighbouring Karpathos.

What must be stressed about Kasos is its maritime power, which was already apparent in 1779 when a French traveller, visiting the island, described it as "a small maritime state, maintained by shipping and trade, particularly with Syria".

When the Revolution of 1821 against the Turks began in Greece, Kasos provided 22 three-masted warships and 60 merchantmen, most of which were armed. This fleet, which anchored in summer at the islet of Armathia and in winter at Tristomo on Karpathos , began to be a serious harassment to the Sultan and Ibrahim Pasha, who after one failed attempt, succeeded in taking the island on 7 June 1824. Very few of the inhabitants escaped the slaughter which followed, and the whole of Kasos was burnt. This was the Holocaust, the anniversary of which is observed by the people of Kasos in a body each year. The subsequent history of the island is that of the rest of the islands of the Dodecanese. Kasos's union with the Greek state took place in 1948.

Getting to know the island

Fri. This is the island's capital and its only port. The ferry ties up at the jetty, alongside the **little harbour of Bouka**, which is crammed with boats and fishing-caïques.

Beaches for bathing: at Fri, Ayios Konstantinos, 2 km. south-west of Fri, and at the famous sandy beaches on the nearby islet of **Armathi**a.

Ayia Marina. This is a beautiful village with noteworthy churches and traditional houses, approximately 1 km. south-west of Fri. At a distance of 1.5 km., the **Ellinokamara cave** is of archaeological and historical interest and served as a place of refuge for the islanders during pirate raids.

The **Selaï cave** with its fine stalactites is 3 km. away.

Fri, the small harbour of Kasos.

Arvanitochori. This village stands almost in the centre of the island.

Emboreios. this is the island's old commercial harbour, less than 1 km. east of Fri. This is the site of the early Christian church of Our Lady, the biggest on the island. Next to the church is the baptistry and some ancient marble columns.

Panayia. 1 km. east of Fri. Worth seeing is the Church of Our Lady 'tou Yorghi', dating from 1770.

Poli. The old capital of the island, 2 km. south-east of Fri. On the nearby hill are remains of the ancient fortress. The Church of the "Holy Trinity", with its blue walls and orange domes, is particularly beautiful.

Hadies. This is an area at the south-western end of the island, 12 km. from Fri. This is the site of the **Monastery of St George**, which has a large guesthouse, and, futher south, of the **Helandros bay**, which is a good place for swimming.

Kastelorizo

RO

KASTELLORIZO (Megisti)

Galazia (Fokiali)

STROGYLI

This is Greece's eastern extremity, 72 miles from the port of Rhodes. It is only one mile from the southern coast of Turkey, and 150 miles from Cyprus. This is a small and rocky island, and yet at the beginning of the present century it had 15,000 inhabitants. Today, of all this nothing remains except its houses, in ruins as the result of fire and bombing. Those close to the harbour have been repaired and are gleaming white with their doors and window-frames painted in bright colours.

Today, the permanent residents, who number just over 200, are mostly fishermen.

Most of the people have emigrated to Australia.

Kastelorizo can be reached from Rhodes by boat or air.

HISTORY

Kastelorizo has been inhabited since Neolithic times. Its ancient name, still used today, was Megiste. The presence of the Myceneans on the island has been confirmed by the finding of Mycenean tombs. The Dorians who came later built an acropolis on the low hill next to the harbour and the fortress at Palaokastro, west of the harbour.

In 1306, the island passed into the possession of the Knights of St John, to be taken in 1440 by the Sultan of Egypt and in 1450 by the King of Naples, Alfonso I of Aragon. The long Turkish occupation began in 1512 and came to an end in 1920, when the Italians became rulers of the island. It was then that the gradual emigration of the population began.

Kastelorizo was bombed in the course of the Second World War and the fire which this caused resulted in a further diminution of the population.

*Kastelorizo,
one of the most picturesque
harbours in the Dodecanese.*

Getting to know the island

Kastelorizo. Perhaps the most picturesque harbour in the Dodecanese. Kastelorizo has its houses - of two or more storeys - grouped in a semicircle. On the left as we enter the harbour is the **Fortress of the Knights of St John**, built in the 14th century on a hill with red rocks - the 'Castello Rosso' or 'Red Castle'. It is from this that the island's more modern name of Castellorizo is derived. At the back of the harbour, on the slopes of the mountain, is the white path which zig-zags up to the Monastery of **St George** ('Ai Yorghi'). To the east is a second little harbour, **Mandraki**, and above it on a kind of platform, the famous church of **St Constantine**, the cathedral, built in 1833. Its roof is supported by 12 granite columns, brought from the Temple of Apollo at Tatara, in Lycia on the opposite shore.

The **Archaeological Museum** has been housed since 1984 in a bastion of the Fortress of the Knights, which has been altered to fit it for this purpose.

Close to the Museum and about 20 m. from the sea is a magnificent **Lycian Tomb**, carved in the rock, of the 4th - 3rd century BC, similar to ones which have been found in Lycia on the mainland opposite. The churches of **St Nicholas**, of the 11th century, below the fortress (in ruins), Our Lady 'of the Fields' and St Mercurius are noteworthy. Virtually all the inhabitants of the island live in the town of Kastelorizo.

The Blue Cave (Fokiali). This is said by some to be more beautiful than Capri's Blue Grotto. It is on the south-eastern coast of the island and can be entered by boat only when the sea is calm.

Monastery of St George. Built in 1759, it has a catacomb. The view from the path up to it towards the harbour is uniquely fine.

Palaiokastro. This is the Dorian acropolis to the west of the harbour. Parts of the wall remain. **Cyclopean Walls**. These are to be found at various points on the island. Perhaps the most impressive are those near **Kambos**, between Palaiokastro and Mounta hill.

Neighbouring islands. To the south-east is the islet of **Strongyli**, whose sole inhabitants are its lighthouse-keepers.

The islet of **Rho**, near Kastelorizo, had until a few years ago a single inhabitant, who guarded it and ran up the Greek flag every morning. This was Despina Achadioti, the Lady of Rho, as she was known. The Lady of Rho died in 1982 at the age of 92.

Above: Part of harbour of Kastelorizo.

Below: Mandraki with the church of St. Constantine.

140

THE ISLANDS AND ISLETS OF THE DODECANESE

RHODES
Prasonisi............................S Rhodes.
Makry, Strongyli............W Rhodes.
Chtenies..........................SW Rhodes.
Karabolas.........................SW Rhodes.
Strongyla.........................W Rhodes.

SYMI
Nimos.....................................N Symi.
Chondro...............................N Symi.
Platy.....................................N Symi.
Oxya.................................NW Symi.
Diavates.............................W Symi.
    Didyma.............................W Symi.
    Gi.......................................W Symi.
    Megalonisi.....................W Symi.
    Karavonisi......................W Symi.
    Marmaras.......................W Symi.
Seskli.......................................S Symi.
Troumbeto............................S Symi.
Strongylo...............................S Symi.
Ayia Marina.....................E harbour.

HALKI
Nisa.......................................E harbour.
Krevatia.........................SE harbour.
Alimia.................................NE Halki.
Ayios Theodoros.............NE Halki.
Tragousa................................E Halki.

TILOS
Antitilos................................SE Tilos.
Gaidoros............................NE Livadi.
Nisi.....................................NW Tilos.

KOS
Kastri...................Op. Ayios Stefanos.
Prasso...............................N Kefalos.

NISYROS
Yiali.....................................NE Nisyros.
Ayios Antonios......................E Yiali.
Strongyli...................................E Yiali.
Pacheia.............................W Nisyros.
Pergousa..........................W Nisyros.
Kandeliousa.....................SW Nisyros.

ASTYPALAIA
Diaporia.................Bay of Maltezana.
Ligno......................Bay of Maltezana.
Chondro................Bay of Maltezana.
Nisia Ayias Kyriakis..S Maltezana.
Koutsomyti...................SE Maltezana.
Kounoupoi.....................SE Maltezana.
Fokionisia......................N Astypalaia.
Panormos.....................NW Astypalaia.
Katsagreli......................NW Astypalaia.
Pontikousa.....................E Astypalaia.
Ofidousa.........................E Astypalaia.

KALYMNOS
Karavros.........................S Emboreio.

Ayios Andreas..............S Kalymnos.
Nera......................................S Kalymnos.
Safonidi...............................S Kalymnos.
Kalolimnos.......................NE Kalymnos.
Pitta.....................................NE Kalymnos.
Prasolo..............................NE Kalymnos.
Limnia.................................NE Kalymnos.
Saronisi...............................E Kalymnos.

TELENDOS
Apano Nisi..................NW Telendos.
Ayia Kyriaki....................S Telendos.

PSERIMOS
Plati.....................................W Pserimos.
Zouka.................................N Pserimos.

LEROS
Archangelos.........................NW Leros.
Faradonisia.........................NW Leros.
Strongyli....................................N Leros.
Plakousa...................................N Leros.
Trypiti..N Leros.
Petalioi.....................................N Leros.
Ayia Kyriaki...................SE Pantelios.
Piganoussa............................SE Leros.
Glaronisia.................................S Leros.
    Velona.....................................S Leros.
    Gaviani....................................S Leros.
    Diapori....................................S Leros.

PATMOS
Kentronisi.............Bay of Kambos.
Ayios Georgios......Bay of Kambos.
Ayia Thekla............Bay of Kambos.
Sklava......................................E Skala.
Sklavopoula.........................E Skala.
Xeropouli................................E Skala.
Pilafi.......................................E Sapsila.
Tragonisi...................Bay of Grigos.
Prasonisi..............................S Patmos.
Mersini.........................Bay of Lefka.
Anydro..............................NW Patmos.
Petrokaravo...................NW Patmos.

LEIPSI
Arefousa...............................NW Leipsi.
Voreia Aspronisia.........NW Leipsi.
Notia Aspronisia..............E Leipsi.
Kalapodia..............................SE Leipsi.
Kyra.........................Bay of Katsadia.
Makry..S Leipsi.
Kalavres...................................S Leipsi.
Sarakianos.............................S Leipsi.

ARKI
Marathi....................................SW Arki.
Stronglylo...............................SW Arki.
Marathos................................SW Arki.
Makronisi................................SE Arki.
Kalovolo..................................SE Arki.
Kamaros...................................N Arki.

AGATHONISI
Psathonisi.................N Agathonisi.
Strongyli.....................N Agathonisi.
Mera.............................N Agathonisi.
Glaros........................NE Agathonisi.
Kouneli........................S Agathonisi.

KARPATHOS
Saria..............................N Karpathos.
Prasonisi.....................N Karpathos.
Sokastro.....................W Karpathos.
Diakoftis....................SW Karpathos.
Prasonisi.....................SE Karpathos.
Moira............................Se Karpathos.

KASOS
Armathia.............................NW Kasos.
Litra.......................................NW Kasos.
Pontikonisia.....................NW Kasos.
Makronisi...............................N Kasos.
Koufonisi.................................N Kasos.
Koskino....................................N Kasos.
Kalofonas............................NE Kasos.
Strongyli...................................E Kasos.
Platy...W Kasos.
Kouroukia...............................W Kasos.

KASTELORIZO
Ro...............................W Kastelorizo.
Strongyli...................SE Kastelorizo.
Proradia...........................E harbour.
Ayios Georgios..............E harbour.
Polyfados..........................E harbour.
Psomi.................................E harbour.

OTHER ISLETS
Farmakonisi......................NE Leros.
Megalo Livadi..............E Amorgos.
Mikro Livadi..................E Amorgos.
Kinaros...................................SW Leros.
Glaros.....................................SW Leros.
Mavra......................................SW Leros.
Levida......................................SW Leros.
Syrna...................................SE Astypalaia.
Katsikoulia........................SE Astypalaia.
Tria Nisia..........................SE Astypalaia.
    Plakia......................SE Astypalaia.
    Meso........................SE Astypalaia.
    Stephania..............SE Astypalaia.
Nisia Zafora.......................SE Astypalaia.
    Meg. Sofrano........S Astypalaia.
    Mikro Sofrano........S Astypalaia.
    Karavonisia............S Astypalaia.
    Avgonisi..............NW Karpathos.
    Adelfes.................W Karpathos.
Chamilonisi..................W Karpathos.
Astakida.......................NW Karpathos.
Astakidopoula.........NW Karpathos.
Divounia......................W Karpathos.

A narrow channel only 40 meters wide separates Euboea from mainland Greece. Between them is a sea current that frequently reaches speeds of 8 miles an hours. The strange thing is not the speed but that every six hours the current changes direction. This back and forth movement has gone on for thousands of years non stop. This is the famous strait of Evripos, 80 km. north of Athens, which many ancient sages as well as modern-day researchers have studied, finally concluding it is a tidal phenomenon caused by the moon's attraction. There is a drawbridge over Evripos which opens to let the boats pass through and connects the island to the mainland by road. Beyond the bridge is the lovely town of Chalkida, the capital of Euboea, which lends its own special tone to the landscape. Right and left, further than the eye can see, this long, narrow island stretches for more than 175 km.

Euboea is mountainous with abundant flora and its landscape features abrupt changes. Very hilly in its interior it is also full of firs and pines with picturesque villages clinging to the slopes, ravines choked with plane and chestnut trees and murmuring streams, followed by fertile plains covered in fruit trees. There are leeward shores with gorgeous sand beaches, but also steep cliffs battered by the waves of the Aegean; quaint fishing harbours but

The Petalioi islets, south of Euboea

ALONISSOS
SKIATHOS
SKOPELOS
EVIA
SKYROS
Chalkida

also modern tourist installations to satisfy any whim a visitor might have.

North of Euboea are the Sporades, an island complex we will speak of below.

South of Euboea are the charming Petalioi islets. You can see them from the road winding high above. The coast sparkls in the sun-bright sea. Arriving you see they are stark but with pure white sand beaches.

There is a large number of small islands besides the Petalioi islands and rocky out-croppings of which we mention a total of 55, giving their special "mark". Of these, including Euboea itself, only 9 are inhabited.

Euboea

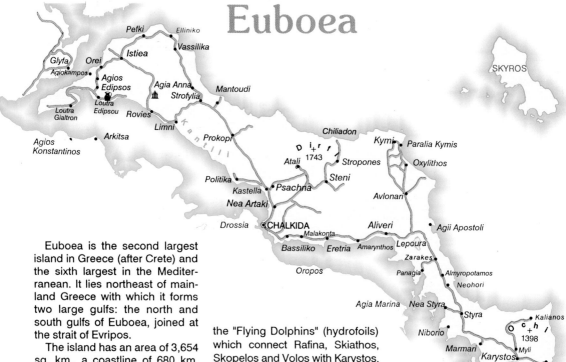

Euboea is the second largest island in Greece (after Crete) and the sixth largest in the Mediterranean. It lies northeast of mainland Greece with which it forms two large gulfs: the north and south gulfs of Euboea, joined at the strait of Evripos.

The island has an area of 3,654 sq. km., a coastline of 680 km. and a population of 185,000. Its main mountains are Kantili (1,246 m.) looming over the waters of the north Euboean gulf, the imposing Dirfys (1,743 m.) in the center of the island, the Euboean Olympos (1,172 m.) a little further south, and Ochi (1,398 m.) at its south - eastern tip.

The main products produced on Euboea are olive oil, cereals and figs. It also produces mineral products, primarily magnesite which is one of the richest sources of magnesium. Animal husbandry and poultry farming are also quite well-developed on the island.

You can reach Euboea by bus or in your own automobile, going over the old bridge at Evripos or the new suspension bridge. You can also go by ferry boat on the following routes:

From Oropos, Attica to Eretria, Euboea; from Rafina, Attica to Karysto and Marmari; from Ayia Marina, Attica to Styra and Alymropotamos; from Akritsa to Aidipsos, from Glyfa in Phthiotis to Ayiokambos. There are also connections from the Sporades, mainly Skyros to Kymi.

In the summer the schedules of the ferry boats are augmented by the "Flying Dolphins" (hydrofoils) which connect Rafina, Skiathos, Skopelos and Volos with Karystos, Marmari, Styra, Chalkida, Gregolimano, Aidipsos and Pefki. (The last seven are all harbors on Euboea).

You can also reach Chalkida from Athens by train.

HISTORY

Euboea has been inhabited since the end of the Neolithic period. Finds which belong to the third millenium B.C. show that most of its settlements were then concentrated in the center of the island and along its western coast. During that period it developed trade with the Cyclades and many Mycenean settlements appeared during the second millenium.

Homer refers to Euboea by name, though the island formerly had other names as well such as Makri and Dolchni. It is also mentioned that it took part in the Trojan War (12th century B.C.). At the end of the second millenium, Thessalians and Dryopians came to the island and settled there, mainly in north and south Euboea respectively, and were followed by the Ionians and the Dorians.

Euboea reached its greatest historical height in the 8th and 7th century B.C. Then two of its many independent towns stood out: Chalcis and Eretria. Both of them were rich from trade which they had developed with practically the entire ancient world, and powerful because of their war fleet; they created colonies in Chalkidiki, Thrace, the Sporades, Sicily and southern Italy. Between the two towns, which are no more than twenty kilometres apart, lay (and still does) the most fertile plain on the island, the Lilantine plain which is split by the Lilas river. This plain was the cause of not only the frequent conflicts between the two towns over its possession, but also the declaration of war between Athens and

Above: The waterfront of Eretria with the small peninsula called the Isle of Dreams.

Below: Impressive suspension bridge at Chalkida, joining the island to the Greek mainland.

became a member of the Athenian Alliance. In 371 B.C. the island came under the authority of Thebes and in 350 B.C. the Macedonians. In 194 B.C. the Romans became the rulers of Euboea. This was followed by the long Byzantine period up to 1205 A.D. when the Franks appeared. Then the ruler of the island was the King of Thessaloniki, Boniface de Montferrat, who in agreement with the feudal system divided Euboea into three baronies. The Venetians seized the island in 1336. They were the ones who, in honour of the famous bridge of Evripos, renamed the island Negroponte (Black Bridge). In 1470 Euboea was captured by the Turks, who were to hold on to it for more than 350 years.

Chalcis. During this war, in 506 B.C., Chalcis was defeated and the Athenians shared out the contested plain to thousands of settlers. Then came the Persian wars and the pillaging of Eretria by Darius, the King of the Persians only to have the Athenians return after the withdrawal of the Persians.

Near the end of the Peloponnesian War, Euboea was occupied by Sparta, but in 378 B.C. it

During the Greek War of Independence of 1821, the people of Euboea played their part and many battles were waged on the island till it was finally liberated in 1829.

Chalkida

The capital of Euboea is this pretty and modern town with 45,000 inhabitants, built on the site of ancient Chalcis of which only a few traces remain. Just as in ancient times, this site is still the key to the strait of Evripos and it has played an important role in its development. The largest part of the town lies east of the bridge, on the island itself. But there is also a smaller section which developed recently on the coast opposite, in Boeotia. Near it, on the peak of a hill, is the commanding Turkish fortress of **Karababas** built in 1686 on the ruins of fortifications from the 5th century B.C.

The view from the fortress toward the town and the Gulf of Euboea is unique. Opposite and southeast of the bridge is the neighborhood of **Kastro**, at the entrance to which is the old **mosque of Emir Zade**, with a marble fountain in front. Near the mosque, which houses a museum with medieval and Byzantine exhibits, is **Ayia Paraskevi**, the oldest church in Chalkida. This is a basilica from perhaps the 5th century which has been subjected to many alterations and additions, first by the Franks and then the Venetians. The interior decoration is impressive.

On El. Venizelos Avenue is the **Archaeological Museum** with important finds from throughout Euboea. A section from the pediment of the Temple of the Laurel-Crowned Apollo, from Eretria, is outstanding.

In Chalkida one can also visit the Folk Museum, the Municipal Gallery and the medieval aqueduct. But what one must really not miss is a stroll along the picturesque harbour with its cafes and restaurants all in a row and the famous **bridge of Evripos** which was first built in 441 B.C. and was followed by three more structures, the last one in 1962.

There, on the bridge, the visitor who watches the sea current racing through the channel, is bound to speculate on it, as all researchers have speculated, at least those who have occupied themselves with this strange phenomenon which we have already spoken about at the beginning of the chapter.

Town of Chalkida with channel of Evripos.

Statue of Antinoos, from Archaeological Museum of Chalkida.

EXCURSIONS

1. Chalkida - Strofylia - Istiaia - Aidipsos (155 km.)

On this excursion you will come to know a section of central Euboea, but above all northern Euboea with its lovely pine forests and endless sand beaches.

You take the coast road which heads north from Chalkida.

8 km. Nea Artaki. A large, coastal settlement with restaurants and fish tavernas. The turn-off from here right goes to the picturesque village of Steni which is described on page 149.

15 km. Psachna. A market town in the center of a fertile valley. 8 km. NE is the convent of Panayia Makrymalli.

From the crossroads at Psachna a turn-off left from the main excursion leads after 9 km. to **Politika**, a small town near the sea. In the summer it is very active around Politika because of its extensive sand beach.

Church of Ayios Ioannis Rosos at Prokopi.

52 km. Prokopi. A small settlement nestled in dense vegetation with a beautiful church, **Ayios Ioannis Roso** in which the saint's holy relic is housed.

You reach this village after a marvelous drive alongside a ravine full of plain trees. From Prokopi a turn-off right leads after 11 km. to the coastal village of Peli. From Prokopi the road to Mantoudi goes along the river Kireas which is shrouded in ancient plane trees.

60 km. Mantoudi. A large village with deposits of magnesite nearby. Its port is **Kymasi**.

64 km. Junction. The road right leads after five km. to the coast at **Krya Vrysi** with a vast beach of brown sand and strange rocks which at some point form a small natural bridge over the sand.

68 km. Strofylia. A Mediterranean village from which the road left leads to **Limni**.

75 km. Ayia Anna. A turn-off from this village right leads after 4 km. to **Agali**, a seaside settlement with a spacious sand beach.

86 km. From here a turn-off right leads after 6 km. to the well-known beach of **Kotsikias** with a most lovely coloured sea.

98 km. Vasilika. A village surrounded by greenery, 10 km. from Papades. Its harbour is the waterfront of **Psaropouli**.

122 km Pefki. A tourist center on a bay with a superb sand beach and pine trees in the surrounding area. In summer one can take small boats from here to Koukounaries on Skiathos. You reach Pefki after passing through the villages of **Ayriovotano**, **Gouves** and **Artemisio** which sunk in greenery, survey the sea from on high.

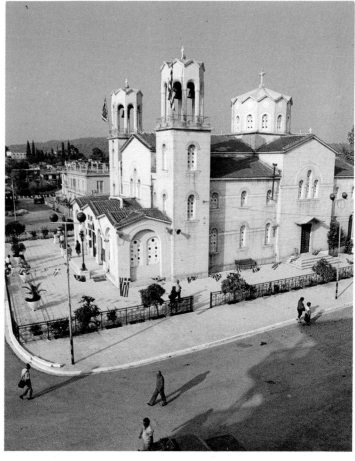

133 km. Istiaia. The capital of one of the three provinces of Euboea (the other two are Chalkida and Karystos) with more than 5,000 inhabitants. It is mentioned by Homer as *"rich in grapes"* because of its production of grapes, the quality of which is still renowned today. In Istiaia there is a small museum with a local hunting collection of stuffed animals and birds from the region as well as an archaeological collection housed in the Mayor's Office, and a Folk Museum.

139 km. Oraioi. The harbour of Istiaia is the channel that separates Euboea from Magnesia and Phthiotis. In the summer it is connected to Volos and Trikeri. On the adjacent hills are the ruins of two acropolises and a medieval castle.

144 km. Junction. A road right goes after 1 km. to **Ayiokambos** a picturesque seaside settlement, with the clearest of seas. There are daily ferry boats from Ayiokambos to Glyfa opposite in Phthiotis.

Views from the cosmopolitan spa of Aidipsos.

155 km. Aidipsos. The largest bathing-resort in Greece which developed because of its warm, medicinal springs, suitable for the treatment of many complaints, mainly arthritis and sciatica. Concerning these springs (which were known in antiquity) Greek mythology states that Hercules drew strength from them. During Roman times they were visited by Roman emperors as well as General Sylla for the treatment of his gout. Ruins of the "Sylla hot-springs" with their vaults still exist today. It goes without saying, that someone who has no need of warm springs can still enjoy the sea and the social life this bathing-resort has to offer. Aidipsos is connected by ferry boat to the harbour of **Arkitsa** opposite, which shortens the trip to Athens a great deal.

From the village of Aidipsos (3 km. N) a coast road going west passes through **Loutra Gialtron** (15 km.) and the gorgeous site **Gregolimano** ending at the sand beach of **Ayios Georgios** (25 km.) and the village of **Lichada**.

2. Chalkida - Strofylia - Limni - Aidipsos (117 km.)

68 Strofylia. Follow excursion 1 and at Strofylia go left.
87 km. Limni. Pretty little town built amphi-theatrically above the sea, with a thick pine forest all around it. 8 km. NE of Limni is the **Convent of Galataki** and nearby a marvellous sand beach. Wall paintings from the 16th century can be found in the main church of the convent.

From Limni you take the road heading NW, next to the sea.
97 km. Rovies. A seaside village with pine trees, fruit trees and a crystal-clear sea.
117 km. Aidipsos.

Stone fountain at Steni, Euboea.

3. Chalkida - Steni - Stropones (46 km.)

On this excursion you will come to know the picturesque Steni nestled in greenery and will reach the refuge of Dirfys, the highest mountain on Euboea.
8 km. Nea Artaki. From here you go right.
23 km. Kathenoi. A village with a view of the imposing Dirfys. Here you meet the road coming from **Attali, Triada** and **Psachna**.

31 km. Steni. It is built in a lush, green ravine through which flow the waters of springs near the village.

It has hotels, quaint little tavernas and restaurants under the plane trees. The stroll along the road that goes up toward Dirfys among the chestnuts and fir trees is very enjoyable.

The same road goes over the pass of Dirfys from which the refuge (1,150 m.) is 1 km. distant. From the refuge the ascent to the summit of Dirfys (1,743 m.) can be done in about two hours. The view of the sea from the usually snow-capped peak of the mountain is spectacular.

The road, not always in prime condition, heads down the defile to the Aegean, passing through a dense forest.

46 km. Stropones. An isolated village on the north side of Dirfys. From here a road goes to a beach with large pebbles, crystal-clear water and impressive rocks. Near the beach is the old **Monastery of Chiliadous**.

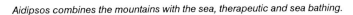

Aidipsos combines the mountains with the sea, therapeutic and sea bathing.

4. Chalkida - Eretria - Kymi (91 km.)

You take the road that goes NE for Eretria.

10 km. Vasiliko. An extensive settlement on the fertile Lilas plain. From here the road right goes, after 2 km., to Levkanti, a much frequented seaside settlement.

18 km. Malakonta. An area with large hotels, camping and a sand beach.

22 km. Eretria. A market town whose tourist development is owed to the ravishing beach, its antiquities and its site (here is where the ferry boats from Oropos, Attica, dock). It was one of the two powerful towns on ancient Euboea. Among the ruins of ancient Eretria are those of the **theater**, the sanctuary of Dionysos, the ancient Gymnasium, sections of the wall of the acropolis and the temple of the Laurel-Crowned Apollo.

The **Archaeological Museum** is worth a visit as well as the small peninsula, Isle of Dreams, which is near the harbour.

31 km. Amarynthos. A lovely, seaside town. 7 km. away is the village of **Gymno** on the slopes of Euboean Olympos.

48 Aliveri. A small town with 5,000 inhabitants, 2 km. from the sea.

56 km. Lepoura. In this village you will go left toward the north. The road right goes SE to south Euboea.

67 km. Junction. The road right leads after 1 km. to the traditional village of **Avlonari** with a medieval tower and the church of Ayios Dimitrios (11th century) and 7 km. later the village of **Ochthonia** (alt: 420 m.). Just before Ochthonia, on the right, in a beautiful site full of poplars, is the **Lefka Monastery**, one of the oldest monasteries on Euboea.

91 km. Kymi. This marvelous balcony on the Aegean is a small town of 2,700 inhabitants. Known since antiquity, it has retained its naval tradition right up to the present as many of its inhabitants are sailors. All the environs are dense with greenery and the view of the sea is superb. The ferry boats leave for Skyros from the sea-front of Kymi, 4 km. away.

Near Kymi is the site **Choneftiko**, with its plane trees and celebrated spring, the water of which is recommended to people with kidney ailments and gallstones. South of Kymi is the beautiful sand beach of **Platanas** and the village of **Oxylithos** under the pointed peak of the like-named mountain.

5. Chalkida - Karystos (129 km.)

You take excursion 4 up to 56 km., at Lepoura, and then go right, to the NE.

59 km. Krieza. From this village a branch left leads after 5 km. to **Petries** and 4 km. further to the beach of **Ayioi Apostoloi**, of the finest sand.

79 km. Almyropotamos. The port of this village, **Panayia**, is connected by ferry boat to Ayia Marina, Attica, on the opposite coast.

87 km. Junction. You leave the main road and go right toward Nea Styra.

Eretria with its archaeological sites and the Isle of Dreams right.

92 km. Nea Styra. A beautiful tourist centre in a bay protected from the winds by the small island of **Styra**, which lies opposite. Its rapid development is due to its splendid sand beach and its proximity to Athens. The ferry boats from the shores of Ayia Marina opposite dock in its harbour.

97 km. Styra. This village is on the main road to which you return and continue south.

100 km. Kapsala. From here a turn-off right leads to the picturesque bay of **Niborio** with clean water and a small settlement.

116 km. The road right goes, after 6 km., to **Marmari**, a coastal settlement with beautiful sand beaches. It is very active in summer. It has regular connections with Rafina, Attica by ferry boat which shortens the journey a great deal. Opposite Marmari are the charming private islets called **Petalioi**.

129 km. Karystos. A lovely little town to the rear of a horseshoe-shaped bay. It is on the south end of Euboea, beneath Ochi, the second largest mountain on the island. It is considered to be one of the most important summer

Karystos from Kokkino Kastro.

resorts on the island. Next to the harbour is the Venetian fortress of Bourtzi, and north of the town, on the luxuriant slopes of Ochi, the traditional villages of **Myloi** and **Grabia**. Near the latter, and on the peak of a hill, is the ruined **Kastello Roso** (Red Castle) with a breathtaking view of the sea. That is where ancient Karystos was built, known from prehistoric times for its powerful commercial and military fleet.

From Karystos one can visit the beautiful sand beach of **Bouros** and explore the villages which begin at the picturesque **Platanisto** and stretch all the way to cape Kaferea (Kavo Doro) fabled for its storms.

Sand beach of Marmari.

THE SPORADES

The most charming, the most enchanting islands in the Aegean. The abundant greenery and the emerald water around the shores is reminiscent of neighbouring Pelion. Skiathos is the nearest to this beautiful mountain and is the most highly developed of the islands touristically, with some of the most dazzling sand beaches in Greece. Further east is Skopelos with its luxuriant mountains and picturesque Aegean harbour. Next to it is Alonissos with a dense pine forest and a incredible underwater world. This island and its neighbouring islands are the last refuge for the small Mediterranean seal. Near Euboea is Skyros with its traditional Chora perched on a barren hill, and its celebrated folk art - Skyrian furniture and ceramics.

The trip to Skiathos, Skopelos and Alonissos is by a small ferry boat or the speedy hydrofoils from Ayios Konstantinos and Volos. Skyros is reached from Kymi, Euboea. There are also connections by plane from Athens to Skiathos and Skyros. Finally it should be noted that there are a host of small islands and rocky outcroppings around the four main islands which number more than 700. We describe (or simply fix the location of) a total of 73, of which only 9 are inhabited.

Lalaria, Skiathos:
one of the most beautiful
beaches on Greece

Skiathos

Skiathos was one of the first of the unknown paradises to be discovered. Until then it was known only from the short stories of Papadiamantis. Upon first seeing it travellers must think: "how can such a small island have all this beauty?"

Luxury hotels slowly began to be built along its lovely sand beaches, tourist activity continually grew and Skiathos became one of the most cosmopolitan islands in the Aegean.

Life on Skiathos has changed a great deal since the days when it was discovered. But its celebrated beaches are still beautiful and the narrow lanes of Chora are still as picturesque as ever. On one of them is the house of Papadiamantis, serious and severe, untouched by the passage of time, reminding one of other periods, which the great prose writer wrote about.

Skiathos is the first island one meets east of Pelion. It lies 41 nautical miles from Volos and 44 nautical miles from Ayios Konstantinos. It low hills are covered with pine trees and there are many small and large bays with wonderful sand beaches. It has an area of 48 sq. km., a coastline of 44 km and a population of 4,200.

You go to Skiathos by plane from Athens. You can also go by ferry boat or the fast hydrofoils from Ayios Konstantinos, Volos, Alonissos and Skopelos. In summer you can also go from Kymi, Euboea, Skyros and other islands.

Papadiamantis house.

HISTORY

Skiathos took part in wars against the Persians and in 478 B.C. became a part of the Athenian Alliance. Later it was

occupied by the Macedonians and then the Romans.

During the Byzantine period it sank into oblivion. In 1204 it was conquered by the Venetians and in 1538 by the Turks. It was then that the inhabitants of the old town, built on the site of present-day Skiathos, abandoned it and constructed on the north side of the island the famous Kastro, perched on a nearly invisible rock.

During the Greek War of Independence of 1821 many warriors from Thessaly opposite took refuge on the island. Skiathos was liberated in 1823. In 1830 the Skiathians left their historic Kastro and rebuilt Chora, which one visits today.

The great short-story writer Alexandros Papadiamantis (1851-1911), who was born on Skiathos, revitalizes through his stories interesting pages from the history of the island.

View of the harbour of Skiathos.

Lovely Bourtzi.

Skiathos or Chora

Chora was built around 1830 on the site of the old, abandoned town. Its picturesque, narrow lanes are filled with vitality in summer. Here is the home of the great prose writer **Alexandros Papadiamantis**, which operates as a museum and contains much of his furniture and other personal belongings.

Between the two harbours of Chora is the small peninsula of **Bourtzi** with pine trees and the ruins of a wall from an old castle. Chora also has some interesting churches. Among them **Treis Ierarches**, the cathedral church in the upper part of the town, stands out.

Near Chora is the settlement of **Ftelia** and the beach **Megali Ammos**.

4 km. Achladies. A small bay with one of the finest sand beaches on the island and a settlement which has developed into a modern summer tourist resort.

4.5 km. Tzaneries. A more enclosed bay than Achladies, which also developed into a modern summer tourist resort.

4.5 km. Kanapitsa. A settlement south of the bay of Tzanaries.

8 km. Troullos. Settlement at the junction with the road that leads to the monastery of **Panayia Kounistra**.

11 km. Koukounaries. At this point begins the most beautiful beach in Greece. It is shaped like a horseshoe and has golden sands surrounded by lofty and deep green pine trees. A stream flows past the beginning of the sand and a small bridge connects you to the marvellous beach. Behind the pine forest a lake completes this site of rare beauty.

East of here are the beaches of **Banana, Krassa** and **Ayia Eleni** and north, after a dense pine forest, the exotic **Mandraki** with its high sand dunes which end in a steep descent to the sea.

155

Excursions by caïque

Going round the island by caïque you will see the following sites: **Galazia Spilia** (Blue Cave) on the north part of the island and **Skotini Spilia** (Dark Cave), near Galazia Spilia. When you get used to the dark the spectacle is breathtaking.

Lalaria and **Trypia Petra**. This is an impressive beach with white, round pebbles of various sizes. At its end, a rock forms a bridge over the emerald water of the sea.

Kastro. An imposing rock on the northermost part of the island near Lalaria. In the 16th century the Skiathians built their castle up there containing three hundred houses and thirty churches. There they waged their battle against the Turks and the pirates that Papadiamantis writes about. Unfortunately, only two churches are left. One is **Christos** with a wooden iconostasis from 1695 and many wall paintings.

After the visit to Kastro the caïque heads southwest and passes by **Aselino** and **Mandraki** (or the harbour of Xerxes) to return to Chora via Koukounaries.

Tsougrias. A very pretty, lush green little island with a pure white sand beach opposite Achladies. It is private property but one is allowed to visit it.

Monasteries

Ayios Charalambos Monastery.
It is about 5 km. north of Chora,
between the Evangelistria monastery and Lalaria. This is where the
Skiathian short story writer Alexandros Moraïtidis, spent the final
period of his life.

Evangelistria Monastery. It is 4
km. north of Chora. It is the
historical monastery of Skiathos
on which the Greek flag was
raised for the first time in 1807 - in
its final form with the white cross
and its present-day colours. On
the 15th of August the ceremony
of the Interment of the Virgin takes
places in this monastery, a custom unique to Greece.

Kechria Monastery. An isolated
and, one would say, forgotten
monastery on a like-named bay
on the NW side of the island. It **is**
about 8 km. from Chora.

Panayia Kounistra Monastery. A
turn-off right at the 8th km. of the
road Chora-Koukounaries (to
Troullos) leads after 9 km. to this
Byzantine monastery with a beautiful, carved, wooden iconostasis.

Above left: Skiathos.
Center: Historic Kastro on north
end of island.
Right: Evangelistria monastery.
Below famed Koukounaries beach.

Skopelos

Skopelos lies between Skiathos and Alonissos and is 58 nautical miles from Volos. A lush green island whose highest mountain is Delphi at 680 m., it has an area of 95 sq. km., a coastline of 67 km. and a population of 4,500.

The tourist development noted on the island the past few years has not affected its intensely traditional character.

The island is famed for its folk art, above all its cermaics as well as for the production and the quality of its damask-work.

You go to Skopelos by ferry boat or on the fast hydrofoils from Ayios Konstantinos, Volos, Skiathos and Alonissos. During the summer you can go from Kymi, Skyros and other islands.

HISTORY

Skopelos was known in antiquity by the peculiar name of Peparinthos. It was a colony of Minos, the Cretan king and is said that the first settler and king there was the mythical Stafylos, son of Dionysos and Ariadne. A tomb discovered in 1927 at Ornos Stafylos is thought to be his. Among the lavish grave offerings found in it was a sceptre of solid gold which is in the Archaeological Museum of Volos and a large gold hilt from a sword which is in the Archaeological Museum of Athens.

It took the name Skopelos during the Hellenistic period. This was followed by the Roman period at the end of which the patron saint of he island, Ayios Reginos was martyred there.

Skopelos is the largest island in the Sporades after Skyros. It is a lush green paradise which encloses within its embrace the picturesque harbour of Chora. As soon as you see the white houses from the boat, the whole town clinging to the top of the hills, you want to go for a stroll along its beautiful waterfront and go up and down its narrow lanes. And after you arrive in Chora and absorb what it has to offer, you set out to get to know the rest of the island. To go to Stafylos, the bay of which took its name from the mythical general of Minoan Crete, the one who built Skopelos and became its first king.

His tomb was also found there with its pure gold sceptre and the other lavish grave offerings. From Stafylos you will go to the bay of Agnontas and to the idyllic Panormos with a lush green little island at its entrance. Then the famous Milia with its seemingly endless sand beach. The asphalt road will take you to Elios and then up to Glossa to end at Loutraki which is the second harbour on the island. Thus, you will have seen all the southwest coast of Skopelos and the northeast will be left with its steep ravines and rocks battered by the **meltemi** winds. You can only visit this by caïque. The famous monasteries of Skopelos still remain with their rare wall paintings, icons and carved wooden iconostases. The monasteries are built high up on the lush slopes with superb views of the sea.

During the Byzantine period Skopelos was used as a place of exile. In 1204 it was occupied by the Venetians to be re-occupied later by the knight Lokarios of the Byzantine emperor Michael VIII Palaeologus and it remained in Greek hands until 1453 when Constantinople fell. This was followed by renewed Venetian occupation until 1538 when the Turkish admiral Barbarossa occupied the island and slaughtered all its inhabitants. Skopelos was deserted for many years and only during the 17th and 18th century did it begin to be inhabited once more; it then became organized and also took part in the Greek War of Independence of 1821 and acquired its freedom in 1832, along with the rest of the Sporades.

Left: Gorgeous Skopelos. Above two of its many and lovely churches.

Getting to know the island

Skopelos or Chora

Its white houses built amphitheatrically on the slopes of the hills many years ago had roofs of stone slabs. The whitewashed niches on these roofs stood out like a white line and all Chora had a fairy-tale look. Today the stone slabs have been replaced by tiles and the white niches on the ridges of the roofs are now rare. Despite this change, Chora, Skopelos, continues to be one of the loveliest settlements in the Aegean. Its beauty is complemented by the rich vegetation all around it and its famous churches which number over 100. Prominent among them are Zoodochos Pigis, Archangelos Michael, Christos and Ayios Athanasios in the ruins of Kastro.

It is worth a visit to an old Skopelian home to see the interior arrangement of the space and the decoration which consists of weavings, embroideries and ceramics, all products of local folk art.

Excursion by automobile

Stafylos. From the main road a narrow turn-off left at the 5th km. leads to this dazzling bay with its sand beach; it is very closely tied to the island's history.

Agnontas. A leeward bay 8 km. S of Chora. When the strong **meltemi** winds are blowing, it is used by the hydrofoils instead of the harbour at Chora. A road left, after Agnontas, leads to Limnonari, a deep bay with a sand beach and wild beauty.

Panormos. The most beautiful bay on the island, 16 km. from Chora. The landscape is idyllic. There is a glorious sand beach and opposite a lush green little island.

Milia. The most beautiful and the largest sand beach on Skopelos and certainly one of the finest in the Aegean. Straight, framing a stunningly coloured sea, it magnetizes you when you see it from on high through the pine trees which descend steeply to the shore. From the main road one goes down to Milia by making a small detour.

Opposite Milia is the conical, lush islet of **Desa**.

Elios. Another sand beach, NW of the road, 21 km. from Chora.

Klima. A village near Glossa, a short distance from the sea. It is 24 km. from Chora.

Glossa. A large village, nestled in greenery, built high up with a beautiful view of the sea, 26 km. from Chora. Its inhabitants still retain their old manners and customs and many women still wear their local costume.

28 km. Loutraki. The harbour of Glossa. It is the second port on the island and is quite active in the summer.

Excursion by caïque

By caïque you can get to know all the above coastline and even the deserted shores to the north-east which cannot be reached by car. A trip to the **Trypiti** cave is particularly rewarding, about 30′ from Chora.

Monasteries

There are many monasteries on Skopelos - more than a dozen - built on beautiful, lush green sites with remarkable churches, old icons, and wall paintings. The main ones are:

Ayios Reginos Monastery. It is about 3 km. S of Chora. This is not a frequently visited monastery. Despite that, it is of great historical and religious importance since here lies the tomb of Ayios Reginos the patron saint of the island who was martyred on Skopelos in 362.

Episkopi Monastery. It is called simply Episkopi and is only 10′ from Chora. It was the seat of a bishopric (Episkopi=bishopric).

Evangelistria Monastery. One of the most important monasteries on the island, about 3 km. east of Chora. Built in the 18th century by the Skopelitan scholar Depante. There is a fabulous carved wooden iconostasis in its main church.

Metamorphosis Monastery. It is also east of Chora. Its main church is cruciform with wall paintings and an extraordinary iconostasis.

Prodromos Monastery. 6 km. NE of Chora. Built in the 17th century. There are important relics there.

The beach Elios in the coast of the island.

"Panayia tou Pyrgou" in the end of the harbour.

Alonissos

Alonissos has the most amazing sea bottom of any of the islands in the Aegean. Imagine white, marble rock with red veins descending into emerald water forming columns and above the rock a dense pine forest. You will encounter this image along most of the island's coast but the most beautiful spot is Votsi, the bay that lies north of the harbour (Patitiri).

The old capital - Chorio or Liadromia, as the locals call it - is built high up on the summit of a hill and is still far from the bustling tourist world. Up there, despite the damage from the earthquake of 1965, some of the old traditional houses still survive and have been renovated by their new owners, while others have been left to the merciless wear and tear of time. Most of the inhabitants of the village left it after the earthquake and sold their houses to foreigners, building a new village of cement further down, near the sea.

There is a host of beautiful little islands near Alonissos. These little islands with their marine caves have been chosen as refuges by the last Mediterranean seals and there has been an appeal to make a marine park for their protection. But will it be in time to save these last Mediterranean seals from extinction?

Alonissos lies very near Skopelos and is 62 nautical miles from Volos. The island is covered with pine trees which often hang over the sea; it has an area of 64 sq. km., a coastline of 64 km. and a population of 1,500. None of its mountains is over 500 meters high. Its road network is limited to a short, paved road which serves only the south part of the island, its northern part being practically uninhabited.

You go to Alonissos by ferry boat or on the fast hydrofoils from Ayios Konstantinos, Volos, Skopelos and Skiathos. In the summer you can also go from Kymi, Euboea.

HISTORY

It appears that ancient Alonissos was either on the small island of Kyra-Panayia or, more probably, the small island of Psathoura, where there are ruins of an ancient town in the depths of the sea. Both of these lay north of Alonissos, though they were once joined to it.

The island was inhabited during prehistoric times. The ancient town of Ikos, at the site Kokkinokastro, was of importance and sections of the walls of the classical acropolis still survive.

There was considerable friction between the Athenians and Philip of Macedonia in the 4th century B.C. for the possession of Alonissos. The island was of greater importance than Skiathos but less than neighbouring Skopelos. It was, indeed, dependent on the latter and was tied to its fortunes. In the second century B.C. it was occupied by the Romans. This was followed by the Byzantine period during which the walls of the castle of Chorio were built and in 1207 the Venetians occupied it under the Ghizzis. The Turks seized it in 1538 and it was unified with Greece in 1830.

Girls in traditional costume in Chorio.

Patitiri. The harbour of the island and the port of Chora. Its houses are built amphitheatrically on the rocks and there is a dense pine forest all around it.

Alonissos. (Old Chorio or Liadromia). It lies about 4 km. from the port on the summit of a steep hill with a beautiful view.

The earthquake of 1965 destroyed most of the houses.

Some sections of the old Byzantine wall still survive on the rim of the steep hill which was later repaired by the Ghizzis, the Venetian conquerors. The churches that survived the earthquake are of interest.

Votsi. 1 km. NE of Patitiri. A settlement clinging to the slopes above the most picturesque bay on the island with a little lake below.

Chysi Milia. One of the finest sand beaches on Alonissos, 4 km. NE of Patitiri. It is reached by caïque (about 20′ from Patitiri).

Kokkinokastro. A sand beach beneath a steep gorge with red earth and pine trees on top. Near it are the ruins of the walls of an ancient town which is thought to be the renowned **Ikos**. It lies NE of Patiri.

Kokkinonisi or **Vrachos**. A small island opposite Kokkinokastro. Tools were found there from the Paleolithic period which are considered to be the oldest traces of a human presence in the Aegean.

Tzortzi Gialos. 5 km of Patitiri a beautiful sand beach right after Kokkinokastro. It is believed to be the port of ancient Ikos.

Leptos Gialos. A small, lovely bay with pure white sand and crystal-clear water, 30′ by caïque, 6 km. NE of Patitiri.

Steni Vala. A settlement built in a narrow opening which seems like a small fjord. It has developed into a limited summer resort area. It lies 12 km. NE of Patitiri.

Marpounta. Summer resort settlement with two exotic beaches and rocks at the southernmost point of Alonissos, 3 km, from Patitiri.

Picturesque corner of Marpounta.

SMALL ISLANDS
NEAR ALONISSOS

Gioura. A mountainous island with difficult terrain, known for the remarkable **cave of Cyclops** with its stalagmites and stalactites, located on the west side of the island. You need a guide to go into the cave. A rare kind of wild goat lives on the island, resembling the kri-kri of Crete. Gioura lies NE of Alonissos, by Kyra-Panayia and Psathoura.

Dyo Adelfia. Two small islands lying east of Patitiri. They are between Alonissos and Skantzoura.

Kyra-Panayia (Pelagonisi). The most interesting and the largest of the small islands around Alonissos. According to one account ancient Alonissos was located on this island. It has three bays: southwest is **Ayios Petros** with beautiful sand beaches, to the north **Planitis**, with a marvelous, enclosed natural harbour and a smaller one to the east where there is also the **Monastery of the Panayia** probably built in the 16th century; the main church is a single-aisled basilica with cells, refectory and a guest house. The monastery is a monastic estate of the Megisti Lavra Monastery on Mt. Athos.

Kyra-Panayia has a few inhabitants who are employed at animal husbandry. The island, which lies 12 km. NE of Alonissos, is reached by the excursion caïques from Patitiri.

Peristera (Xero). The island nearest Alonissos and the largest after Kyra-Panayia. It has various bays with sand beaches and a few inhabitants.

Piperi. A luxuriant, green island in the middle of the Aegean, the one furthest from Alonissos and buffeted by the weather. That is why the caïque that goes to Kyra-Panayia rarely goes to Piperi.

The island has a rare kind of small-bodied cow, coloured cinnamon and black, which belongs to the short-horned breed, as it is called.

Pappous. A small island with a charming old chapel. It is between Kyra-Panayia and Gioura and next to the islet of **Prasso**.

Skantzoura. The island is known to fishermen and, above all, to spear-fishermen. It lies 13 nautical miles SE of Alonissos, has wonderful beaches and a monastery with a guest house. It is inhabited only by shepherds.

Psathoura. The northernmost of the little islands, not only of Alonissos but all the Sporates. It is so low it is difficult to spot from afar. But at night, its lighthouse, built on its volcanic rock, makes its presence keenly felt to passing boats.

On the south part of the island, near the harbour and between Psathoura and the small island of **Psathouropoula** is a sunken ancient town which is identified by some with ancient Alonissos.

The sea caves of islets of Alonissos are inhabited by the Mediterranean seal "Monachous Monachous".

Skyros

Skyros is the largest island of the Sporades with the imposing Chora clinging to its rock on which there is also the Byzantine monastery of Ayios Georgios and the ancient castle. It is the island where, according to mythology, King Lykomidis hid the young Achilles dressed up like a girl to keep him out of the Trojan War, but he was discovered by Odysseus who took him away.

A large sand beach stretches out beneath Chora and there is a dense pine forest which covers practically half the island and ornaments its picturesque bays.

But what really makes Skyros stand out among the islands of the Sporades is its traditional folk art: the ceramics and the embroideries with their fabulous designs and the celebrated carved wooden Skyrian furniture. In addition, there are the deeply-rooted manners and customs which have been preseved unadulterated right up to the present.

A kind of small horse, no more than one meter high, still survives on the island. Thirty years ago there were around 2,000 of these ponies, but today there are only 150 left. The interest of the Minicipality and the State has been turned toward protecting them. Will they be able to save these rare ponies?

Skyros lies practically in the center of the Aegean, 22 nautical miles from Kymi on Euboea. Its northern section is covered with pine trees while its southern section is barren. The latter also contains its highest mountain, Kochylas (792 m.) The island has an area of 209 sq. km., a coastline of 130 km., and a population of around 2,800.

A good, paved road traverses the northern section of the island and local buses, on a regular schedule, connect the harbour of Linaria to Chora and its beach.

Skyros with its sunny and cool climate is a ideal place for quiet holidays You can go there by ferry boat from Kymi, Euboea and (only in summer) from Skiathos and other islands. In summer you can also go by plane from Athens or on the speedy hydrofoils from Volos, Skiathos, Skopelos and Alonissos.

HISTORY

One of the most interesting islands in Greek mythology, connected to Achilles and Theseus. The former was mentioned in the introduction while the latter sought refuge there at the Court of Lykomidis. But Lykomidis lured him on a walk, pushed him off the cliffs and killed him.

The Athenian general Kimon occupied Skyros in 468 B.C. and it is said found the tomb of Theseus and removed his bones to Athens, placing them in the Theseion.

In 322 B.C. the Macedonians conquered Skyros and in 196 B.C. the Romans made a gift of it to Athens. The Byzantine period followed and in 1204 the Venetian occupation; the island was then occupied by the Turks in 1538 and was liberated in 1832.

Chora with castle and wide sand beach.

Chorio or Chora. It lies in the northeast sector of the island, 11 km. from the port of Linaria. It is built amphitheatrically on the slopes of an enormous rock which at its peak has the **castle** of the Homeric king Lykomidis.

Sections of the wall of the classical acropolis (5th century) still survive while much older traces have been found that go back to the Bronze Age. But what the visitor sees today are for the most part Byzantine and post-Byzantine structures.

Of interest is the church of **Koimiseis Theotokou** (The Assumption of the Virgin) built in 895 in the castle and the famous monastery of **Ayios Georgios Skyrianos** which according to tradition was founded in 960 by Ayios Athanasios (or Nikephoros Fokas). The view of Chora from the monastery is unique. One is impressed by its houses; they are like cubes and their roofs (all those that have not been replaced by cement ones) are covered with a kind of grey-blue earth (**meligi**).

The important churches outside the castle are **Archontopanayias** and **Ayios Yiannis**.

On the north end of Chora is a spacious square from which there is an excellent view of the sea and **Magazia**. At the end of it is the quaint little church of Ayia Triada and the bronze statue of the English poet **Rupert Brooke** who died on Skyros in 1915 and was buried at the site Treis Boukes. Below the square is the **Folk** and **Historical Museum Faltaïts** which bears the name of the Skyrian philosopher and student of the history and folklore of the island, Manos Faltaïts.

Near Brooke Square, next to the narrow lane which goes down to the Magazia, is the **Archaeological Museum**.

Besides the visit to the museums it is also worthwhile visiting private houses on Skyros. Their interiors are decorated exclusively with products of traditional folk art (carved wooden furniture, ceramics, embroideries and wall hangings).

Aspous. A settlement with a sand beach and a taverna, 4 km. north of Chora. Near the bay of **Achilli**.

Atsitsa. A picturesque bay with pine trees on the northwest side of the island. You can go there by car.

Kalamitsa. A large, hoseshoe-shaped bay with a beautiful sand beach, east of Linaria. Beyond Kalamitsa the dirt road goes to **Ayios Mamas**, and **Nifi**, with its spring and plane trees, and ends at **Treis Boukes**.

Linaria. The port of Skyros where the ferry boat docks, 11 km. south of Chora on a bay protected from the **meltemi** wind. Opposite are the small islands of **Valaxa** and further west **Skyropoula**, both uninhabited. Next to Linaria is **Acherounes**.

Magazia. The first settlement that was built below Chora on a marvellous and enormous beach.

Molos. The continuation of Magazia with a small fishing-cove.

Pefkos. A very picturesque bay with a sand beach and taverna, east of Linaria. It can be reached by automobile or caïque (excursions are often arranged from Chora to Pefkos).

Spilies. These caves lie on the steep coastal cliffs of **Kochylas**, NE of Chora. The approach is by caïque from Molos and of course the weather must be calm.

Treis Boukes. A lovely bay in the south section of the island. Its entrance is impeded by two small islands, leaving three passages. The grave of the English poet R. Brooke is in the area. A small cave (Glyfada) with a stunning sand beach, lies on **Sarakiniko**, one of the two islands in the bay.

The monument to Brooke can be reached by car. But to really enjoy the excursion as a whole you should do it by caïque. These excursions are frequently organized from Chora.

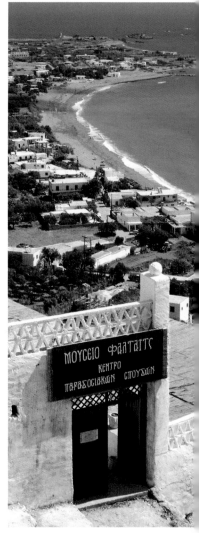

Above: Characteristic Skyrian embroidery.

Below: View from Faltaits Museum to Magazia.

ISLETS AROUND EUBOEA

NORTH EUBOEA

Monolia.............. W Ayios Georgios.
Lichades............ W Ayios Georgios.
Strongyli............ W Ayios Georgios.
Atalanti..................... Bay of Atalanti.
Ayios Nikolaos....... Bay of Atalanti.
Gaidouronisi........... Bay of Atalanti.
Ayios Georgios. ....NE Larymna.
Ktyponisi. ....E Chalia.

SOUTH EUBOEA

Pasantasi. .... S Chalkida.
Kolonna. .... S Chalkida.
Griniarou. .... S Chalkida.
Patsi.................................E Eretria.
Pezonisi..............................S Eretria.
Ayia Triada.......................SE Eretria.
Aspronisi.........................SE Eretria.
Feidonisi............................ S Aliveri.
Boufos.....................Bay of Boufalos.

Kavaliani. ..... Bay of Almyropotamos.
Ay. Dimitris.. Bay of Almyropotamos.
Batherista. ... Bay of Almyropotamos.
Dimakos. ...... Bay of Almyropotamos.
Styra...................................W N. Styra.
Kouneli. ....N Stouronisi.
Fonias..........................N Stouronisi.
Tigani. ....N Stouronisi.
Ayios Andreas........... W Stouronisi.
Vergoudi...................... W Stouronisi.
Petousa. .... S Stouronisi.
Akio.................................. SE Nimbori.
Elafonisi. .... E Marmari.
Petalioi...........................Se Marmari.
   Megalo Nisi............ SE Marmari.
   Chersonisi.............. SE Marmari.
   Tragos. .... SE Marmari.
   Founti......................... SE Marmari.
   Lamberousa. .... E Marmari.
   Avgo.......................... E Marmari.

Makronisi. .... E Marmari.
Praso. .... SE Marmari.
  Louloudi.................. SE Marmari.
Paximadi...................... S Karystos.
Ayia Paraskevi.............. S Karystos.
Mandilou.....................SE Karystos.
Raftis........................... E Porto Raftis.
Dipsa.............................. W Nimbori.

AEGEAN COAST

Pontikonisi. ....NE Agriovotano.
Mirmigonisi............. E Agriovotano.
Levkonisia...................... E Kotsikia.
Tria Nisia.................... N Chiliadous.
Chiliodonisi............... N Chiliadous.
Chili. .... N Kymi.
Platy. .... N Kymi.
Prasouda............................E Kymi.
Karvouno. .... E Ochthonia.
Doros. .... E Kavo-Doro.

THE ISLANDS AND ISLETS OF THE SPORADES

SKIATHOS

Daskalio. ....E harbour.
Marangos.....................SE harbour.
Argos.............................SE harbour.
Repi.................................SE harbour.
Tsougrias. .... SE Achladi.
Tsougriaki. .... SE Achladi.
Psarou. ....E Kanapitsa.
Marines............................ S Troulos.
Tourlonisia....................... S Troulos.
Lefteris.................... E Koukounaria.
Eleni........................ E Koukounaria.
Kastronisia.......................N Kastro.
Ano Myrmigonisia. ....E Skiathos.
Aspronisos....................E Skiathos.
Myrmigonisia...............SE harbour.

SKOPELOS

Ayios Georgios........... E Skopelos.
Mikro............................. E Skopelos.
Dessa.................................. W Milia.
Strongylo............................ W Milia.
Plevro..................................... W Elia.
Kasidas................................. W Elia.
Paximadia.....................SW Loutraki.

ALONISSOS

Skopelos...........................SE Patitiri.
Vrachos.................. S Kokkinokastro.
Peristera. .... E Alonissos.
Lykorrema. .... E Alonissos.
Pedimoules....................N Alonissos.
Moromoules. ....N Alonissos.
Manoulas. .... W Alonissos.
Stavros........................... W Alonissos.
Kyra-Panayia...............NE Alonissos.
Pelerisa. .... W Kyra-Panayia.
Praso. .... NE Kyra-Panayia.
Koumbi................. NE Kyra-Panayia.
Pappous............... NE Kyra-Panayia.
Gioura.................. NE Kyra-Panayia.
Psathoura........................N Gioura.
Psathouropoula. ....N Gioura.
Piperi.........................E Kyra-Panayia.
Dyo Adelfia. .... E Patitiri.
  Adelfia............................ E Patitiri.
  Adelfopoulo. .... E Patitiri.
Kambria.............................. E Patitiri.
Polyrichos........................SE Patitiri.
Gaidaros........................SE Patitiri.
Skantzoura.......................SE Patitiri.

Lazofitonisia............NW Skantzoura.
Strongylo................. W Skantzoura.
Praso. .... W Skantzoura.
Skantili. .... SW Skantzoura.
Korakas. .... SW Skantzoura.

SKYROS

Valaxa..............................SW Linaria.
Erinia. .... W Skyros.
Skyropoula. .... W Skyros.
Lakkonisi. .... W Skyros.
Ayios Fokas. .... W Skyros.
Thaleia............................. W Skyros.
Salagi................................ W Skyros.
Koulouri. .... W Skyros.
Myrmingonisia..............NW Skyros.
Atsitsa..............................NW Skyros.
Katsouli...........................NW Skyros.
Notio Podi........................ N Skyros.
Voreio Podi...................... N Skyros.
Vrikolakonisia....................NE Chora.
Sarakiniko. .... S Skyros.
Platy................................... S Skyros.
Exo Diavatis. .... S Linaria.
Plaka............................... S Linaria.
Mesa Diavatis.................. S Linaria

There are 11 main islands, real pearls of the Aegean, and a host of islets set the one below the other, forming a zig-zag line starting in Kavala, Macedonia and ending in the Dodecanese. Several of them, Lesbos, Chios and Samos in particular, are very close to Asia Minor, so close that you often can see, across the strait that separates them, the roads, the houses and the fields of the East. The most northerly of all of them is **Thasos** with its lofty pines opposite the shores of Macedonia while south of Thrace is **Samothraki** the island where the famous Winged Victory which ornaments the Louvre Museum was found. Even further south is **Limnos**, the island of Hephaestus, and **Ayios Efstratios** in the middle of the Aegean. This is followed by **Lesbos** a large, verdant island with beautiful bays and a petrified forest and

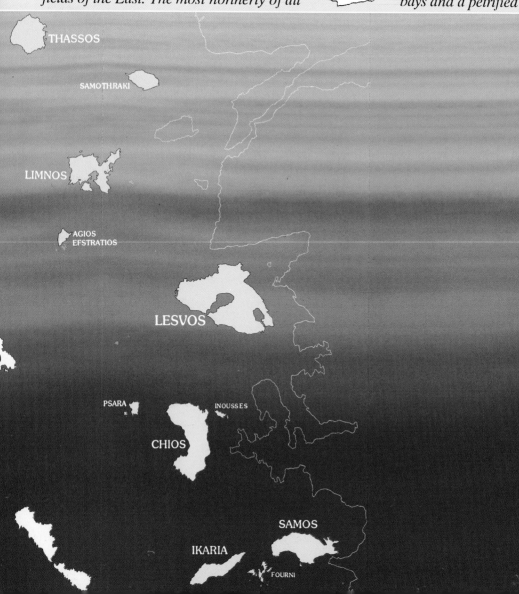

THASSOS

SAMOTHRAKI

LIMNOS

AGIOS EFSTRATIOS

LESVOS

PSARA

INOUSSES

CHIOS

SAMOS

IKARIA

FOURNI

*further down **Chios** the island with the fragrant mastic trees and the medieval villages. Opposite it is the small **Oinouses** with its ravishing beaches and further away the illustrious **Psara**. South of this is the lovely **Samos**, the island of Pythagoras, covered in forests with dazzling white, sand beaches. To the west is **Icaria**, a lush, mountainous island with a primitive kind of beauty and between Samos and Icaria the islets of **Fourni** with their its picturesque fishing harbours. You can go to Limnos and Lesbos by plane from Athens and Thessaloniki but only from Athens to Chios and Samos.*

We note the main ferry-boat lines to the islands in the introduction to each one. We spoke of a host of islets that surround the main islands of the north and east Aegean. In this chapter, along with the islets and the rocky outcroppings of Chalkidiki and the Pagasitic Gulf, we describe (or simply fix the location of) 82 of them, 20 of which are inhabited.

Thasos

Thasos is a large island with lofty pine trees. The pines are a special kind with a white and perfectly straight trunk, good for the making of ships' masts. It lies 17 miles from Kavala in Macedonia and only 4 miles from Keramoti. It is a truly beautiful island with a high mountain, Ypsario or Psario (1,203 m.) in the middle and a lace-like fringe of beaches with pure white sand and pine trees, often literally hanging over the sea. The beauty of the spot is frequently complemented by rocks made of white marble.

Thasos has rapidly grown into a large tourist center. A good paved road rings the island and branches lead into the interior, ending at picturesque villages. This road network is also used by the local buses which connect these villages to the coast and the capital, Limenas or Thasos.

All of this guarantees the visitor a comfortable and pleasant stay and in addition there is the ease of choosing between a social life at the large, tourist centres and the tranquility of an isolated corner on one of the island's endless sand beaches.

Thasos is the northermost island in the Aegean, with an area of 379 sq. km., a coastline of 95 km. and a population of 13,000. You reach Limenas by ferry boat from Kavala or Keramoti while Prinos, the second port of Thasos opposite the oil wells, can be reached only from Kavala.

Limenas, capital of Thasos.

HISTORY

Thasos was already inhabited at the end of the Neolithic period, most probably by Thracians. At the beginning of the 7th century B.C. Parians set off on an expedition to conquer the island. Their aim was the mineral wealth of Thasos and specifically the gold and marble. This expedition in which the popular Parian poet, Archilochos took part, as described in one of his poems, was in the end crowned with success and the Parians became the rulers of Thasos. The island began to flourish from that period. A colony was founded on the coast opposite, the town of Thasos was fortified and developed commercial relations with Athens, Corinth, the Cyclades and Ionia. This prosperity was momentarily interrupted by Persian pillaging which the island suffered twice: in 490 B.C. when Darius tore down the walls of the town and in 480 B.C. under Xerxes. During the Peloponnesian War the domination of the island alternated between Athens and Sparta. In 477 B.C. it became a part of the Delian Alliance and in 340 B.C. it was occupied by the King of Macedonia, Philip II. The island flourished under Roman rule in the 2nd and 1st century B.C. Though the deposits of gold had been exhausted, Thasos still had marble and wine to export. The long Byzantine period followed which was interrupted by the appearance of the Franks to be continued approximately 50 years later, lasting until the 15th century when the Gattiluci became the rulers of Thasos, staying on the island for about 40 years. The Turkish occupation lasted from 1460 to 1912 (with a four year period of Russian rule, 1770-1774) when Thasos was liberated and then united with Greece.

Ancient theater of Thasos.

Getting to know the island

Limenas or Thasos

The capital of the island, with 2,400 inhabitants, it is built on the site of the ancient town within an idyllic bay, nestled in greenery. During the summer this town, as is natural, garners most of the visitors to the island. The greatest amount of activity is late in the afternoon when the vacationers take their stroll or sit at little tables on the harbour to enjoy the magnificent sunsets.

The archaeological space lies next to the harbour, (which in antiquity was used as a naval yard) and is very close to the town's houses. East of this harbour are the ruins of a sanctuary to Poseidon, the sanctuary of Dionysos (both from the 4th century B.C.) and the Agora. Further east, on the slope of a pine-covered hill can be seen the ruins of a **theater** (3rd century B.C.). This theater, in which performances are still given in summer, underwent alterations at the hands of the Romans. The **acropolis** commands the summit of the hill. The surviving walls are medieval and were built on the site of the ancient walls. The descent from the acropolis can be made to the south-west, following the wall. In this case, the visitor will pass successively through the Gate of Silenus, the Gate of Hercules and Dionysos and finally the Gate of Zeus and Hera. The ruins of the sanctuary of Hercules, the island's protector, lie north of the Gate of Hercules and Dionysos.

Near the ancient harbour is the **Archaeological Museum** with noteworthy finds from the island.

Limenaria characterized by its picturesquesness and large sand beach.

EXCURSIONS

1. Limenas - Panayia - Potamia - Limenaria (54 km.)

3 km. East of the port is the enchanting bay of **Makryammos** with a large hotel complex and a picturesque islet-rock to the right. Further on are the idyllic shores of Ai-Yiannis with the pine trees above the sea and the white marble.

7 km. Panayia. A village where the houses have retained their traditional Macedonian style. Among its sites are the Church of the Panayia and Drakospilia (a cave). A turn-off from the village left leads to the famous **Chrysi Ammos** beach (Skala Panayias).

9 km. Potamia. A village below the peak of Psarios, the highest mountain of Thasos (1,203 m.), surrounded by a lovely pine forest.

12 km. Junction. From here a turn-off left leads to **Chrysi Akti** beach (Skala Potamias) a resort centre with a sand beach.

20 km. Koinyra. A small settlement touristically developed in a peaceful and idyllic area with a like-named small island opposite. It serves as a link between the gorgeous rocks, the pine trees and the sea.

31 km. Alyki. Near here are the ancient marble quarries. Further on, near **Thymonia** and on the steep slope of a mountain, is the monastery of the **Archangelos Michael,** the island's patron saint.

45 km. Psili Ammos, Astrida. Two adjacent, lovely summer resort settlements.

50 km. Potos. A summer resort center. From here a turn-off right leads after 10 km. to **Theologos**, one of the most beautiful villages on Thasos with old mansions and eminent churches.

54 km. Limenaria. One of the largest tourist centres on Thasos with an enormous sand beach sheltered from the **meltemi** winds. Between Potos and Limenaria is **Pefkari** with a equally beautiful sand beach.

2. Limenas - Prinos - Skala Marion - Limenaria (41 km)

4 km. Glyfada. A very picturesque bay with a sand beach. It collects a lot of people because of its short distance from Limenas.

12 km. Skala Rachoniou. A seaside settlement with a sand beach, the port of the village of Rachoni.

16 km. Prinos. This is the port of **Mikros** and **Megalos Prinos**, which are in the interior. Prinos developed significantly after the discovery of oil and the drilling of oil wells in the sea near it. It also has a superb sand beach with trees.

21 km. Skala Sotira. The port of Sotira with crystal-clear water. **Skala Kallirachis** is nearby.

30 km. Skala Marion. It is in the southwest corner of Thasos and is the port of Maries which is 13 km. from there.

41 km. Limenaria.

Samothraki

connection and it is also connected, to Kavala and less frequently to Limnos. It has an area of 178 sq. km., a coastline of 58 km. and a population of 2,900 occupied with farming, animal husbandry, tourism and fishing. The island is considered to be one of the best fishing spots in Greece.

HISTORY

When you enter the Louvre Museum in Paris, the first thing you see as you climb the stairs is the **famous winged victory of Samothrace**, with its large, widespread wings. This statue was found on Samothrace. This fact predisposes one to thinking of the island as being of great archaeological interest. This is what you expect and you are not disappointed as you roam the ruins of Palaiopoli and the famous temple of the Great Gods. But what you did not expect and which can startle you is the unqiue, wild beauty of the island.

Above all else there is the imposing mountain of Fengari, the Saos of the ancients, which at 1,611 meters is the highest in the Aegean. Homer mentions that Poseidon sat on its peak to watch the unfolding of the Trojan War, 200 km. away.

From the rocky and sheer peaks of this majestic mountain descend lush green gorges which tumble so steeply into the sea that waterfalls are common, Sometimes small pools are formed at the base of these waterfalls. Huge plane trees hang over the pools along with brambles and myrtle. Whatever beauty nature has to offer.

Samothrace is famed both for its crystal-clear, sparkling clean water and its medicinal springs. The island still lies far from the major tourist activity, despite the enormous archaeological and natural interest it presents.

Samothrace lies 29 nautical miles southwest of Alexandroupoli with which there is a daily ferry boat

Samothrace has been inhabited since the end of the Neolithic period. In the 11th century B.C., Thracians from the coast opposite, came to the island and along with the locals established the religion of the Great Gods, which contained the much discussed mysteries of the Cabiri. There are some similarities between these mysteries and the mysteries of Eleusis, just as there are a number of parallels between the Great Gods and Greek divinities. Thus, the Great Goddess Axieros is compared to the goddess Demeter while Axiokersos and Axiokersa, the gods who assisted the Great Goddess, are compared to Hades and Persephone, the chthonian Greek divinities. Finally, the two Cabiri have some similarities with the Greek Dioskouri. In any case, in what concerns the Cabirian mysteries, whatever our hypotheses may be, it is clear we do not understand what they involved because all those who were initiated (and more than a few illustrious Greeks of that time have been mentioned as initiates) kept their lips sealed. Tradition says that the King of Macedonia, Philip II met the Epirot Princess Olympia at the mysteries. What is known is that Alexander the Great was born of their union. Along with these mysteries, festivals were held every year during which the pilgrims endowed the sanctuary with impressive edifices such as the Arsinoeion, the Ptolemaeion and the famous statue of the Winged Victory of Samothrace.

The Winged Victory of Samothrace.

These ancient festivals established the island as a religious center of the north Aegean and brought it wealth and prosperity. The Aeolians of Lesbos and Asia Minor came to the island at the end of the 8th century B.C. From then on the island began to rise and was flourishing in the 5th century B.C. reaching its peak during the Hellenistic period (3rd century B.C.) which carried over to the Roman period. Samothrace would finally fall into complete oblivion by the 4th century A.D. when the emperor of Byzantium, Theodosius, forbade idolatrous festivals at the temple of the Cabirians.

During the Byzantine period the old town was abandoned and the inhabitants gathered in the interior of the island and founded Chora. The Genoan Gattiluci would become the rulers of the island in 1430, would fortify Kastro and would remain until 1457 when the Turks came. The liberation of the island and its union with Greece finally occurred in 1912.

Kamariotissa. The port of Samothrace. Along with Chora it has the most activity on the island.

Chora. The picturesque capital built amphitheatrically beneath the medieval castle. All of its houses are traditional ones with tile roofs. It is 6 km. from the port.

Palaiopoli (7 km. NE of Kamariotissa). Next to the Xenia hotel is the archaeological site of ancient Samothrace which was founded in the 7th century B.C. Among the ruins the **Sanctuary of the Cabiri** (or the Great Gods) stands out, on a beautiful site with pine trees and an excellent view of the sea. This is the temple you see with the five reconstructed columns. Near here are the ruins of the theater and the site on which the **Winged Victory** sat.

In the **Archaeological Museum**, which is further to the north, are important finds from the area around the temple, models of buildings and a plaster likeness of the Winged Victory of Samothrace.

Therma. A settlement 15 km. to the east of Kamariotissa in an area with running water and luxuriant greenery. It lies 1 km. from the sea and owes its development mainly to its medicinal springs.

Gria Vathra Waterfall (Fonias). It is formed by a river which ends near the Tower of Fonias, 4 km. east of Therma. At its base is a pool surrounded by plane trees. This can be reached by automobile, up to the mouth of the river, and then it takes about 30′ on foot along the river.

Profitis Ilias. A picturesque village with traditional houses and a marvellous view of the sea. It is 15 km. NE of Kamariotissa. The village of **Lakkoma** comes before it, at the 11th km.

Pacheia Ammos. Certanly the most beautiful sand beach on the island. You reach this after quite a few kms. over a dirt road, which starts after Lakkoma and passes next to the picturesque church of **Panayia Krimniotissa** which was built on the top of a pointed rock with a marvellous view of the sea and the plain.

East of Pacheia Ammos is the famous beach of **Vatos** with its crystal-clear water, fine sand, tall rocks, and caves and even further east is **Kremastos waterfall** which comes down from the peak of Saos and spilling over the bare, sheer rock, plunges straight into the sea. You can reach both these sites by caïque from Kamariotissa.

Also impressive is the beach of **Kipos** on the NE corner of the island, which can be reached by automobile or caïque.

Above: Sanctuary of Cabiri at Palaiopoli.
Below: Fonia waterfall and pool.

Limnos

In antiquity the island was covered with a thick pall of smoke licked by fiery tongues of flame. These were the fires of its two volcanic mountains. According to tradition Zeus had hurled Hephaestus into one of them, Mosychlos, to live there outcast from Olympus, the home of the other gods.

The centuries rolled on, the volcanoes grew quiet and as the smoke disappeared an island came into view, which looked like a large, open plain. A dry plain with a clayish kind of soil, thirsting for water. Nothing recalled the cosmogony of all that had passed. Only in the west, near Myrina, was there anything strange and it was what we see even today.

The enormous black rocks gathered into large piles next to the pure white sand. The steep hills which rise up threateningly above the blue sea. There the tranquil plain in linked to the rough mountain. The merry and protected seashore of Myrina mingles with the wild rock on which the Genoan castle sits. This is what makes Limnos so beautiful and what the visitor finds impressive. This is where the lacy coastline, the bays and the superb sand beaches, the dry climate, the sun, the marvellous wine and the hospitality of the inhabitants all work together.

Limnos, which lies northwest of Lesbos, can be reached by plane from Athens, Thessaloniki and Lesbos or by ferry boat from Piraeus, Rafina, Mytilini, the Thessaloniki and Kavala.

Limnos has an area of 477 sq. km., a coastline of 259 km. and a population of 16,000. It is 186 nautical miles from Piraeus and its capital is Myrina.

Castle and sand beach of Myrina.

Homer mentions the first inhabitants of Limnos as the mythical Sindians. They looked after the exiled and crippled god of fire Hephaestus, whom Zeus had cast on their island, and to pay them back Hephaestus taught them the art of the blacksmith. According to mythology, Thoas was the first king of Limnos, who took Myrina, the daughter of the king of Iolkos for his wife. During the time of Thoas, the women of Limnos, led by the king's daughter, Ypsipyli, took revenge on their husbands who were neglecting them, by getting them drunk and killing them all, except for Thoas. Later they married the Argonauts who had come to the island on their return from Colchis. Indeed, Ypsipyli married their leader, Jason. From the union of the Limnian women with the Argonauts, it is said that the Minyans were born.

Excavations carried out in the south-east uncovered the ancient town of Poliochni whose life is dated from the fourth millinium B.C. to approximately 1600 B.C.

Around 1000 B.C. the island was inhabitaed by the Pelasgians or the Tyrrhenians. Then two more towns began to be created on the island, ancient Hephaestia and Myrina. During the Persian wars Limnos was seized by the Persians and after the Persians were defeated it became an ally of Athens which then awarded land on the island to its own people.

The island was successively occupied by the Macedonians, the Romans and the Byzantines, finally falling under the domination of the Venetians and the Genoans. In the 15th century the Turks came to the fore. During one of their attempts to capture the island, around 1475, the Limnians, heartened by the courageous resistance of the young Maroulas, successfully repulsed the invader. But it finally fell into Turkish hands in 1479 and was liberated by the Greek fleet only in 1912.

Harbour of Myrina from Kastro.

Getting to know the island

Myrina. This is the port and the capital of the island built on the site of the ancient town and with the same name. It spreads out before two beaches which have a rocky and sheer peninsula between with the imposing **Kastro** (castle) on its peak. The stroll along the waterfront and the beautiful sand beach of Myrina is very enjoyable. The climb up to the Genoan castle with its marvelous view of the town and the sea is the best that Limnos has to offer.

You must not forget to visit the **Archaeological Museum** which has noteworthy finds.

Platy. A stunning, enclosed bay with gorgeous sand below the village of the same name. It is 2 km. from Myrina.

Thanos. A village of dense greenery, 2 km. SE of Platy. At the bay of Thanos, which is about 1 km. from the village, there is a beautiful sand beach and restaurants.

Kontias. One of the largest villages on Limnos with old mansions, lovely streets and the wonderful church of Christos. It is 7 km. from Thanos and 1 from Myrina. In the bay of Kontias you will find perhaps the best leeward sand beach of Limnos.

Kaspakas. A village 6 km. north of Myrina. A seemingly endless sand beach spreads out beneath Kaspakas. Large sheer rocks rise up from one part of it, like Meteora in miniature.

Kotsinas. A fishing harbour at the back of the bay of Bournias, on the north coast of the island, 25 km. from Myrina with a medieval castle. Near Kotsinas is Mount Despotis which is thought to be the ancient **Mosychlos** volcano.

Hephaestia. The largest town of ancient Limnos which began to be built in 1000 B.C. and lasted for over 2000 years.

You will go to Hephaestia (35 km. from Myrina) from the village of Kontopouli which lies near the island's two lakes.

Cabirian Sanctuary (Chloe). Ruins from a complex of buildings from the 7th and the 6th century

B.C. which was a place of worship for the Cabiri. In the exceptionally large chambers which were called Telestiria ("ceremonial halls") the Cabirian mysteries were held, as on Samothrace. You will go to the Cabirian sanctuary, which is 35 km. from Myrina, on the left branch which goes from **Kontopouli** to Plaka.

Poliochni. The most important archaeological site on Limnos. This is the oldest Neolithic settlement in the Aegean which began to be built in 4000 B.C. (see History). Poliochni is in SE Limnos and is 33 km. from Myrina and 9 km. from Moudros.

Moudros. The second largest harbour and former capital of the island with a beautiful church of the Evangelismos Theotokou (The Annunciation). It is 27 km. from Myrina and lies to the rear of a like-named bay. This bay is thought to be one of the most secure in the Mediterranean.

Ayios Efstratios

AGIOS EFSTRATIOS •

This is a small island in the middle of the Aegean, between Limnos, Skyros and Lesbos. In the "middle of nowhere". It seems it was discovered by sailors who landed there and settled. They tilled the earth, took up fishing and...

Time passed. In the 9th century Ayios (Saint) Efstratios lived and died in exile here, giving his name to the island. In 1968 an earthquake shook Ayios Efstratios badly. More than half the houses collapsed. Many people left the island. But most stayed. They built new homes, returned to the fields, went out to sea once more.

Ayios Efstratios lies 16 nautical miles from Limnos, has an area of 43 sq. km. and a population of 296. You can reach the island by ferry boat from Piraeus, Rafina, Chios, Mytilini, Kavala and Thessaloniki (via Limnos).

HISTORY

The Mycenean ruins of the ancient town of Neai, which was built on an elevation, show that the island was inhabited in antiquity. During the Middle Ages it was deserted for a period from fear of pirates.

Getting to know the island

The small harbour of **Ai-Stratis** is on the NW coast of the island. The village, built amphitheatrically, goes up a hill. Ai-Stratis is a volcanic island with a steep coast, many marine caves but also beautiful sand beaches. Administratively it belongs to the province of Limnos in the prefecture of Lesbos. The harbour nearest the island is Myrina in Limnos.

Lesbos

It is difficult to describe in a few words a large and beautiful island such as Lesbos. What should one say first? Should one speak of the Gulfs of Yera and Kalloni? Its seemingly endless sand beaches and its castles? Or should one speak of Sigri and the petrified forest? Or the picturesque Molyvos, Ayiassos and the folk painter Theophilos? Or the folkloric festivals with their ancient roots? That you can be satisfied with what you see today without needing to go back to the time of Sappho and Alcaios? But can you not refer to those who then sang on Lesbos their famous poems and left behind such a great spiritual heritage? The heritage that has been carried on in Lesbos for many centuries and has reached our own time, the time of Eftaliotis, Myrivilis and Venezis.

And should one not speak of the living Nobel prize winner, Odysseus Elytis?

Sapphós fatal leap from the rocks of Lefkas (copperplate).

Lesbos lies between Chios and Limnos, very near the Turkish coast. The third largest island in Greece it has an area of 1,630 sq. km., a coastline of 370 km. and a population of 89,000. It is 188 nautical miles from Piraeus.

There are ferry boats to Lesbos not only from Piraeus but also Thessaloniki, Kavala, Limnos, Chios, Samos and the Dodecanese. It is connected by plane to Athens and Thessaloniki.

The island is verdant with pine and olive trees and has a gentle ridge of mountains that never exceed 1,000 meters in height. It has a good road network and a satisfactory tourist substructure. Lesbos is famed for the production and the quality of its olive oil and cheese. It is also famed for its ouzo, its sardines fished from the Bay of Kalloni and its folk art, such as ceramics, wood carving and woven articles.

HISTORY

The island was first inhabited around 3000 B.C. by people from the neighboring East, who were centered in Troy. The Aiolians came to the island around 1000 B.C. It was then the six ancient towns on the island began to develop: Mytilene, Methymna, Arisvi, Antissa, Eressos and Pyrra. Its intellectual blossoming began later. At the end of the 8th century B.C. and the beginning of the 7th the island brought forth three important personalities of the intellect and art. There was Arion the lyra player, the poet Alcaios and the famous lyric poetess Sappho.

This great intellectual thriving was cut off with the capture of the island by the Persians in the middle of the 6th century B.C. In 479 B.C. after the Persians were defeated, the island was incorporated into the Athenian Alliance, but from the outbreak of the Peloponnesian War up to the 4th century B.C. with the appearance of the Macedonians, Lesbon sometimes belonged to Athens and other times to Sparta. In 84 B.C. the Romans assumed control of the island, but granted it autonomy. This led the island to renewed prosperity.

During the Byzantine period, a landmark in the history of Lesbos was the ceding of the island by the emperor John Palaeologus to his Genoan brother-in-law, Francesco Gattiluci as a dowry for his marriage to the emperor's daughter Maria. By this transfer the sovereignity of the Gattiluci was consolidated which lasted until 1462 when the island was seized by the large army of Muhammed II, carried out with massacres and looting.

The Greek population suffered great hardships throughout the Turkish occupation and only after the Russo-Turkish War of 1774, did it acquire some freedom in the exercise of its religion. During the Greek War of Independence of 1821, the island rose up but without success and suffered severe reprisals by the Turks. Liberation finally arrived in 1912.

Work of folk painter Theophilos.

Getting to know the island

Mytilini

A beautiful town, rich in local colour. Today it has around 30,000 inhabitants and is the capital of the Prefecture of Lesbos which contains Lesbos, Limnos and Ayios Efstratios. As you look at it for the first time from the boat, you see on your right, on a pine-covered hill, the historic fortress and before you the main harbour with its pier, the polychrome caïques, the large sailboats, the shops and the hotels. The church of Ayios Therapont dominates the area with its impressive architecture and stately domes. Behind the town and all around it are its mountains densely carpeted in pines and olives.

There is a great deal for one to see in this town. And for a start, next to where the ferry boats dock, is the **Archaeological Museum**. North of the museum is the neighbourhood of **Kioski** with its old mansions which goes up the hill toward the fortress.

The imposing **Fortress of Mytilini** was an old Byzantine fort but was renovated by the Genoan Francesco Gattiluci in 1373. Northwest of the Fortress is the old harbour of the town, the "North One" as it is called. Between the two harbours is the Cathedral Church of **Ayios Athanasios** from the 17th century. On the first street parallel to the quay, the market street, is the magnificent church of **Ayios Therapont** from the 19th century with the **Byzantine Museum** in its enclosure. On the quay is the two-storey **Folk Museum** with a very interesting collection. Besides the folklore exhibits there also several pieces from the petrified forest. Northwest of the town, on an elevation, are the ruins of an **ancient theater** which was one of the largest in ancient Greece.

South Suburbs

Vareia (4 km.). The home of the folk painter Theophilos, which is why the Theophilos Museum is located there. Next to this is the Museum of Modern Art of Eleftheriadis-Teriad.

Vigla (5 km.). The most beautiful beach in this area.

The airport (8 km.).

Kratigos (12 km.). A beach with crystal-clear water.

Kountouroudia (11 km.). One kilometre after Skala Loutron. From here you can take small craft to pass through the channel at the entrance to the gulf and go to **Perasma** opposite. Sailing in this area as well as in the Gulf of Yera, is very enjoyable.

Ayios Ermoyenis (14 km, via Loutra, 20 km. via Kratigos).

A picturesque bay at the entrance to the Gulf of Yera with a fine sea for swimming.

Overall view of Mytilene. Historic fortress to the rear.

1. Petrified Forest - Sigri (92 km.)

You head out of town west toward the Gulf of Kalloni.

7 km. At this point you have descended to the lovely **Gulf of Yera**, which is so enclosed it seems like a lake. It is a lush landscape.

12 km. Junction with the road that goes left to Plomari. You go straight ahead.

14 km. Junction with the road that goes left to Agiassos and Polichnitos. You go straight ahead.

31 km. You arrive at the second, and larger, gulf on the island, the **Gulf of Kalloni** with quaint fishing harbours and sand beaches.

37 km. From here a turn-off right leads after 4 km. to the market town of **Ayia Paraskevi**. The famous Bull Festival is held here at the end of May.

39 km. Arisvi. Above the village are the ruins of ancient Arisvi.

40 km. Kalloni. The capital of the province of Methymni on the largest gulf on Lesbos with heavy commercial traffic. From Kalloni a turn-off right leads after 4 km. to **Skala Kallonis** with a sand beach and fish tavernas.

From the junction of Kalloni, which is at the north entrance, you take the road to Molyvos (Methymna).

41 km. A branch right, goes to Petra and Molyvos. You proceed left to Sigri.

45 km. Leimonos Monastery. This is the most important monastery on Lesbos, built in 1523. It was the spiritual center of the island and its "secret" school during the Turkish occupation. Its museum and library contain works of unbelievable value.

76 km. Antissa. The main village in the area, handsomely spread out on the slopes of a mountain above the road. Its port is **Gavathas** (9 km.). Ancient Antissa lies east of Gavathas, next to the sea.

78 km. Junction. From here a turn-off from the main route left leads after 10 km. to **Eressos** and 4 km. later **Skala Eressou** with its glorious, huge sand beach. Near Skala Eressou are the ruins of **ancient Eressos** and two Early Christian basilicas from the 5th century.

80 km. From here a turn-off leads you after 2 km. to **Ypsilos Monastery**, the old Byzantine monastery that was built around the 9th century on the peak of Mt. Ordymnos and later repaired. It has important ecclesiastical relics and a marvelous view.

You return to your main route and head west.

85 km. The Beginning of the Petrified Forest. This parched and wild land which spreads out to your left is a "forest" as far as the eye can see. Do not expect to see trunks of trees, the one on top of the other. But what you will en-

Petrified tree trunk.

counter when you follow the dirt road that meanders left for many kilometers is certainly something very worthwhile. There are isolated petrified trees, with a diameter of over three meters and over ten meters high. But it is difficult to find them. So you will find smaller ones. They have the form of a tree trunk but are nothing more than a stone, a stone trunk which were formed more than a million years ago by volcanic activity.

92 km. Sigri. The western corner of Lesbos. The magic of a bay which is commanded from above by a castle and below by a calm sea full of rocks and a lot of boats. The settlement, which has a good deal of tourist activity, lies next to the castle. There are petrified trees on the little island opposite, **Nisiopi**, as well as on the bottom of the sea.

*Sigri hides
a special charm.*

2. Ayiassos - Polichnitos - Vatera (61 km.)

You take the previous route up to the 14th km. and then turn left. **22 km**. Ayiassos junction. From here a turn-off left leads after 4 km. to **Ayiassos**, one of the most picturesque villages on Lesbos, clinging to the lush green slopes of Mt. Olymbos at a height of 450 m. All the roofs of the houses are the same, tile-covered, and the lanes narrow, uphill and flagged, the houses old, most with wooden balconies and decorated with flowers. Near the center of the village is the commanding church of the Panayia with its tall bell tower. It was built in 1170 as a triple-aisled basilica and took its present form in 1815.

*Wide sand beach
at Eressos.*

In the building complex around the church is a Byzantine museum and a folk museum with notable displays.

Folk art is more developed in Ayiassos than in any other part of Lesbos. Its inhabitants speak a strong Lesbos dialect. Ceramics and wood carving make up a tradition three millenia old. It is likely that during the town's festivals you will hear the old *samb-touri* played by one of the best players on the island, most of whom come from Ayiassos.

From the junction of Ayiassos (4 km.) you go on your way to Polichnitos.

45 km. Polichnitos. A small town known for its hot springs. Near Polichnitos is **Skala Polichnitou** (4 km.) with a beach and **Nyfida** with a gorgeous sand beach. Both of these are on the Gulf of Kalloni.

53 km. Vatera. The most beautiful sand beach on Lesbos which begins at the settlement and goes east up to the cape of Ayios Fokas. Near the cape is a temple of Dionysos.

3. Thermi - Mantamades - Skala Sykamias (51 km.)

You take the coast road which after the old harbour heads north.
9 km. Pyrgoi Thermis. Formerly there were many towers here (pyrgos = tower), but only a few still survive. Left of the road, on an elevation, is the Byzantine church of the Panayia Tourloti, one of the oldest churches on the island. Near the sea at Pyrgoi Thermis was discovered an **ancient settlement** originally built around 3000 B.C. Later settlements were built on the ruins of the first one.
11 km. Paralia Thermis. A large tourist center with a magnificent sea. Together with **Thermis** it makes up a municipality with the official name of Loutropoli (spa) Thermis. It took the name Thermis ("warm") from its warm, therapeutic springs. Southwest of Thermis, 3 km. away, is the **Convent of Ayios Raphael.**
16 km. Mystegna. A short distance on the right is Skala Mystegnon with a nice strand.

21 km. Skala Neon Kydonion. The port of Neoi Kydonies with very clear sea water.
23 km. Xambelia. A beautiful beach with tavernas, next to the sea.
31 km. A short turn-off right leads to the beach of **Aspropotamos** and 2 km. later to one of the most important Byzantine churches on the island, Ayios Stephanos.

37 km. Mantamados. A large village famed for its livestock products. Noteworthy is the Monastery of the Taxiarchon next to the village.
48 km. Sykamia. It is also called Sykaminea. A picturesque village with a lot of greenery and a spectacular view facing the sea. It was the home of the writer Stratis Myrivilis. His paternal home bears a built-in plaque.
51 km. Skala Sykamias. The most picturesque fishing harbour on Lesbos with the church of the Panayia Gorgona ("Gorgon") built on rock at the entrance to the harbour.

4. Pappados - Ayios Isidoros - Plomari (41 km.)

12 km. Follow Excursion 1 and then turn left to Plomari.
24 km. Pappados. The main village in the area with a prominent church to the Taxiarchs.
25 km. Right, at 1 km., the appealing village of **Skopelos** and left after 5 km. **Perama** which is at the entrance to the Gulf of Yera. You can take a boat from Perama to **Kountouroudia** opposite and from there you can return to Mytilini by bus (11 km.). You will go straight ahead at the crossroads at the 25th km.
38 km. Ayios Isidoros. A settlement with an attractive strand.
41 km. Plomari. The second largest town on the island with strong local colour but also with new houses, built on a hill. The harbour is just below the hill and there is a spacious square. The beach is at **Ammoudeli.** Plomari is famed for its ouzo.

Sykamia, one of the more beautiful corners in Mytilene.

The coastline from Plomari to Vatera is of great interest.

Close to Plomari, **Melinda**, the port of **Palaiochori**, has a dazzling sand beach. **Panayia Kryfti** is another beautiful site, a chapel hidden to the rear of a cover full of rocks.

5. Kalloni - Petra - Molyvos (Methymna) (63 km.)

If you only have one day to see Lesbos then you must set that aside for a trip to Molyvos.

After Kalloni, at the 41st km., you turn right.

57 km. Petra. This lovely fishing harbour, which has developed into a tourist center, took its name from an enormous rock (petra= rock) which stands out from afar on the verdant plain, next to a marvellous sand beach. At the peak of the rock is the church of Panayia Glykofiloussa from the middle of the 16th century. More than 100 steps lead you to the top from which their is a fabulous view.

Strange rock of Petra.

Plomari.

MOLYVOS (Methymna). *This is perhaps the most picturesque place that Lesbos has to offer. This is also why it developed into the leading tourist center on the island. It contains everything. The traditional architecture of the multicolored houses which are built around the steep hill, the famous castle at the top of the hill, the enticing fishing harbour and the crystal-clear sea.*

Among the sights you will see at Molyvos are the house of the poet Argyris Eftaliotis, the house of the *"Shool-teacher with the Golden Eyes"*, the heroine of a novel by Myrivilis, the archaeological collection of the Municipality, the public library and the art gallery which is an annex of the School of Fine Arts.

Molyvos has been declared a traditional settlement. East of Molyvos, at a distance of around 4 km., is the sand beach of Eftalou. From Molyvos you can take a caique if the weather is good, to Skala Sykamias, the fishing harbour with the church of Panayia Gorgona. The caique passes by Eftalou.

Chios

Map labels: Agio Gala, Kampia, Nagos, INOUSSES, Melanios, Marmaro, Trypes, Kardamyla, Pelineo, Oros, Pirama, 1186, Agia Markella, Volissos, Limnia, Sidirounda, 796, DASKALOPETRA, Vrontados, Anavatos, Karyes, Nea Moni, Avgonyma, CHIOS, PELAGONISSOS, Agios Minas, Karfas, Kalimassia, Limani Meston, ORIAS, Mesta, Katarachtis, Armolia, Taxiarches, Olympi, Nenita, Pyrgi, FANA, Emporio

It has been confirmed from finds in a cave in northern Chios that the island has been inhabited since the end of the Neolithic period (4000-3000 B.C.). According to tradition, Homer, who is thought to have most probably come from Chios, taught at Dascalopetra, a large rock near the sea at Vrontados.

The Ionians came to the island in the 9th century B.C. from Euboea. A period of development began then which reached its height in the 6th century B.C. Ancient Chios was one of the 12 towns of Ionia. It was highly developed in trade, shipping and the arts. Its prosperity was halted by the conquest of the Persians in 545 B.C. After the defeat of the Persians, Chios became a member of the first Athenian Alliance of Delos in 477 B.C. and the second in 378 B.C. while in 331 B.C. it was occupied by the Macedonians. They were followed by the Romans and Mithradates, before the beginning of the long Byzantine period, a period that was fraught with the raids of pirates, soliders of fortune and others. In 1045 at the command of the emperor Constantine IX, Monomachus, the famous Nea Moni was built.

In 1272 Chios was seized by the Venetians and in 1346 by the Genoans. The Genoans then set up the first company, Maoria, for the exploitation of mastic. In 1566 the Turks conquered the island which they ceded, however, numerous privileges; they would also become interested in the trade in mastic. In 1822 Chios would rise up in quest of freedom. This revolt would fail and the Turks would take cruel revenge. This was to be the greatest slaughter in the years of the Turkish occupation. A slaughter that would move Europe and would inspire the great French painter Delacroix to produce his famous painting, "The Slaughter on Chios" and Victor Hugo to write the poem "The Child of Chios". Chios was finally liberated in 1912. During the years of its turbulent history Chios has produced many great names in the arts and letters.

There is an old tradition on Chios that says when the Romans were led to the execution of Ayios Isidoros, he, unrepentant, but in agonizing pain, wept all the way along the road and the tears that fell on the earth became the fragrant mastic.

That is how a strange phenomenon is explained: how is it that a tree, the lentish, which exists in many places in the Mediterranean, only makes mastic on Chios? Nowhere else. So the people believe this is a gift from their patron saint, Ayios Isidoros. But Chios is not just mastic. There are the famous medieval villages such as Olymbos and Mesta, which still survive untouched by the passage of time. There is Pyrgi, the traditional village with the strange wall decoration, the "xysta" which cannot be found anywhere else in Greece. There is Nea Moni ("New Monastery"), the renowned Byzantine monastery with superb mosaics. There is even the famous "Seat of Homer", the Dascalopetra.

And along with all that it has always been closely tied to its own history. From ancient times until the relatively recent past. Until 1822 when it rose up to claim its freedom and was answered by a Turkish slaughter. A slaughter that left Chios characterized as the most martyred island in Greece.

The trip to Chios is easy. You can go by ferry boat from Piraeus, Thessaloniki, Kavala, Limnos, Lesbos and Samos or by plane from Athens.

Chios lies just off the Turkish coast between Samos and Lesbos and makes up the Prefecture of Chios with Oinouses and Psara.

A mountainous island, the highest peak being Mt. Pelinaios with many pine forests, it has an area of 842 sq. km, a coastline of 213 km. and a population of 50,000. Many of them, who live in the south section, are employed at the production of mastic which is one of the main products of the island.

Chios, or **Chora** as the locals call it, lies on the east coast of the island opposite the shores of Asia Minor.

It is the capital of the island with a population of 24,000. It was built on the site of the ancient Ionian town of which only a few traces of a theater and a wall have survived. The old Turkish neighborhood is north of the harbour, as is the large **castle** which was first built by the Byzantines and enlarged by the Genoans. Proceeding from there into the heart of the town, you can visit the **Archaeological Museum** and further on the **Koraïs Library**, one of the largest in Greece-it contains more that 130,000 volumes-and the fine Folklore Museum, Philippos Argentis, which is housed in the same building. Right next to it is the Cathedral of Ayioi Viktoroi, built in 1881.

1. Kambos - Ayios Minas - Nenita (21 km.)

You follow the road which heads south of the town. In a while you will find yourself in the area of Kambos, which extends 6 km. south with its old mansions and large gardens, full of citrus and other trees. Among them the property of Philippos Argentis stands out.

4 km. A turn-off left after 3 km. to the beach at **Karfas**.

5 km. Junction. Go left to Kallimasia.

10 km. **Ayios Minas**. A short distance from the road of your main route is this historic monastery on the left. Here in 1822, 3,000 Chiotes from the area were slaughtered, after seeking refuge in the monastery.

13 km. A turn-off left past **Kallimasia** leads after 2 km. to the seashore of **Ayios Amilianos**.

17 km. Katarachtis. Picturesque seaside settlement.

21 km. Nenita. The church of the village, Ayios Tryphon, has an exquisite carved wooden iconostasis. Near Nenita is the **Monastery of the Taxiarchon**.

2. Pyrgi - Mesta - Harbour of Mesta (41 km.)

At 5 km of Excursion 1 turn right to Pyrgi.

13 km. Tholopotami. It is in the area of the **Mastichochoria** ("Mastic-Villages"). All the villages south of Kambos are called Mastichochoria. There are mastic trees left and right of the road. Each mastic tree produces about 200 grams of mastic a year.

21 km. Armolia. A village with a pottery tradition. On the hill and 30′ on foot is the Genoan **Castle of Oria** or **Apolychnon**, from the 15th century.

25 km. A branch 5 km. long left leads to the attractive little harbour of **Emborio** where the ruins of a prehistoric settlement were discovered on the hill of Profitis Ilias.

South of the harbour is the impressive bay of **Mavra Volia**, one of the most stunning beaches on Chios.

You return to your main route and head west.

View of harbour of Chios

26 km. Pyrgi. The medieval village which began to be built around an original tower (pyrgos = tower). Here later developed the traditional decoration of the exterior walls with greyish-white geometrical shapes which the locals call **xysta**.

Noteworthy in the village is the Byzantine church of Ayioi Apostoloi which has striking wall paintings and the basilica of the Koimiseis Theotokou (The Assumption).

Heading west from Pyrgoi to **Olymbos**, you have the bay of **Fanes** on your right for around 5 km. with a beautiful sand beach.

33 km. Olymbos. Another medieval village built with the same construction system as Pyrgi.

37 km. Mesta. Yet another medieval village, the best preserved and the most impressive. There are five entrances to it. If there were not any arrows to show you the right direction you could easily get lost in the narrow, circular lanes which are covered with arches. A church of the Megali Taxiarchi ("Great Taxiarch") was built at the site of a central fortified tower.

Near the church is the delighful village square.

The church of the Palaios Taxiarchis ("Old Taxiarch"), at the north end of the village, is worth seeing.

41 km. Harbour of Mesta (Pasalimani). A settlement that is developing. From here the trip to Rafina, Attica, by ferry boat (when it is in service) takes only 6 hours.

3. Nea Moni - Anavatos

You follow the road going west and uphill.

5 km. Karyes. A village with a fine view of Chora and the sea.

10 km. You turn left.

13 km. Nea Moni. The Byzantine monastery built in a luxuriant, green valley. It was founded around 1045 by the emperor Constantine IX Monomachus to house the miracle-working icon of the Virgin which had been found in the area.

Pyrgi. Village with traditional wall decorations.

Archangel Michael from the fabulous mosaic at Nea Moni.

The architecture of the church is unique and in all of Greece is found only on Chios. This type of church is called octagonal because its dome is supported on eight niches which give it greater height and volume and make it more majestic. Unfortunately, the original dome collapsed during the earthquake of 1881 and the one you see today is a reconstruction. It is mentioned in the descriptions of travellers that its mosaic of the Pantokrator was the most beautiful in the world. But the mosaics that have survived are still the best that Byzantine art has to offer. Nuns now live in the monastery. After the visit to the monastery you return to the main road and go even further west.

25 km. Avgonyma. At Avgonyma you turn right.

30 km. Anavatos. This impressive but ruined and deserted village was built on a colossal rock which has sheer sides and can only be reached from the north.

Stairs take you up to its half-ruined houses and from afar it looks like a castle in a fairy tale. Anavatos was one of the refuges where thousands of Chiotes went in 1822 to escape slaughter by the Turks, unfortunately in vain.

4. Monastery of Ayia Markella - Ayio Gala (64 km.)

You depart Chios heading northwest, leaving Vrontados on your right.

32 km. Junction with the road going to Sidirounta. You head right.

42 km. Volissos. A village built on the slopes of a mountain which has a medieval castle at its sum-

Imposing Anavatos.

mit. From Volissos a road leads after 6 km. to the picturesque **Monastery of Ayia Markella** with an unspoiled sea. Another road goes after 2 km. to the port of Volissos, **Limnia**, with a gorgeous sand beach. **Psara** is only 17 nautical miles from here.

From Volissos you head northwest to make a tour of **Mt. Amani** passing through the villages of **Trypes** and **Melanios**.
64 km. Ayio Gala. This remote little village in the northwest corner of Chios with the strange name got its reputation from the cave near the village.

5. Vrontados - Kardamyla - Kambia (48 km.)

You follow the coast road heading north.
3 km. Near Leivadia is the basilica of **Ayios Isidoros**, the patron saint of the island. The earliest structures of the church as well as a few mosaics are dated to the 5th century.
6 km. Vrontados. It is a municipality with 4,500 inhabitants, many of whom are sailors. At **Lo Bay** there is an organized beach and installations for water sports.
6.5 km. Dascalopetra. Just outside Vrontados near the shore amid dense flora called **Vrysi tou Pasa** ("Pasha's Fountain") is an enormous carved rock which according to tradition is where Homer sat and taught. That is also why it is called "**Homer's Seat**".
26 km. Kardamyla. The main village in the area with 2,500 inhabitants which is the third municipality on the island.
28 km. Marmara. The port of Kardamyla, at the back of a bay.
32 km. Nagos. A picturesque bay and one the finest beaches on Chios.
48 km. Kambia. From the village (alt: 340 m.) as well as from **Spartounta** (alt: 530 m.), which is futher south, the ascent is made in about three hours to the summit **Profitis Ilias** (alt: 1,297 m.) of Mt. Pelinaios, the highest mountain on Chios. The road from Kambia heads south and passing through the villages of **Fyta** and **Diefcha**, meets the road to Volissos.

Oinousses

When twilight comes, far off to the northwest of the harbour of Chios some distant lights appear which reflect off the surface of the sea. This is the small island of Oinoussa. You can see it better from the ship which passes by it on the way to Lesbos. You can even make out the houses which are sparking white and well-built.

This island seems to have a lot of activity in summer. It is the season when the Oinousian sailors - many of them shipowners - gather there for their summer holidays. For all the visitors who would like to enjoy its beautiful coves the places to stay are limited to a small hotel.

Next to Oinoussa are other, even smaller, uninhabited islands which make up the complex called Oinousses with a total area of 14 sq. km., and a population of 500. It is 9 nautical miles from the harbour of Chios with which it has daily connections.

HISTORY

The island has been known by its present name since antiquity. Its position in the strait which separates Chios from Asia Minor stirred the interest first of the Venetians and then the Turks who used is an a base. From time to time it was used for the same thing by pirates.

Its only settlement is a municipality. It has old houses and many new ones, Captains' mansions. It also has several noteworthy churches and chapels. There is a naval museum on Oinousses.

To the northwest and at a distance of 3 km. is the **Evangelismos Monastery** while in the approximate middle of the excursion is the old Castle. The chapel of Zoodochos Pigi, which is on the small island of **Pasas**, is worth seeing.

Psara

Kimissi
Theotokou

ANTIPSARA

DASKALIO

PSARA

KATONISSI

Psara lies 44 nautical miles northwest of the main harbour of Chios to which it is connected by a small ferry boat. But the nearest harbour to the island is Limnia on Chios (17 nautical miles).

Psara is a barren island of 40 sq. km with a population of 460. Together with neighboring **Antipsara** and a few other uninhabited little islands, such as **Daskaleio, Kato Nisi** and **Ayios Nikolaos**, it makes up a small island complex.

HISTORY

In antiquity the island was known by the name of Psyra. But the most brilliant period of its history occurred during the Greek War of Independence of 1821. It was one of the first islands to rise up against the Turks and it was then the third largest naval power in Greece after Hydra and Spetses. Its fleet, with the daring Psarian fireship captains, Kanaris, Papanikolis and Pipinos, was the scourge of the Turks. That is why the Turks decided to annhilate them. Thus in 1824 they attacked with 140 ships and 14,000 Janissaries. A fierce but uneven battle ensued which resulted in the victory of the Turks who seized the island. All those who managed to escape with Kanaris, later built Nea Psara ("New" Psara) on Euboea. Many preferred to die, blowing up the gunpowder magazines on the island.

The rest were slaughtered or taken prisoner and Psara was set ablaze. The destruction of Psara was a terrible blow to Hellenism and inspired the great Greek poet, Dionysios Solomos, to write his famous poem:

> "*At Psara striding*
> *the pitch-black crest*
> *Only Glory all alone...*"

Psara had to wait until 1912 to become a part of Greece.

View of Psara.

Getting to know the island

The visitor to the island will enjoy its tranquil life and the beautiful shores with their pristine sea.

In the charming little harbour of Psara you will find and a few rooms to rent.

You can visit the modest Archaeological Museum and **Palaikastro** which was built in the 15th century.

In the north part of the island and on the slopes of the highest mountain, Profitis Ilias (530 m.), is the **Monastery of the Koimiseis Theotokou** with a distinguished library which contains many books, some of which were printed in Venice.

Oinousses.

Samos

This island, which is closer to Asia Minor than any other Greek island and constitutes the bridge between Greece and the East, managed because of its power to remain independent, frequently and for many years, while at the same time flourishing despite the battles that were waged to conquer it. Was that perhaps one of the reasons that caused Samos to produce so many men of genius and great artists?

Pythagoras (580-490 B.C.) the famous philosopher and mathematician, Rhoikos and Theodoros (6th-5th century B.C.), architects of the Temple of Hera and the first to employ brass-founding, Mandrocles who built for Darius the floating bridge on the Boshorus in 513 B.C., Evpalinos from Megara who built a famous aqueduct at Pythagoreio, the so-called Evpalineios Tunnel, digging out the mountain simultaneously from both sides, the sculptor Pythagoras who is said to have been the creator of the Charioteer at Delphi and Aristarchos (320-250 B.C.) the greatest astronomer of antiquity, were all born or lived on Samos.

In the pitch-black nights of winter, when the fishermen pass by the wind-buffeted and sheer slopes of Mt. Kerkis, the highest mountain on Samos, they tell how they see a light up on the peak which like a lighthouse guides them on a safe course during a storm. They even say that the light is the spirit of Pythagoras.

Pythagoras was born on Samos nearly 2,000 years ago and benefitted the world with his philosophy and mathematics. He still lives on in the hearts and souls of the fishermen of Samos.

This large, Aegean island is a gorgeous, verdant place which at one point is no more than 2 km. from Turkey. It is covered with pure white sand beaches, picturesque villages and fishing harbours. You can reach Samos from Athens by plane or by ferry boat from Piraeus, Kavala, Icaria, the Dodecanese, Crete and other islands. Samos lies east of Icaria and is 174 nautical miles from Piraeus. It has an area of 475 sq. km. a coastline of 159 km. and a population of 40,000. The island is famed for the production and the quality of its wine, the sweet variety of which has an international reputation.

Statue of Pythagoras.

The island has been inhabited since the third millenium B.C., proven by finds near Pythagoreio. The Ionians came to Samos around 1000 B.C. Hera had been worshipped on the island since ancient times; she was believed to have been born on Samos. The Ionians continued this old tradition. In the 7th century B.C. they built, near Pythagoreio, the famous Temple of Hera, on the ruins of an earlier prehistoric temple. Samos reached its pinnacle during the period it was governed by the tyrant Polycrates (532-522 B.C.). It was then that Samos grew into a great naval power and founded its own colonies. A new kind of ship was constructed in the shipyards on the island with 50 oars, the celebrated **samaina**. The Samian fleet with 100 such ships was an awesome force for the period.

The beginning of the end of this brilliant period for Samos came with the death of Polycrates. This mighty tyrant was tricked by a Persian satrap and assassinated. The despotic government on Samos continued but now with Persian assistance until the defeat of the Persians at Salamis and the intervention of Athens, which imposed a democratic regime and made the island part of the Delian Alliance (478 B.C.).

Later it passed into the hands of the Macedonians and then the Romans who originally ceded it to the Kingdom of Pergamon only to take it themselves later with a flurry of destruction and looting.

The Byzantine period followed. But the rule of Byzantium was so loose that the island was left exposed to the attacks of Goths, Huns and pirates. In 1204 the Franks assumed control and after the fall of Constantinople, the Turks. In 1475 the island was destroyed by a powerful earthquake and abandoned. Nearly 100 years passed before it was colonized again. Then after all the privileges the Turks ceded to the Christians, many Samians returned to the island along with other Greeks from various parts of Greece who founded settlements bearing the names of their homelands, some of which still exist today, such as Mytilinioi, that is, with people from Mytilini, Lesbos.

The years marched on and 1821 arrived, a year of the uprising of all Hellenism against the Turkish oppressor. Samos rose up as well led by Lykourgos Logothetis and his fellow warrior Captain Stamatis. They managed to drive the Turks from the island and to keep them at bay for many years despite their enraged counterattacks. But regardless of the Samians success, in 1830 the Great Powers decided to give Samos to Turkey. The only consolation was that the island was able to retain some of its autonomy.

Thus, Samos began the period of the Hegemony. The Prince was a Christian but appointed by the Sultan. This period lasted until 1912 when Themistoklis Sophoulis landed on the island with a force of volunteers, joined up with the local rebels and definitively drove the Turks from Samos. It was officially united with Greece at the beginning of 1913.

Archaeological site of Heraion.
To the rear left, the only remaining column of the Temple of Hera.

Vathy, lovely capital of Samos.

Getting to know the island

Samos or Vathy

To the rear of a picturesque and lush green bay is the town and the harbour of Samos, which today has around 5,000 inhabitants. It is called Vathy from the name of the old settlement which was built high up above the sea. Then there were only a few warehouses near the harbour. But the harbour slowly developed into a lovely town and united with Vathy, which is the capital of the island today.

When you have disembarked from the boat and have taken your stroll along the delightful waterfront avenue, you will encounter on your left the large **Pythagoras Square** with its marble lion. Further along you will turn left to go to the historic church of St. Spyridonas, to the old mansion of the **Parliament** which today houses City Hall and the public library and next to City Hall you will visit the Archaeological Museum with distinguished finds from throughout Samos, mainly from the Heraion.

Near the **Archaelogical Museum** is also located the interurban bus station where there are buses to the main villages and the finest beaches on the island. Opposite the quay where the ships dock but a bit further on and next to the church of Ayioi Theodoroi, is the **Byzantine Museum** with beautiful icons of Christ, the Virgin and the Crucifixion from the 17th century, old Gospel books and holy vestments among which is the cope worn by the Patriarch Gregory V.

Near the town you will swim at the beach **Gangos** which is to the north, about 1.5 km. away.

Kokkari, renowned fishing - harbour of Samos.

EXCURSIONS

1. Samos - Karlovasi - Pythagoreio - Samos (84 km.)

This excursion, the 84 km. of the main route along with a swim and a meal, can be done in one day. But there is no possible way it can be done if the secondary excursions are also made, which are directly connected to the main one.

Take the coast road toward Karlovasi.

10 km. Kokkari. The most picturesque fishing harbour on Samos, which has now developed into a large tourist center. A small peninsula full of houses which climb up to the top of the hill with a small harbour on one side and a superb sand beach on the other. The tavernas, the cafes and the shops make for a unique image.

12 km. Lemonakia. One of the most dazzling, small, lush coves on Samos with a marvellous sand beach.

12.5 km. Tsamadou. A great sand beach next to Lemonakia.

16 km. Avlakia. A sand beach, touristically developed.

17 km. A turn-off left leads you after 5 km. to the village of **Vourliotes**, a true balcony on the sea at height of 340 meters. At a distance of 2 km. from the village is the **Monastery of Panayia Vrontiani** (alt: 480 m.), the oldest on Samos. It was built in the 16th century. From here it is about 3 hours on foot to the summit of **Mt Karvouni** (1,153 m.).

20 km. Platanakia. A lovely seashore with plane trees and country restaurants. From here a turn-off left leads after 1 km. to the verdant gorge of **Aedonia** with attractive country inns. The walk there, under the enormous plane trees and next to the running water, is pure pleasure. The road goes up, ascending through many curves to arrive 3 km. later at the village of **Manolates** at a height of 380 m. with an incredible ravine to the west.

20.5 Ayios Konstantinos. A seaside village which is quite active in summer.

From here a turn-off left takes you after 4 km. to the charming village of **Ambelos** and 1 km. later to the village of **Stavrinides**. Both of these are dense with flora and have a marvelous view of the sea.

28 km. Ayios Dimitrios. A branch here leads after 1 km. to the village of **Kontakeïka**.

31 km. A turn-off left leads after 5 km. to **Ydrousa**, a village with abundant water.

33 km. Karlovasi. The second largest town and harbour on Samos. All the ships that go to Samos stop first at Karlovasi.

Verdant Karlovasi.

Bay of Marathokambos.

It is made up of three areas, New, Middle and Old Karlovasi. A very pretty town, particularly in the area of the verdant hill of Ayia Triada with houses clinging to the slopes and the like-named church at the top. In Karlovasi you will see old mansions and abandoned tanning factories. Tanning flourished there many years ago but today there are only a few light industries dedicated to ceramics, wall decorations and weaving.

Karlovasi was the home of Lykourgos Logothetis, the rebel from 1821 and the Governor of Samos.

Four km. west of Karlovasi is **Potami**, one of the most beautiful beaches on Samos. The walk through the ravine that ends at the sea is very relaxing.

From Karlovasi you can make lovely excursions which include hiking, mountain climbing, and a visit to mountain villages and astonishing monasteries on Mt. **Kerkis** (1,433 m.), the highest mountain on Samos.

One of these excursions is the visit to the village of **Kosmadaioi**, which is 13 km. from Karlovasi and 600 m. high, followed by the **Monastery of the Koimiseis Theotokou**. Most of this journey

is done under lofty pines and lasts about one hour. A half an hour from the monastery you arrive at a noteworthy cave passing through the Kakoperato Gorge.

Another excursion from Karlovasi is to the village of Kastania which is 8 km. away and very high up with abundant water and chestnut trees.

To continue your tour of the island leave Karlovasi and head south.

41 km. Junction. From here a turn-off right leads after 5 km. to the village of **Marathokampos**. The **Bay of Marathokampos** is 4 km. away. This is a summer resort area with a vast sand beach. 3 km. further west is **Votsalakia**, one of the best beaches on Samos. Even further west is the beach of **Psili Ammos** (one of many sand beaches on Samos with this name). The road continuing on in its westerly direction, climbs high above the sea and goes around Mt. Kerkis passing through the villages of **Ayia Kyriaki, Kallithea** and **Drakaioi**. Between the two last ones, a small road descends to the Bay of **Ayios Isidoros**.

44 km. You are again on your main excursion, coming from the

junction at Marathokambos. At this point a turn-off left leads after 3 km to the mountainous and verdant **Platanos**.

47 km. New junction. From here a turn-off right leads after 3 km. to **Koumeïka** and its bay and 4 km. further to **Skoureïka** and its shores.

52 km. Koutsi. A fabulous site with plane trees, water and a stupendous view.

55 km. Pyrgos. A large village renowned for its production of wine, grapes and apples. It is also known for its weaving and its woollen, handmade rugs.

Two very interesting excursions start from Pyrgos.

The one goes to the north and ascends Mt. Karvouni ending at the mountain village of **Pandrosos** (5 km.), 630 m. high while the other heads south passing through the colourful village of **Spatharaioi** (6 km.) and then descending to the sea at Limnonaki. From **Limnonaki** you can take a small boat to the charming little island of **Samiopoula** which has two sand beaches.

Panoramic view of Pythagoreio, to the center left the Heraion.

59 km. Koumaradaoi. A village with a pottery-making tradition.

63 km. Junction with the road that after 1 km. goes to the **Monastery of the Timios Stavros**, from the 16th century with important relics and 2 km. later the village of **Mavratzaoi** where many of the inhabitants are involved with pottery-making like those in Koumaradaioi.

66 km. Chora. The old capital of the island in the Middle Ages.

From Chora a turn-off from the main excursion north leads after 4 km. to Mytilinioi, a market town with 2,500 inhabitants and a very interesting Paleontological Museum in which are displayed finds from prehistoric animals which were discovered near Mytilinioi. Among the exhibits the bones of the so-called Samotherios, the small horse of Samos with three toes on each hoof and a skelton more primitive than today's wild animals.

To continue your tour of the island return to Chora and go to the south-east.

68 km. Junction. From here there is a very important turn-off which leads to **Myloi** (8 km.), the village next to the ancient river **Imvrassos** at the main village in the area, **Pagonda** (12 km.) and to the most noteworthy archaeological site on Samos, the famous **Heraion** (6 km.) as well as the coastal settlement of Heraion (7 km.) one of the largest tourist centers in Samos, with a splendid sand beach.

It was believed that the goddess Hera was born at Heraion and that is why there has been a temple there since prehistoric times, the first one probably made of wood. After its destruction a second one was built in the 7th century B.C. But that was also destroyed, by the King of Persia, Cyrus. On its ruins the architect Rhoikos built the third temple in the 6th century which was also destroyed by the Persians. Finally, Polycrates assigned to the son of Rhoikos, Theodoros, the task of building the fourth temple, larger and more magnificent. Herodotus wrote that it was the largest and most magnificent temple he had ever seen. Only one of its columns survives today.

71 km. Pythagoreio (formerly called Tigani). This is a picturesque tourist center with a harbour in exactly the same cove as the ancient one. Its quay with the yachts, small boats and shops full of tourists bustles with activity and not only during the summer - it is lively in spring and autumn too. Pythagoreio is also the starting point for many sea excursions.

Small ships leave from here, as from Samos, for Patmos, Agathonisi, Samiopoula and Kusadasi in Turkey.

There is a modest **Archaeological Museum** in Pythagoreio with finds from the surrounding area. Of the sites you will visit, the Tower of Logothetis, which is at the top of the hill above the harbour, and the Church of the Metamorphosis next to it which he himself built in 1824 after the miraculous repulsion of the Turkish attack, stand out. Then you will visit the ruins of the ancient walls and an ancient theater which are north of the town and on the slopes of the mountain.

Even further away you will see the **Evpalineios Tunnel**, a tunnel more than 1 km. long and 2 meters high, on one side of which there is a deep trench for running water. This tunnel which passed

Lovely Pythagoreio, starting point for many interesting excursions.

The Monastery of Panayia Spiliani.

through the mountain and supplied the ancient town with water is said to have been dug simultaneously from both sides.

At the end the two shafts met somewhere in the middle of the mountain and were almost exactly aligned. This tunnel was one of the great works of Polycrates and was built by the famous engineer from Megara, Evpalinos in the 6th century B.C. Near the ancient theater is the **Monastery of Panayia Spiliani**. The like-named church lies to the rear of a cave which is said to be the oracle of Photo. The beach at Pythagoreio is west of the harbour. Even further west is the beach of **Potokaki**.

From Pythagoreio you take the road that ascends to the northeast.

83 km. Samos. This completes the tour of the island.

2. Eastern Samos

Kalami - Ayia Paraskevi. You take the coast road to the northwest and then turn east. Ayia Paraskevi is a delightful bay with a chapel of the same name.

Monastery of Zoodochos Pigis - Mourtia (7 km). Proceed east. At the crossroads you will meet after 2 km., you go left. (The road right goes to the Monastery of Ayia Zoni after 1 km.). After 4 km. you arrive at the **Monastery of Zoodochos Pigis**, from the 18th century with a magnificent main church. A road just before the monastery to the right leads to the gorgeous, lush bay of **Mourtia**.

Palaiokastro - Poseidoni (11 km.). You follow the road from Psili Ammos to the southeast and at Treis Ekklisies (2 km.) you turn left for Palaiokastro. Poseidoni is a small and tranquil circular bay opposite the coast of Turkey.

Psili Ammos (9 km.). You follow the road for the preceding excursion and at Treis Ekkliseis go right. Psili Ammos, which can also be reached by bus, is one of the most beautiful beaches on Samos and is about 1 mile from the coast of Turkey.

"Fisherman at Midday", 1982.
Oil on canvas (90 × 110)
Work of the painter
K. Grammatopoulos.

Icaria

(map of Icaria showing: Fanari, Kionio, Monokampi, Katafygio, Mavrikato, Armenistis, Kampos, Evdilos, Akamatra, Agios Dimitrios, Christos, Frantato, Dafni, Xylossyrtis, AGIOS KIRIKOS, Monte, Chrysostomos, Vrakades, NIKARIA, Lagada, Amalo, Pezio, Maganiti, Plagia, Vardarades, Karkinagri, Trapalo)

Most people know of Icaria because of its therapeutic springs. Where people of a certain age go for a "cure". No one believes it has anything besides springs, but that is a great mistake! All you have to do is go up the winding road above Ayios Kirykos and survey the landscape from up there and you will immediately understand. You will see before you a pretty little village, nestled in greenery. The roofs of the houses are all made of slate, like the ones on Pelion but even more handsome. The mountain is covered in wild, almost primitive vegetation and as far as the eye can see before you, is the sea gleaming under a blazing sun that also warms your bones. This is the Icarian Sea. The sea into which the mythical Icarus fell and drowned when the sun melted his wax wings.

This will be your first impression of Icaria and it will be followed by others. When you have passed over the ridge of the high mountain and begin to descend to the north coast then you will see the remote ravines full of slate rock ending down at the sea in breathtaking bays. And later, when you have visited Evdilos and have gone to Armenistis you will encounter some of the most ravishing sand beaches in the Aegean, Yialiskari and Mesakti.

Icaria has a primordial beauty blessed by the warm hospitality of its inhabitants. You can reach Icaria by ferry boat from Piraeus, Samos, the Cyclades and the Dodecanese. Icaria lies west of Samos and is 142 nautical miles from Piraeus. It has an area of 255 sq. km., a coastline of 102 km. and a population of around 8,000.

The island is ideal for peaceful holidays.

HISTORY

Icaria owes its name to the mythical Icarus who, according to mythology, escaped from the Labyrinth of Crete along with his father flying with wings which were attached to his body with wax. Entranced by his flight, Icarus spurned the advice of his father and flew high up toward the sun; the wax wings melted from the heat and he fell into the sea and drowned. Thus, this sea came to be called the Icarian Sea and the island Icaria.

The Ionians settled on the island around the end of the 9th century B.C. Later Icaria became a part of the Athenian Alliance. After a long period of oblivion, at the beginning of the 13th century it was conquered by the Venetians and in 1524 by the Turks.

In July 1912 it revolted, four months later uniting with the rest of Greece.

The beach of Therma.

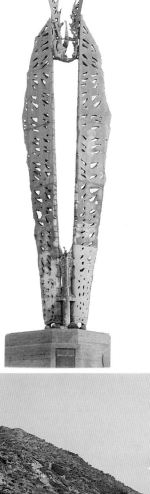

Fishermen in the harbour of Evdilos.

The Area of Ayios Kirykos

Ayios Kirykos. The capital of the island and its main harbour. There you can visit the church of Ayios Kirykos and the small **Archae-ological-Folklore Museum**.

2 km. Therma (Loutra). NE of Ayios Kirykos is one of the two spas on Icaria with therapeutic springs and a beach. There are the ruins of an ancient acropolis near Therma.

Therma (Loutra) Lefkadas (2 km.). SW of Ayios Kirykos is the second spa on Icaria. There are therapeutic springs and a beach here as well. Near Lefkades is the **Monastery of the Evangelismos** (The Annunciation).

7 km. Mavrato. A pretty, verdant village on the slopes of the mountain above Ayios Kirykos. The roofs of the houses, made with stone slabs, and the dense vegetation of the surrounding area make it seem like a Pelion village.

8 km. Oxea. Another village like Mavrato, but higher up.

22 km. Mileopos. One of the loveliest villages in northern Icaria in a resplendent gorge above the sea, rich in flora.

38 km. Evdilos. The former capital of the island and today its second most important harbour, with its neoclassical houses. Some of the ferry boats stop at Evdilos rather than Ayios Kirykos. It has a pleasant beach.

40 km. Kambos. Here are the ruins of ancient Oinoe and the **Archaeological Museum**. Before the village are the beaches of **Fytema** and **Kambos**.

52.5 Yialiskari. A small seaside settlement.
Near there is the small island of **Diapori** with the Church of the Assumption. From there on stretch out the most glorious sand beaches on Icaria, **Mesakti** and **Livadi**.

54.5 km. A turn-off left leads after 7 km. to the lovely mountain village of **Christos tis Raches**. The road goes on to **Profitis Ilias** and **Pezi** which is at a high elevation and is a natural balcony with a superb view of the sea.

55 km. Armenistis. One more little harbour on Icaria at the end of a promontory.

From Armenistis a road goes high above the sea and parallel to the coast leading after 3 km. to the charming **Bay of Na**.

There are ruins of walls there and the **Temple of Artemis Tav-ropolis** ("Bull-goddess").

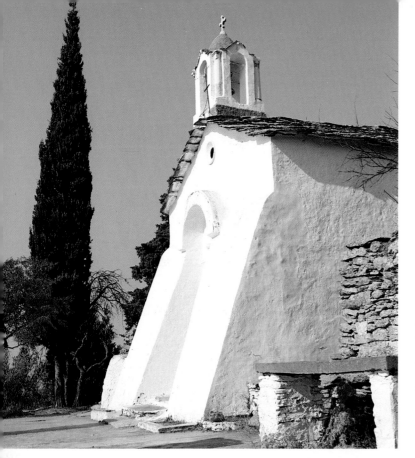

Fournoi

There are some small islands lying between Icaria and Samos with a lacy coastline that few people know about. These are Fourni, all of them together, Left is the leeward Chrysomilia and right the small island of Thymaina. Before you is Fournoi, the picturesque little harbour with about 1,000 inhabitants, most of them fishermen.

This is a fantastic place to relax and enjoy the sea. Just do not be too demanding. Be satisfied with a simple room and a fish-tavern. It is enough if you like to spend the evening at a cafe talking to the fishermen of Fourni.

Fourni lies between Icaria, Samos and Patmos. They have an area of 40 sq. km. and a coastline of 125 km. They are connected to Ayios Kirykos, which is 11 nautical miles away, both by a small, local boat and by a ferry boat which goes from Piraeus to the Cyclades, Icaria, Fourni and Samos. There are no cars on the island.

Getting to know the island

The things to see on Fourni are its magnificent bays, many of which have small harbours. On the same island there is also the leeward bay of **Chrysomilia** with a small village. On the neighbouring island of **Thymena** is a small fishing village with the same name. The third little island of **Ayios Minas** lies to the east and is uninhabited.

Above, the church of Ayia Theoktisti and below, picturesque Na on Icaria.

Images from Fourni.

THE ISLANDS AND ISLETS OF THE NORTH AND EAST AEGEAN

THASOS
Thasopoula.............*N Thasos.*
Koinyra....................*E Thasos.*
Panayia. ....*S Thasos.*

SAMOTHRAKI

LIMNOS
Diavates................*SW Myrina.*
Sergitsi....................*N Limnos.*
Koukonisi. .... *Bay of Moudros.*
Ayios Nikolaos. ....
.... *Bay of Moudros.*
Alagonisi....... *Bay of Moudros.*
Kombi. ....*S Moudros.*

AYIOS EFSTRATIOS
Ayioi Apostoloi......................
............................*N Ay. Efstratios.*
Velia............. *E Ayios Efstratios.*

LESBOS
Nisiopi........................*W Sigri.*
Sidousa....................*SW Sigri.*
Fanes............................*S Sigri.*
Pochis.............. *NW Lesbos.*
Ayios Georgios.........*W Petra.*
Panayia. .... *NE Lesbos.*
Barbalias. .... *NE Lesbos.*
Aspronisos........... *NE Lesbos.*
Tsoukalas.............. *NE Lesbos.*
Prasologos. .... *NE Lesbos.*
Kydonas.................*E Lesbos.*
N. Pamfyllon.........*E Lesbos.*
Mersinia.................*SE Lesbos.*
Garnias............ *Gulf of Kalloni.*

CHIOS
Margariti. ....*N Chios.*
Strovili. ....*N Chios.*
Ayios Stephanos..................
.... *NE Pantoukia.*

Venetiko......................*S Chios.*
Ayios Stephanos. ....*N Mesta.*
Pelagonisi... *N harbour Mesta.*

OINOUSES
Prasonisia...........*W Oinouses.*
Pasas.................... *E Oinouses.*
Pontikonisos.... *SE Oinouses.*
Vatos................... *SE Oinouses.*

PSARA
Antipsara..................*W Psara.*
Ayios Nikolaos........ *W Psara.*
Katonisi................*S Antipsara.*
Mastroyiorgis........ *NW Psara.*
Prasonisi. .... *NW Psara.*

SAMOS
Ayios Nikolaos. ....*N Vathy.*
Prasonisi. ....*N Vathy.*
Makronisi. ....*N Vathy.*
Petra. .... *S Heraion.*
Samiopoula. ....*S Samos.*
Aspros Vrachos. ....
......................................*SW Samos.*

ICARIA

FOURNI
Thymaina.................*W Fourni.*
Thymainaki. ....*W Fourni.*
Kesiria........................*W Fourni.*
Ayios Minas...............*E Fourni.*
Mikros Anthropofas............
....*SE Fourni.*
Megalos Anthropofas. ....
....*SE Fourni.*
Makronisi. ....*S Fourni.*
Plakaki.......................*S Fourni.*
Plaka........................*S Fourni.*
Strongylo...................*S Fourni.*
Prasonisaki.............*S Fourni.*

OTHER AEGEAN ISLANDS

ISLETS OF CHALKIDIKI
Amoliani.....................*S Trypiti.*
Diaporos......... *N Bourbouros.*
Kelyfos. .... *SW N. Marmaras.*

ISLETS OF THE PAGASITIC GULF
Palaio Trikeri...... *S Pagasitic.*
Strongyli. .... *S Pagasitic.*
Pythou.................*S Pagasitic.*
Nisos Psathion... *S Pagasitic.*

Alatas. .... *SW Milina.*
Kykinthos.......*NE Amaliapolis.*
Argyroniso........... *S Pagasitic.*

ISLETS OF THE WEST AEGEAN
Velopoula............................
.........*22 nautical miles N Hydra.*
Falkonera...............................
........*25 nautical miles NW Milos.*
Karavi.....................................
..........*25 nautical miles W Milos.*

The Ionian Islands (or Heptanesos, the Seven Islands) have stood apart since days of old: fertile land, a mild climate and forested mountains. Lofty, white cliffs above a blue sea but also tranquil shores with snow-white beaches where you can easily anchor your boat and find refuge. That is one reason they were inhabited so early. Archaeological finds show that the first inhabitants came there in the Stone Age and the area flourished during the Mycenean period. Then the Greeks set off for the Trojan War and along with them Odysseus, Homer's hero, who had his kimgdom on one of these islands: Ithaca. Homer also speaks of two other islands, Lefkada and the rich and beautiful land of the Phaeacians, which is none other than Corfu. Corinth colonized Corfu in the 8th century B.C. and Lefkada in the 7th. It wanted these islands as stations for its commercial fleet on the way to Sicily and the rest of the West. But Corfu acquired power and allied itself with Athens which was the cause of the Peloponnesian War between Athens and Sparta in 431 B.C. The Ionian Islands came under Roman rule in 146 B.C. and later Byzantium. The Venetians occupied them in 1386 and stayed for 400 years. But the islands always remained Greek, cultivated letters and had

CORFU

Kerkyra

PAXI

LEFKADA

ITHAKI

KEFALONIA

KYTHIRA

ZAKYNTHOS

distinguished writers, among them the great Greek poet, Dionysios Solomos. They also cultivated the fine arts, painting and music in particular. The Venetian occupation ended in 1797 after the triumph of Napoleon and the occupation of the islands by the French. In 1799 the Russo-Turkish fleet took the islands from the French and in 1800 a treaty was signed for the formation of the "Septinsular Republic". It was the first time the islands acquired autonomy. It was called "Septinsular" because there are seven main islands. The Septinsular Republic only lasted for 7 years and the French returned; in 1815 a treaty was signed which recognized the "United States of the Ionian Islands" under a British protectorate. Unfortunately the "protectorate" turned out to be just another occupation and thus the dream of liberation was lost for the moment. But the inhabitants did not give up the struggle. When the time came for Greece to rise up against the Turks, the islands offered a significant amount of assistance, despite the opposition of the British. The chieftains of the Greeks War of Independence of 1821, took their oath on the Ionian Islands. The first Governor of free Greece was John Kapodistrias from Corfu. But the Ionian Islands themselves stayed under British domination until Union finally came in 1864. An earthquake in 1953 destroyed three of these islands: Zakynthos, Cephalonia and Ithaca. Traditional houses and old mansions collapsed and old churches were devestated. "The crevices opened by the earthquake immediately filled with flowers", Solomos once wrote. Though he did not say it about this earthquake, his words were still prophetic because the islands were quickly rebuilt.

In this chapter we refer to 123 islands (including the 7 major ones) found scattered throughout the Ionian Sea and the Gulf of Corinth. Only 28 of them are inhabited.

Corfu

There is even one product that is produced only on Corfu. Nowhere else in Europe. This is the cumquat, the very small orange of Chinese derivation which is made into a sweet or a liquer.

We spoke above of the great tourist development on Corfu. Much has changed on the island under the assault of tourism.

But what has not changed at all, fortunately, is the old town of Corfu. Squeezed in between the Old and the New Fortress it remains almost like it was 200 years ago. The traditions also have not changed nor the manners and customs. The Corfiots love their homeland. They leave it with difficulty. They stay there and go on celebrating life the way their ancestors celebrated it.

Visitors are fortunate who happen to be on Corfu for Easter or the brilliant processions of St. Spyridonas, the patron saint of the island.

There is a small bay on Corfu with pure white sand and all around it a mountain with thick vegetation. A stream flows past and empties into the sea. According to tradition, on this sand beach, Nausica, the daughter of King Alcinous, found the ship-wrecked Odysseus and tended to him. This bay, Ermones, is like the one described by Homer in the Odyssey where he speaks to us of the final stop of Odysseus in the land of the Phaeacians, Corfu.

Thus, known since the time of Homer, Corfu later became even better known, as royalty adopted it for their summer residence, such as Elizabeth of Austria, the famed Sissy who built a palace there which was later purchased by Kaiser Wilhelm II of Germany. Since then more and more travellers have visited the island and spoken with enthusiasm about the natural beauty of Corfu and the politeness and culture of its inhabitants.

Thus Corfu has slowly gone from being an island of a mainly farming population, to an international tourist center.

But besides its natural beauties, Corfu also owes its development to its geographical position. It is the northernmost island in the Ionian Sea and the nearest to the West. It lies opposite the coast of Epirus and Albania and is the second largest of the Ionian Islands with an area of 592 sq. km, a coastline of 217 km. and a population of over 100,000.

The gentle lines of its mountains which descend smoothly toward its western shores, form idyllic bays with sand beaches. The eastern shores are steeper and the beauty wilder but with no fewer sand beaches than in the west. The highest mountain, Pantokrator at 906 m., commands the northern section of the island.

The vegetation consists mainly of olive and cypress trees. There are fewer cypress groves than olive groves and they appear like strong brush-strokes on a painting where green is dominant. Olive oil is the chief product of the island and is considered to be among the best in Greece. Other products are milk, butter, Gruyère cheese, white wine and processed meats.

Traditional folk art continues to be cultivated on the island. Its products are woven items, rugs, wickerwork, silverware and jewellery.

Music is a special tradition among the Corfiots which has deep roots there flourishing especially during the 18th and the 19th century when Italian operatic companies frequently performed in the town of Corfu.

The love the Corfiots have for music also shows in their devotion to the dance. You should certainly attend one of their dances and see young men and women from Corfu wearing the striking local costume and dancing their traditional dances, so full of grace.

Women in traditional Corfiot costume.

Everything mentioned till now is a guarantee of a pleasant and restful holiday, on this island of politeness and traditional hospitality.

You go to Corfu by plane from Athens or Europe (in summer). Ships go from Patras (132 nautical miles), Igoumenitsa (18 nautical miles) or Sagiada as well as from Italy (Bari, Brindizi, Ancona, Otranto) and the former Yugoslavia (Bar, Dubrovnik, Split). By road you can go from Athens or Thessaloniki by way of Igoumenitsa.

From Corfu there are the following local connections: by ship from Paxi (31 nautical miles), Antipaxi (34 nautical miles), Ithaca (91 nautical miles), Sami, Cephalonia (91 nautical miles) and the small islands of Ereikousa, Mathraki and Othoni. By plane you go to Aktio and Argostoli - Zakynthos (only in summer).

The captivating town of Corfu.

The island, whose ancient name was Corcyra, appears to have been inhabited since the Paleolithic period while a human presence has been confirmed to the Bronze Age (2000 B.C.), on its western coast at least . In 734 B.C. it was colonized by the Corinthians who built the present-day Analipsi, the ancient town and its acropolis. Corfu developed into an important commercial center, acquired a powerful fleet, its own colonies and did not hesitate within seventy years from its foundation to revolt against Corinth itself and to acquire autonomy.

But not only Corinth was interested in this island. The large rival towns of Athens and Sparta both had their eye on it. Thus, in 432 B.C. Corfu became the cause for the outbreak of the Peloponnesian War. After the victory of Sparta, Corfu passed under the authority of the Spartans.

This was followed by the Syracusian occupation, King Pyrrhus of Epirus and the Illyrians, ending with Roman rule.

During the Byzantine period the fortifications of the new town began with the walls of the Old Fortress (8th century) in an endeavor to confront the attacks of the island's enemies, particularly the Normans. During this period the name Coryfo prevailed (from the acropolis perched on its peak) (Koryfo=peak, crest). From Coryfo came the Western Corfu, which is what it has been called by foreigners ever since (Kerkyra in Greek, derived from the ancient Corcyra). In 1204 it was occupied by the Genoans and continually changed masters until 1356 when the Venetians took command and stayed until 1797.

In the meantime, the Turks made their appearance starting in 1537 and unleashing their attacks from the coast of Epirus opposite, repeatedly endeavored to conquer the island, but without success.

After the attacks by the Turks, Corfu experienced a flowering in the arts and letters which continued until the 19th century.

In 1797 it was occupied by the French and ten years later by the Russo-Turkish fleet. This was followed by the Anglo-French struggle for the domination of the island. The French held the upper hand in the beginning and due to the resistance of Donzelot controlled the island from 1807 to 1815 when along with the other Ionian Islands Corfu came under the domination of Great Britain.

The union of Corfu and the other Ionian Islands with Greece finally took place in 1864.

The Town of Corfu

One of the loveliest towns in Greece, it is the capital of the island and at the same time the like-named prefecture. It is in practically the middle of the eastern coast of the island at the point where the land projects out, toward the coast of Epirus opposite. At the end of this projection, at Cape Sidero, is built the old Venetian fortress, which is an extension of the older Byzantine fortifications from the 8th century. This **fortress** has been cut off from the mainland by a moat over 25 m. wide, the famous **Kontrafossa**, so that it is completely surrounded by sea. West of this Old Fortress spreads out the largest and most striking square in Greece, the renowned **Spianada** flanked by wonderful old buildings. On the north side of Spianada is the Palace of the English Lord High Commissioner which today houses the **Museum of Asian Art**. On the west side of Spianada is the well-known **Liston**, a building constructed during the period of French occupation with an arched colonnade with cafes and restaurants. The Liston is the best known meeting place for locals and foreigners alike. **Ayios Spyridonas** street begins behind its north end; this is where the church of the patron saint of the island is (16th century) and where his relic is kept. Evgeniou Voulgareos St., which begins at the south end of the Liston, leads in a while to **City Hall**, a beautiful Venetian building (17th century) and the church of St. Jacob, the Catholic Cathedral (17th century).

Near Ayios Spyridonas is Panayia Spiliotissa, the Greek Orthodox Cathedral (16th century). Proceeding from here further north you reach the old harbour from where the ferry boats depart for Igoumenitsa. The ships to Italy and the former

Above: Narrow lane ("Kantouni") on Corfu.
Below: "May - Day on Corfu" (Ionian School of painting, 19th cent.)

Yugoslavia anchor in the new harbour which is further west. Between the two harbours is the commanding New Fortress high on a hill, also built by the Venetians (16th century). The old town is tightly squeezed into the area between Spianada and the **New Fortress**. That is why the houses were, of necessity, multi-storeyed with very narrow streets between them, so narrow that often the clothesline from one house is tied to the one opposite. This pretty picture, which recalls the old towns of the western Mediterranean, you will also see in the "Kantounia" - what the Corfiots call the narrow lanes - which run at right angles to Glyfada St. and lead to Spianada.

The **Archaeological Museum** which contains finds from the whole island is on the south side of Spianada near the shore at the Bay of Garitsa. Even further south is the Monument of Menecrates (6th century B.C.) and near the end of the bay the church of St. Jason and St. Sossipatros (11th century).

Heading even further south you cross a small, verdant peninsula, **Analipsis**, which is one of the most noteworthy places in Corfu, both from an archaeological point of view (ancient Corfu was built here) and a touristic point of view. The most important archaeological finds here were the ruins of the Temple of Artemis (6th century B.C.) and the Temple of Hera, the largest on the island (4th century B.C.). On this peninsula is also located the Mon Repos mansion, once the summer residence of the Greek royal family. On the south end of the hill, despite the fact that the visitor has already been prepared by everything he has heard or read, he is still bound to be impressed. This is the site **Kanoni** which has a marvelous view of the little island of **Vlacherna** where the Monastery of the Panayia is and the renowned **Pontikonisi**, with the Monastery of the Pantokrator (see p. 216-217).

Above: Ayios Spyridonas St.

Below: Carriage in Spianada square.

EXCURSIONS

1. Corfu - Ypsos - Nisaki - Kassiopi (38 km.)

6 km. Kontokali. A tourist area which extends along the shore, on the right side of the road.

8 km. Gouvia. An area with great tourist development on the en-closed bay of the same name, on the right side of the road.

9 km. Junction.

13 km. Dasia. A very pretty area where the installations for the Club Mediterranée are (inter-national camping).

14 km. Ypsos. One of the largest summer resort areas on the island with a sand beach 2 km. long. The beautiful landscape is comple-mented by the mass of **Pantokra-tor** the highest mountain on Corfu which towers above the north end of the coast.

16 km. Pyrgi. A settlement on the north end of the Bay of Ypsos. From here a road goes west passing through the village of **Ayios Markos** while another goes up through many switchbacks to Pantokrator for the villages of **Spartylas** (with a marvelous view of Ypsos), **Strinylas**, the summit of **Pantokrator, Episkepsi** and **Acharavi**.

19 km. Barbati. A beautiful bay with a sand beach.

22 km. Nisaki. Verdant area and a strand with crystal-clear water.

29 km. Kalami and **Kouloura**. A small turn-off right takes you down to the picturesque bay of Kalami in which a small settlement has been created. Further north is the small harbour of Kouloura and a circular breakwater that protects a few caiques. Kouloura, as seen from the road high up, is one of the loveliest landscapes on Corfu. From here it is only 2 miles to the shores of Albania opposite.

32 km. Junction. From here a turn-off right leads after 2 km. to the coast of **Ayios Stephanos**.

36 km. Kassiopi. A lovely, little town with a harbour for small craft on the northwest edge of Corfu. It is a major tourist development because of its sparkling sea and the successive picturesque coves with rocks and sand.

Palaiokastrista

2. Corfu - Palaiokastritsa (24 km.)

21 km. The road right goes up to the village of Lakones with a panoramic view toward Palaiokastritsa and then continues on to historic **Angelokastro**.

24 km. Palaiokastritsa. This is the famed coast of Corfu with its wild beauty. The entire region is full of picturesque coves with dazzling sand, emerald water and marine caves. These caves are sur-rounded by rocky hills and lush vegetation. The crowning point is the Byzantine **Monastery of Theo-tokou** on the peak of a hill.

From the monastery you can admire the superb landscape which has not been spoiled even by the host of hotels, houses and restaurants.

The Achilleio and the statue of Achilles.

3. Achilleio - Ai Gordis - Pelekas - Glyfada (29 km.)

Your road passes just outside the airport.

8 km. The road left leads to the village of **Gastouri** where the renowned **Achilleio** is (see p. 208).

The ground floor of the palace is today a museum, while a casino operates on the first floor.

At the crossroads at the 8th kilometer you turn right and continuing ahead leave on your left the turn for Ayioi Deka and right the turn to Kynopiastes, and proceed toward Sinarades.

16 km. Ai Gordis. A pretty and spacious sand beach before the deep green and sheer slopes of a mountain. A distinctive part of this landscape is the large, conical rock in the sea at the end of the bay.

20 km. You return to Sinarades, go through it and head to Pelekas.

25 km. Pelekas. A village famed for its gorgeous sunsets. The peak of the hill is a wonderful observation post from where you can see practically all of Corfu.

29 km. Glyfada. One of the loveliest shores on Corfu. Six km. north-west of Glyfada is **Ermones** a traditional settlement in an enclosed harbour with wild natural beauties.

4. Corfu - Benitses - Kavas (48 km.)

You follow the road to the Achilleio and at 5 km. turn left.

8 km. Perama. At this point there is a narrow road in the sea which is around 300 m. long and which you can only cross on foot or on a bicycle; it joins this area to the celebrated **Kanoni** by bridge. You move along the coast toward Benitses and find yourself exactly opposite the fabulous **Pontikonisi**.

12 km. Benitses. The most highly developed tourist area on the island, which extends a long way down the coast.

20 km. Moraïtika. A coastal tourist center.

21 km. The road you leave on your left leads after 2 km. to **Mesongi**, another seaside tourist resort.

31 km. A junction before the village of Argyrades with a road right that leads to **Ayios Georgios**. The beautiful sand beach there is 3 km. long.

42 km. Lefkimmi. The largest market town in the south. In its center you will be startled by a bridge and a canal with boats (which is about a kilometer long).

48 km. Kavos. The end of the excursion and the southermost settlement on Corfu with a seemingly endless sand beach and a clean, shallow sea.

5. Corfu - Sidari (36 km.)

You follow the road to Palaiokastritsa and at the 13th km. turn right to Skripero and Sidari.

23 km. Branch. The right part of the road leads after 14 km. to Roda, a coastal settlement with a fine sand beach.

24 km. Arkadades. In this village a road left leads after 10 km. to the Bay of **Ayios Georgios ton Pagon** one of the best sand beaches of Corfu.

25 km. Agros. A village from which a road left leads after 11 km. to the sand beach of **Arilla**.

Above: Much-frequented Benitses.
Middle: Leukimi canal.
Below: Sand beach at Roda.

36 km. Sidari. This renowned shore has a strange kind of beauty. The rocks and the brownish grooves which slide into the sea form small fjord-like formations with shallow blue water and a sandy bottom. One of these fjords is the celebrated **Canal d'Amour**. A large tourist center has been created there because of this natural beauty.

One can visit the **Diapontian Islands** from Sidari.

"Canal d'Amour" at Sidari.

Diapontian Islands

A short distance (3-7 nautical miles) from Sidari, Corfu, are some verdant, small islands with beautiful sandy beaches and crystalline water, **Ereikousa**, **Mathraki** and **Othoni**, better known as the Diapontian Islands. Their total area does not exceed 18 sq. km. and the permanent inhabitants of each of them is around 200.

The only thing clear about their history is that generally speaking they shared the fortunes of neighbouring Corfu, to which they al ways belonged and on which the are completely dependent. B isolated the way they are it is equally certain they experienced the merciless attacks of pirates, without being able to fight back.

Many believe that Othoni, the largest of the islands, is the island of Calypso, the Ogygia of Homer. There Odysseus was shipwrecked and sought refuge. A cave about 20 minutes by boat from the harbour is said to be the mythical cave of the beautiful nymph who kept the shipwrecked sailor on the island for 7 years.

Today 70% of the population it had before the war has gone to America, 10% to Corfu and only 20% spends the winter there. And we say the winter because these by now American-Greeks have not forgotten their islands.

They see no reason to abandon their paradise and in spring they begin to slowly return like swallows.

A small boat connects these islands to the harbour of Corfu twice a week while similar schedules (both regular and special) are run by caïque from Sidari.

On the following page the ravishing Pontikonisi at Vlacherna.

Paxoi

This lush little island, 7 miles south of Corfu, will capture you from the very first glance. Its lofty olive trees which cover practically the whole island, the idyllic coves, the picturesque little harbours, the huge rocks and the marine caves are bound to impress you. And all that on a surface of less than 25 sq. km.

Paxi, the smallest of the Ionian Islands, is 32 nautical miles from the harbour of Corfu and 12 nautical miles from Parga, Epirus, which is opposite. Its eastern shores are peaceful, full of pretty little coves. Its land rises smoothly to reach the rocky and sheer western coast. Its ridge line is gentle, the highest peak being Ayios Isavros at only 250 m. The inhabitants of Paxi, which number around 2,500, are employed at the cultivation of the olive, fishing and tourism. Olive oil, which is of the finest quality in Greece, is the main product and together with tourist revenue make up the main sources of income.

You can go to Paxi by ferry boat from the harbour of Corfu, Mourtos (Syvota) in Epirus and from Patras.

You can also go by bus from Athens via Mourtos and by caïque (only in summer) from Kavos, Corfu and Parga, Epirus. During the summer the island is also connected to Cephalonia, Ithaca and Italy.

Gaios with the verdant islet of Ayios Nikolaos at the entrance to the harbour.

HISTORY

The history is, in general terms, the same as that of Corfu. The Venetian occupation which lasted for over 400 years (14th-18th century) was decisive for the fate of Paxi. It was then that the famous castle was built on the islet of Ayios Nikolaos before the harbour of Gaios (15th century) and the planting of olive trees was expanded until they covered practically the entire surface of the island causing its appearance and life to gradually change. In 1537 the historic naval battle of Paxi took place just off Paxi, between the Christian fleet under Andrea Doria and the Turkish fleet which was defeated; their twelve galleys were captured and towed to Messini.

The Paxians revolted in 1810 against the French and requested the assistance of the British. The revolt failed which led to 7 Paxians being executed and many imprisoned. But finally the British occupied Paxi in 1814 and held it until 1864 when along with the other Ionian Islands it was united with Greece.

Getting to know the island

The harbour of Gaios, which is at the same time the capital of the island, is an impressive one. There are two small, luxuriant islets in front of it, protecting it: **Panayia** with a monastery of the same name and **Ai-Nikolas** which forms a picturesque channel with the mainland opposite, through which the small boats pass to get to the pier to tie up. On Ai-Nikolas is a **Venetian castle** and a windmill. Gaios took its name from a disciple of the Apostle Paul who taught Christianity on Paxi, died and was buried there.

The houses of Paxi, which have retained their traditional Ionian Island architecture, the narrow lanes and the small shops, the bars and the cozy cafes, create a pleasant atmosphere. Near the harbour you will find the Historical Archives, the library and the church of Ayioi Apostoloi with wall paintings. Two small beaches lie southeast of the harbour.

Imposing cliffs on the west coast.

From Gaios a road traverses the island from south to north, passing through the endless olive groves. There are said to be 300,000 olive trees on the island.

To your right, at a distance of 5.5 km. from Gaios, to the rear of a small bay, is the charming little village of **Longos**, nestled in greenery.

At the end of the road you reach **Lakkas**, another picturesque village at the rear of the enclosed bay. Near Lakkas is the beautiful sand beach of **Charamis** and the Byzantine church of Ypapandi.

The visit to the steep western side with its wonderfully coloured sea and the marine caves is done by caïque (as well as the tour of the island). Starting from Gaios and heading southeast you will come to the shores of Ozia, near the islets of **Mongonisi** and **Kaltsionisi**.

From there, going north-west, you will see in turn: **Trypito**, a natural stone bridge, the rocks of **Mousmoulis**, the cave of **Ortholithos**, which has an enormous monolith in front of its entrance, **Erimitis**, the cave of **Kastanidas** at the base of a vertical rock 180 m. high and finally the cave of **Ypapandi** a refuge for seals, 2 nautical miles from Lakkas.

Antipaxoi

It would be a shame if while you were on Paxi you did not visit this small island which is only three miles from Gaios. This is because this small piece of land of 5 sq. km. and 120 inhabitants has the most beautiful sand beaches, the brightest blue sea and of course, the cleanest water.

You will come to **Agrapidia**, you will swim at **Voutoumi** and **Vrika**, you will climb through the vineyards and see the view from on high and in the afternoon you will depart with an ache in your heart for the sudden interruption of so much pleasure. During the summer there are daily caïques from Paxi and Corfu.

Lefkada

at farming, animal husbandry, and tourism. A mountainous island, the highest peak being Mt. Stavrota (1,158 m.), it has dense and varied vegetation, with running water in the mountainous parts and fertile plains on the south and west sides. The island's main products are olive oil and wine.

It also produces very tasty sausage and other preserved meats while the lentils from Eglouvi are thought to be the best in Greece. As for the works of folk art, the traditional Lefkadian weavings, embroideries and lace hold a special place.

Lefkada is the homeland of two of the most important modern Greek poets, Angelos Sikelianos and Aristotelis Valaoritis.

Lefkada is a prefecture which also contains the small neighboring islands of Meganisi, Madouri, Skorpios, Sparti, Kastro and others. The hotel dynamic, the road network, the interurban communications in the interior of the island are at a level capable of insuring a confortable stay for the visitor who has come to enjoy the incredible sand beaches and the crystalline water, or even the charming mountain villages in a few of which the women continue to wear their traditional costumes.

You can reach Lefkada by plane from Athens via Aktios which is 25 km. from the island or by bus which leaves from 100 Kifissou St in Athens. From Nydri on Lefkada there is a local connection with Frikes on Ithaca and Fiskardo on Cephalonia and from Vasiliki with Vathy on Ithaca, Fiskardo and Sami in Cephalonia.

White rocks sit vertically along practically the whole western coast of the island which is why it is called Lefkada ("The White One"). According to tradition, it was from here that Sappho, the greatest poetess of antiquity, hurled herself to her death because of her unfortunate love for Phaon.

Unlike the western, the eastern coast is lush, calm and full of picturesque little bays. One of these, Syvota, which is very like a description by Homer in *The Odyssey* made the German archeologist Dörpfeld insist that the Homeric Ithaca was really Lefkada. Opposite on the eastern coast are the gorgeous islets of Lefkada among which Skorpios holds a special place.

Lefkada was joined to the coast of western Greece opposite and was a peninsula until the 7th century B.C., when Corinthian colonists dig a channel and separated it from the mainland. Today, it communicates with it by a bridge.

Lefkada lies north of Ithaca and Cephalonia from which it is 31 nautical miles and 45 nautical miles respectively. It has an area of 803 sq. km. and a coastline of 117 km. with a population of 20,000, who are mainly employed

Cape Lefkata at "Leucadian Leap".

HISTORY

Lefkada has been inhabited since the Neolithic period as has been shown by archaeological finds on the island. There have also been finds from the Mycenean period. In 640 B.C. the Cortinthians colonized Lefkada, about 100 years after the colonization of Corfu.

In the 4th century B.C. Lefkada was occupied by the Macedonians which was followed by the conquest of King Pyrrhus of Epirus and the Romans. The long and turbulent Byzantine period came to an end in the 13th century when the island passed into the hands of the Franks who built the famous fortress of Ayia Mavra, within the walls of which was founded the monastery of the same name. From the monastery the island itself took the name Ayia Mavra for several centuries.

Lefkada, just a hair's breadth from the shores of western Greece opposite, was bound to succumb to the attacks of the Turks and to suffer their long-term occupation, something which did not happen to the rest of the Ionian Islands.

The Turkish occupation began in 1479 and ended in 1684 when Lefkada was seized by the Venetians. In 1797 the island was occupied by the French and then the Russians while a new attempt by the Turks, under Ali Pasha, to re-take the island, was thwarted by John Kapodistrias who worked in cooperation with Greek rebels from the mainland who had already risen up against the Turks.

The English Protectorate, as it was called in the beginning but which in its turn developed into an occupation, began on the island in 1815. A half century later, in 1864 Lefkada became a part of Greece, along with the other Ionian Islands.

Getting to know the island

The Town of Lefkada

The capital of both the island and the like-named prefecture, it lies on the NE end of Lefkada about a kilometer from the bridge which connects it to the coast of Aitoloakarnania. Near the bridge are the ruins of the **Castle of Ayia Mavra** which was built by the Orsinis and later repaired by the Venetians and the Turks.

The town was rebuilt after the earthquake in 1953. Fortunately, quite a few of the noteworthy churches stood up to the tremors. Thus, one is given the opportunity of visiting Ayios Minas, Ayios Dimitrios, Ayios Spyridonas (17th-18th century), Ayios Ioannis Antzousis, built by d'Anjou in the 14th century and the Pantokrator in the adjacent cemetery where the tomb of the poet Aristotelis Valaoritis is located. The baroque style dominates the architecture of these churches while there are wall paintings in their interiors, mainly by Nikolaos Doxaras, which are representative of the Ionian School of painting.

The small **Archaeological Museum** is worth a visit as are the Gallery of Post-Byzantine Art, the Public Library, the Folklore Museum and the prototypical **Phonograph Museum**.

On a neighbouring hill with a fabulous view of the town and the sea is the **Faneromeni Monastery** which was founded in the 17th century, destroyed by fire and rebuilt in the 19th century at another site. Below the monastery is the well-known white sand beach of Lefkada, **Yyra**, which stretches along for several kilometers.

Calm, shallow sea near the harbour of Lefkas.

EXCURSIONS

1. Nydri - Vasiliki (38 km.)

You will follow the road to Nydri.

2 km. Kalligoni. Ancient Lefkada is located near this settlement. There are sections of a Cyclopian wall and ruins of a small theater there.

6 km. Lygia. A coastal settlement with trees and a sandy beach.

9 km. Nikiana. Village with a small but pretty sand beach.

17 km. Nydri. The largest tourist center on Lefkada with a lot of greenery. Opposite are the luxuriant islets of **Madouri** (the island of Valaoritis) and **Sparti**, **Chelonaki** and **Skorpios** (the property of the Onassis family) and next to it the capivating peninsula of **Ayia Kyriaki** with the home of Dörpfeld at its peak.

Two km. from Nydri, toward the interior, is a **waterfall** after the village of Rachi.

20 km. Vlycho. A coastal village to the rear of a like-named enclosed bay. Opposite Vlycho is the picturesque **Geni**.

25 km. Junction with the road that leads after 2 km. to the village of **Poros** and then, after 4 more km., to the beautiful shores of **Mikros Yialos**.

30 km. Junction with the road that leads after 3 km. to **Syvota** which is to the rear of a fjord-like formation with crystalline water.

38 km. Vasiliki. It competes for tourists with Nydri. It is in the south section of the island to the rear of a large, leeward gulf next to a huge strand with pebbles and sand. This gulf is ideal for wind-surfing.

From here you can visit by caïque the gorgeous shores of **Ayiofyli** and **Pidima Sapfous** near the headland of **Lefkata** from which during antiquity was the sight of the well-known "Leu-cadian leap". This is an enormous vertical cliff against which break the usually raging waves of the Ionian Sea. According to legend, those condemned to death were hurled from this rock. If they survived the terrible fall, they were pardoned. Those who wanted to be delivered of an unrequited love also leapt from here.

2. Ayios Nikitas - Kalamitsi - (Porto Katsiki) - Ayios Petros - Vasiliki (43 km.)

You follow the road toward Ayios Nikitas. After you pass through the village of **Tsouka-lades** (6 km.) a new road de-scends toward a boundless, sandy beach.

12 km. Ayios Nikitas. Up to a few years ago it was a quaint fishing village. Recently it has developed into one of the largest tourist centers on Lefkada.

14 km. A turn-off right leads after 2 km. to the large, sandy beach of **Kathisma**, one of the best on Lefkada. There are tavernas and ample parking there and also many interesting rocks on the north end of the sand beach.

21 km. Kalamitsi. A village at an altitude of 380 m., with olive trees all around. From here a road goes down to lovely, pristine sand beaches.

30 km. A junction which you reach after passing through the village of **Chortata**. From there a paved road right leads after 6 km. to the village of **Athani**. From Athani a road goes after 13 km. to **Porto Katsiki**, one of the most breathtaking landscapes in Greece with a sheer cliff, a wonderful sand beach and a sparkling clear, blue sea. You can go practically every day to Porto Katsiki on a small boat from Nydri or Vasiliki.

36 km. Ayios Petros. Farming settlement on a very beautiful site which faces Vasiliki.

43 km. Vasiliki.

Nydri. Verdant isle of Madouri and Valaoritis' house.

3. Lefkada - Karya - Eglouvi (20 km.)

You follow the road toward Nydri and at 1.5 km. go right to **Lazarata** (10,5 km.) and Karya.

14.5 km. Karya. The main village of this mountainous area and a beautiful one with abundant water and dense greenery which has kept its culture. The famous embroideries of Lefkada are made here.

20 km. Eglouvi. A small mountain village at an altitude of 730 m., which is renowned for the quality of its lentils. It lies beneath the peaks of the highest mountain on Lefkada, Mt. **Stavrota**.

Papanikolis cave on Meganisi.

SMALL ISLANDS NEAR LEFKADA

Meganisi. It is the largest of all the surrounding islands with an area of 20 sq. km. and a population of around 1,300.

It is 12 nautical miles from the harbour of Lefkada and has three settlements, **Vathy, Katomeri** and **Spartochori**. Among the sites on the island is a large marine cave, Papanikolis, the refuge for the submarine "Papanikolis" during the war of 1940-1941.

The little island of **Kalamos**, is east of Meganisi and opposite Cape Mytikas in Aitoloakarnania. It is 20 sq. km. in area and its main settlements are **Kalamos**, the harbour and capital of the island, **Kefali** in the south and **Episkopi** to the north. It has wonderful caves and clean water and mountains, the highest peak at 785 m.

The oblong little island of **Kastos**, which is inhabited, is much smaller than Kalamos and lies a bit further south.

South of Lefkada are the uninhabited rocky islets of **Arkoudi** and **Atokos** while even further south are many other uninhabited islets, the largest of which are **Drakonera, Provati, Petalas, Makri** and **Oxeia**.

East of Lefkada, opposite Athani is the small island of **Sesoula**.

The magnificent seaside at Porto Katsiki.

Ithaca

Ithaca is known throughout the world as the island of Odysseus, the hero of Homer's *The Odyssey*, who after fighting for ten whole years at Troy needed another ten to return to his kingdom and his wife Penelope who was waiting patiently. Thus, Ithaca became a symbol of adventure and at the same time longing for the homeland. And even the symbol of perserverance and conjugal fidelity.

Ithaca is a small island in the Ionian Sea with an area of 96 sq. km. and a coastline of 101 km. It lies northeast of Cephalonia from which it is separated by a strait 3-5 km. wide. It is a mountainous island, quite green, with lovely deep bays. One of them, the Bay of Molos, in the approximate middle of the island, goes even deeper and at this point the dry land forms a neck only 0.5 km. wide, which divides the island in two.

The south section is dominated by Mt. Merovoulos, 552 m. high with both rocks and greenery while to the north Mt. Neritos, 806 m., is covered with arbutus trees and the Monastery of Katharon is

ⲔⲨⲬⲎⲚ
ⲞⲆⲨⳞⳞⲈⲓ

also there. The 3,600 inhabitants are employed primarily at farming, animal husbandry and fishing. Its main products are olive oil and wine.

You can go to Ithaca by bus or with your own car via Patras or Astakos. From Patras and Astakos there is also a connection by ferry boat. Local boats connect Ithaca to Cephalonia, Lefkada, Paxi and Corfu.

HISTORY

Ithaca has been inhabited since the end of the 3rd millenium B.C. The interest of its archeology is focused on the time when the island was ruled, according to Homer, by the wily Odysseus, that is, the 12th century B.C. That was when the Greeks set out to conquer Troy.

This war lasted for 10 whole years and because of the Trojan Horse, that Odysseus dreamed up, Troy fell. But it took another ten years of wandering the seas for Odysseus to get back to his island. Daring the 9th century B.C. the island experienced a period of prosperity when Corinth used it as a commercial station.

In the Archaic, the Classical and the Hellenistic period there was a good deal of activity there. Two acropolises were built (at Aetos and Stavros) pottery was developed and communication with the rest of Greece and the East was continued.

In 1499 A.D. the Venetian period began but immediately afterward the island was destroyed by pirates and deserted. The pirates used it for approximately a century as a base for their assaults

until it was colonized by the neighbouring Cephalonians. But Ithaca has poor soil so many of the inhabitants turned to the sea. The island acquired a naval tradition. In 1797 it was occupied by the French under Napoleon and a few years later by the English. Ithaca along with the rest of the Ionian Islands was finally united with Greece in 1864.

Getting to know the island

Vathy, built to the rear of an enclosed bay that seems like a lake, is the main harbour and the capital of the island.

Its houses which were rebuilt in line with the old, traditional architecture, after the earthquake of 1953, the calm waters of the bay, the surrounding mountains and even the small, lush island of **Lazaretto** in the middle of the harbour, make up a picture of exceptional charm.

In Vathy one can visit the small archaeological museum, the Cathedral Church and the theatrical library.

Perachori, 2 km. S of Vathy, an area full of olive trees and oaks with a lovely view of the harbour. Southwest of the village is the **Monastery of the Taxiarchon** from the 17th century.

The ancient spring **Aretousa** is 5 km. southeast of Vathy.

Near Vathy is the **Cave of the Nymphs** or **Marmarospilia** in which it is said that Odysseus hid the gifts of the Phaeacians upon his return from Troy.

4 km. west of Vathy a branch west leads after 3 km. to **Piso Aetos** a small harbour from which special trips are made to Ayia Efimia on Cephalonia. Above the

Small harbour at Frikes.

road is a commanding hill and the ruins of an acropolis of the ancient town of Alkomenes from the 6th century B.C. which the locals have dubbed "Odysseus' Castle" and which Schliemann thought was the town of Odysseus.

From the junction of Piso Aetos, the the main road heads north along a neck of land to meet the beach on the right, at the **Monastery of Katharon**. This monastery was built at the end of the 17th century. It is at a height of 500 m. on Mt. Neritas which is covered with arbutus trees, with an exceptional view. The road from the monastery heads toward the village of **Anogi** and descends on switchbacks to **Stavros**.

The village of Stavros (17.5 km. from Vathy) and the surrounding area is of the most archaeological interest on the island. A little further north, on the **hill of Pilikata**, finds have proven a human presence on the island by the end

of the 3rd millenium B.C. as well as the existence of a settlement in the middle of the 2nd millenium. Here, in all probability, is where the town of Odysseus was. There is a small archaeological museum in Pilikata.

South-west of Stavros is a bay with the ancient name of **Polis** which has a beautiful sand beach. In the cave **Loizos**, which is on its north side, many clay vessels were found, mainly Mycenean.

The most isolated village on Ithaca, **Exogi**, is 5 km. NW of Stavros on a hill with a splendid view.

Frikes, 21 km. from Vathy, is a small harbour which has ferry boat connections with Fiskardo on Cephalonia and Nydri on Lefkada.

The loveliest shore of Ithaca is next to the road that goes from Frikes to **Kioni** (5 km.), a very picturesque settlement to the rear of a small bay sunk in greenery.

Closed bay of Vathy.

Cephalonia - Ithaca

You can make it out from miles away as you come on the boat from Patras. It is, you see, the largest island in the Ionian Sea with the highest mountain, Mt. Ainos (1,628 m.) and its unique fir trees. It seems to be joined to the smaller Ithaca as if they were one island. The strait which separates the two islands is only 4 km. wide.

This island has many contradictions. Contradictions which have helped forge its special history.

Cephalonia has 27,000 inhabitants today, most of whom are fishermen.

Cephalonia is a wealthy and fertile island, famed for its wine, called **robola**, the production of which cannot keep up with the demand, as well as its honey and a soft **myzithra** cheese. **Mantoles**, a sweet made with almonds is a speciality found in its pastry shops and its cuisine is enlived by meat pies and a garlic sauce which the locals call **aliada**.

It has a rich cultural heritage which is mainly tied to literature and music where western in-fluence, particularly the Italian, is obvious.

The poet Andreas Laskaratos, who lived in the 19th century, was born in Lixouri. The attention that Cephalonias pay to music and choral music in particular, accompanied by a mandolin, is a tradition.

It is said that Cephalonia is the island of paradoxes. The reason for this are the strange geological phenomena observed which are due to major geological disturbances which have occurred from time to time. Near Argostoli, thousands of tons of sea water ceaselessly pour into Katavothres ("Pits") in the earth and disappear. It was discovered, after long years of research, that the water traverses the island underground, coming out at Lakes Melissani and Karavomylos, in the area of Sami. The lake, Avythos or Akolis is so deep that local tradition makes it bottomless. Finally, Kounopetra, southwest of Lixouri, is a rock which made a small, rythmic, non-stop motion. But these quivers came to an end after the earhquake of 1953.

In the middle of the Ionian Sea, Cephalonia lies 53 nautical miles from Patras to which it is connected by ferry boat, both from Argostoli and Sami. The island has an area of 781 sq. km. and a coastline of 254 km. The nearest of the Ionian Islands to the north (except of course for Ithaca) is Lefkada (which has connections with Fiskardo). South of Cephalonia is Zakynthos. There are connections with Zakynthos only in summer. It is also connected to Kyllini in the Peloponnese from Poros and with the coast of Aitoloakarnania opposite (from Ayia Efimia to Astakos). Besides the ferry boats the island also is connected by plane to Athens and in the summer to Zakynthos and Corfu.

HISTORY

A wealth of archaeological finds from Cephalonia have given us valuable information on its history. From a few stone tools found there we known that a human presence on the island can be dated to the Paleolithic period. There are also finds from the Neolithic (6000 - 2600 B.C.); a gap appears in the early Bronze Age after which there is a host of finds again from the Mycenean period such as those from the Mycenean cemeteries at Mazarakata, Metaxata and above all, at Lakkithra.

From these finds its is concluded that during the Mycenean period Cephalonia was flourishing and that the island had connections with neighbouring Ithaca, Lefkada and even the far-off Cyclades. This communication was abruptly terminated in 1500 B.C. probably because of the great destruction caused by the eruption of the volcano on Santorini; it was restored two centuries later when the island began to flourish again.

Melisani. One of the oddities of Cephalonian nature.

From the 11th century B.C. when the Dorians made their appearance until the end of the 7th century B.C., there are few facts. In the 6th century B.C. with the arrival of the Corinthians and the Euboeans in the Ionian area and the colonization of Corfu and Lefkada, intense activity can be observed on Cephalonia. The island was clearly being used as a center for transit trade with Italy and Sicily.

The 5th century B.C. was characterized mainly by the development of four important towns on the island: Krane, near Argostoli, Pali near Lixouri, Pronoi and Sami. The historian Thucydides mentions them all together as Tetrapolis ("Town of Four"). These towns were autonomous, with their own currency, united in the case of a common enemy such as the Persians, but divided during the Peloponnesian War.

Tradition is referring to that period when it speaks to us of the hero Kefalos who came from Attica, fought on the island and gave it his name (in Greek the island is called "Kefalonia").

In 187 B.C. Cephalonia was occupied by the Romans and became subject to Byzantium nearly six centuries later (395 A.D.). In 1082 the Norman baron Guiscard tried, without success, to seize the island and finally died of a fever at Panorma which then took the name of the Norman (the present-day Fiskardo). The endeavors of the Normans were taken up by Venetian pirates until the island finally fell into the possession of the Orsinis in 1185. In 1483 it was destroyed by the Turks and in 1500 recaptured by the Venetians who held on to it until 1797 when it was occupied by the French under Napoleon.

During the Venetian occupation a dramatic role was played by the Castle of St. George 8 km. east of Argostoli which together with the town that contained it, was the capital of the island at that time.

This castle was abandoned in the 18th century after a major earthquake and the capital was slowly transferred to Argostoli. The French occupation was succeeded by a brief Russian and Turkish one until the British prevailed in 1809.

During the Greek War of Independence against the Turks (1823) the Philhellene Lord Byron lived on Cephalonia where he wrote **Don Juan**.

Then he went to Messolongi, which was beseiged by the Turks, and fought on the Greek side, iosing his life there. The British rule of Cephalonia came to an end in 1864 and the island, was united with Greece.

Argostoli

The capital of the island, a new town with 7,500 inhabitants which was rebuilt after the earthquake of 1953 on the site of the old one. It is the capital of the like-named prefecture, to which Ithaca is also subject. Its natural harbour is a safe anchorage in winter.

Argostoli is on the southwest coast of Cephalonia on the side of a bay and next to a salt lake. The English, when they ruled the island, built a bridge with many arches over this shallow sea which shortened the distance to the opposite shore a great deal.

The main sights of Argostoli are the **Archaeological Museum** in which are housed the exciting finds from the excavations on the island, and the Koryialenios Library, in which are housed the Historical Archives, the Folk Museum and a collection of Byzantine icons. The famous **Katavothres** which we spoke of in the introduction, are 2.5 km.

Central square of Argostoli

Platys Yialos.

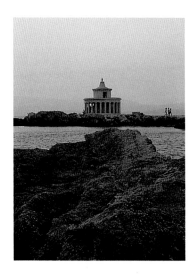

from Argostoli in the area of Lasis. The cave where the patron saint of the island, Ayios Gerasimos lived his ascetic life, is 3 km. south of there.

The ruins of ancient Krane are at the salt lake of Koutavos, 3 km. to the east. The famous beaches of **Makry Yialos** and **Platy Yialos** are 4 km. south.

1. Argostoli - Ainos - Sami - Melissani - Ayia Efimia (35 km.)

You go over the bridge at Argostoli and then head toward Sami.

7 km. Junction. From here a turn-off right leads after 4 km. to the Convent of Ayios Gerasimos, dedicated to the patron saint of the island, where his relic is kept.

12 km. Another junction. The road right (which you do not take) goes up to **Mt. Ainos** and after 15 km. reaches a television substation. The mountain is covered with fir trees of a unique variety that only grow on Cephalonia. The view all around is thrilling. The highest peak, **Megalos Soros**, 1,628 m., is about a half an hour from here.

22 km. A small turn-off leads to the **Drogoratis cave** with stalactite decoration and corridors 300 m. long.

25 km. Sami. The second most important harbour on the island, a new town with a pretty quay. Near it are the ruins of ancient Sami and its acropolis. Just before the entrance to the town the road left goes to Ayia Efimia after going through Karavomylos and Melissani.

28 km. Karavomylos. Idyllic lake surrounded by a great deal of greenery.

Water gushes up from its depths, said to come from the **Katavothres**.

29 km. Melissani. It is a cave-chasm with a lake, the existence of which was discovered when its roof collapsed and the rays of the sun lighted it, showing the beautiful colours of the water. It is visited by boat.

35 km. Ayia Efimia. A market town with a harbour which connects Cephalonia to Astakos on Aitoloakarnania. From here there are special schedules with caïques to Piso Aetos in Ithaca which is opposite. North of Ayia Efimia is the **Monastery of the Panayia Thematon**.

The small harbour of Ayia Efimia

.2. Argostoli - Skala - Poros

You follow the road toward Poros.

8 km. Castle of Ayios Georgios. It dominates the entire fertile plain of **Leivathos**. The medieval capital of the island was here.

14 km. Vlachata. From this village a turn-off right leads after 1 km. to **Lourdata** and then to the shores of a village with a superb sand beach. This region, which lies below the highest peak of the fir-covered **Ainos**, has tropical vegetation.

21 km. Junction with the road that goes, after 7 km., to the spacious sand beach at **Kasteleios** and 6 km. further to **Skala**, a tourist resort next to a sea with incredibly clear water.

25 km. Markopoulos. Each year, between August 6-15, there appear outside this village, the harmless "little snakes of the Virgin" which have a black cross on their head.

36 km. Junction left which goes to Sami, passing through the village of **Ayios Nikolaos** (6 km.). Lake **Avythos** or **Akolis** is located in this area.

40 km. Poros. A harbour with major tourist developments, due to its daily ferry boat connections with Kyllini in the Peloponnese. Near Poros is the old **Monastery of Atros**.

The picturesque Fiskardo.

3. Argostoli - Lixouri - Monastery of Kipouraion

Lixouri. The second largest town on Cephalonia on the Pali peninsula connected to Argostoli by ferry boat. Built in 1534 it was destroyed by the earthquake of 1953 and rebuilt. It is worth a visit to the old mansion of the Iakovates, which houses a library of the same name, the Petritseio Library and the Philharmonic School. Near Lixouria, at the site Palaiokastro, are the ruins of ancient Pali.

4 km. Mantzavinata. A turn-off from this village to the south-west leads after 4 km. to **Kounopetra**.

17 km. Monastery of Kipouraion Passing through the villages of **Chavriata, Chavdata** and by the **Monastery of Tafiou** you arrive at the **Monastery of Kipouraion** built in a luxuriant area in front of a sheer, pure white cliff, a real balcony on the Ionian Sea.

4. Argostoli - Myrtos - Fiskardo (58 km.)

After the bridge at Argostoli, you proceed left.

27 km. The dirt road left goes down to the famed shores of **Myrtos** with its pebbles.

29 km. Panoramic view from on high of the Bay of Myrtos with the wonderful colours of the sea. One of the most beautiful landscapes in Greece.

33 km. Left to Assos.

36 km. Assos. Perhaps the most picturesque village on Cephalonia, built on the neck of a peninsula, at the summit of which is a commanding Venetian castle.

39 km. Back at the junction. You turn left.

58 km. Fiskardo. A well-known fishing harbour, the only village that was untouched by the great earthquake of 1953. Thus the houses have retained their traditional architecture unaltered. The surrounding area is dense with pine and cypress trees. Opposite is Ithaca. During the summer there is heavy tourist activity here.

Myrtos. One of the most beautiful beaches in Greece.
On the following page, a view of Assos.

Zakynthos

The first inhabitants of Zakynthos are thought to have been Achaeans who came to the Peloponnese in the 16th century B.C.

During historical times the island belonged at first to Athens and then to Sparta and later passed on to the Macedonians. The Romans occupied it at the beginning of the 2nd century B.C. and gave it autonomy. This was followed by the long Byzantine period during which it suffered many attacks and much looting.

After the Fall of Constantinople, Zakynthos fell under the domination of the Orsinis until in 1485 it was seized by the Venetians and remained under them for over 300 years.

Since days of old, this island has exercised great charm on visitors. The Venetians called it Zante, the flower of the East. And they did not just mean a place with flowers, but all the flourishing things to be seen on the island, above all the flourishing of the arts and letters.

Two of the greatest Greek poets were born on Zakynthos, Dionysios Solomos and Andreas Kalvos. Painting reached great heights on the island during the 17th century with the creation of a school, the so-called Zakynthos School.

But the true love of the Zakynthians has always been music, above all song. The well-know **cantada** of Zakynthos was sung and continues to be sung on this island.

Zakynthos was famed in the past for its mansions, just as it was famed for its traditional architecture. Its beautiful churches and luxurious mansions were always the objects of admiration. But then the day of the earthquake arrived in 1953 and everything was demolished. Only a few buildings survived.

But the energetic and industrious inhabitants of the island did not give up. They worked hard and rebuilt Zakynthos. What was built may not resemble the old town but instead of decreasing, there are now more visitors than ever. They go to the island to admire the icons and the beautiful wall paintings, to visit the museums but above all to enjoy the marvelous sand beaches, the dream-like caves and the incredible colour of the sea.

Zakynthos is 8 nautical miles south of Cephalonia and 10 nautical miles east of Kyllini in the Peloponnese; it has an area of 402 sq. km and a coastline of 123 km. Its inhabitants, who are mainly employed at farming and tourism, number around 30,000.

The eastern section of the island is for the most part flat with many sandy shores while the western part is mountainous with rocky coasts which descend steeply to the sea, with exceptional views. The highest peak is Mt. Vrachionas (756 m.). The island is covered with olive trees, citrus trees and vineyards.

You can go to Zakynthos by plane from Athens, Corfu and Argostoli. You can also go by bus or train to Kyllini and then by ferry boat. Local boats connect Zakynthos to Cephalonia in summer.

The beautiful town of Zakynthos, the capital of the island.

The long occupation changed the life of the Zakynthos.

The Venetians imposed their own laws and divided the islanders into three categories: the nobles (**nobili**) who were registered in the **Libro d'Oro**, the citizens (**civili**) and the common people (**popolari**).

The terrible oppression of the common people by the nobles led to their revolt in 1630 which in the end was bathed in blood.

In 1797 the French Republicans drove out the Venetians, swept aside the nobles and gave the mayors the authority to rule under the supervision of the French Governor. It was then that the common people, celebrating their liberation from the Venetians, and their allies burned the famous **Libro d'oro** in the Square of St. Mark in Zakynthos.

The presence of the French on the island was a brief one. in 1798 the island came under Russo-Turkish domination until the Republic of the Ionian Islands was founded in 1800 which was the first independent Greek state. In 1807 Zakynthos was seized by the French aristocrats and in 1809 by the British, who placed the capital of the Ionian state at Zakynthos. During the British occupation of Zakynthos a great deal of assistance was afforded Greece, which had been in revolt since 1821, despite the opposition of the British.

Zakynthos became a part of Greece with the other Ionian Islands in 1864.

The Town of Zakynthos

Below a hill thick with pine trees, lies Zakynthos, the capital of the island and at the same time the only harbour. As you come by boat the first thing you will see from afar is the lofty bell tower of **Ayios Dionysios** on the left end of the town. Next to it is the large church built in 1948 which is one of the few buildings that survived the earthquake of 1953. The relic of the saint is housed in the church.

The dock where the boats tie up is further north, on the right end of the town. Near there is also the largest square, **Solomos Square**, with the statue of the great Greek poet in the center. To the rear of the square is the imposing building of the **Byzantine Museum** with its fabulous displays.

The entire right side of the square is occupied by the public library with more than 50,000 books. On the ground floor is located the Museum of the Occupation and the National Resistance and right on the sea **Ayios Nikolaos** at Molos, in which Ayios Dionysios was once the curate. It was built during the Venetian occupation and rebuilt after it was destroyed by the earthquake.

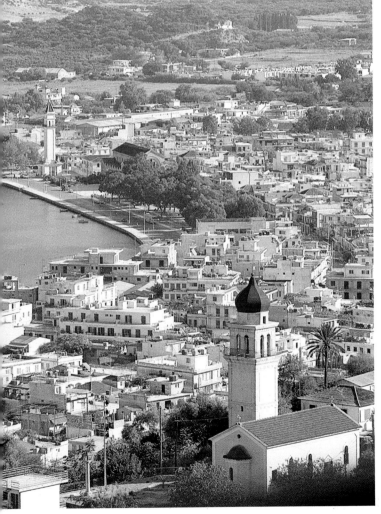

Other important churches in the town are **Kyria ton Angelon** and **Faneromeni**.

Near Solomos Square is the historic **Square of St. Mark** with the Catholic Cathedral, St. Mark, and next to it the Museum of Solomos and other Illustrious Zakynthians.

The **castle** of Zakynthos is at the top of the wooded hill which is above the town. This castle, which was built by the Venetians on the site of the ancient acropolis, can be reached by climbing up from St. Mark Square and passing next to the historic church of **Ayios Georgios ton Philikon** where the members of the **Philiki Etaireia** of Zakynthos took their oath together with the chlieftains of the Greek War of Independence of 1821, Kolokotronis and Nikitaras.

Just above Ayios Georgios is a crossroads. The road left leads to **Bochali** with a splendid view of the town and the sea and then to the castle, while the right leads to the historic **hill of Strani** on which Solomos upon hearing the cannons of the beseiged Mesolongi wrote the Hymn to Freedon which was later set to music by Mantzaros and became the national anthem of Greece.

Crowded beach at Laganas.

EXCURSIONS

1. Zakynthos - Argasi - Yerakas - Porto Roma (16 km.)

You will set off from the waterfront avenue and head toward Ayios Dionysios.

4 km. Argasi. One of the first areas of the island to be developed with an enormous sand beach and a very clear sea.

11 km. a turn-off left leads in a while to the small, pretty sand beach of **Porto Zoros** which has rocks on its right end.

14 km. A new turn-off left leads after 1 km. to the shores of Ayios Nikolaos with a fine sand beach and camping grounds.

15 km. Vasilikos. A village highly regarded for its flora and the beautiful nearby villages. From here a turn-off right leads after 1 km. to the splendid sand beach of Yerakas on the east end of the Bay of Laganas. Here, as in Laganas, is where the sea turtle carette-caretta takes refuge to hatch its eggs.

Southwest of Yerakas is the islet of Pelouzos.

16 km. Porto Roma. A picturesque bay with a sand beach, clean water and a small lake for boats and small craft. It is a true paradise for those who love to sail.

2. Zakynthos - Laganas - Keri (21 km.)

You follow the road to the airport and at the junction with it you keep going straight.

5 km. You turn left.

10 km. Laganas. The most important tourist center on the island with one of the finest sand beaches in Greece.

The sea turtle, **caretta-caretta**, continues to hatch its eggs on the rather congested sand beach of Laganas.

From Laganas you head toward **Lithakia** which is in the interior of the island (west) and just before you reach there you turn left to Keri.

The turtle caretta-caretta.

17 km. Lake Keri. Tar has been noted in this lake since days of old. This created the impression that there oil beneath the surface but drilling showed the little oil there was, was not exploitable.

Opposite Lake Keri is **Marathonisi**.

21 km. Keri. An isolated village built 200 m. above sea level, offering a superb view. The church of the **Panayia Keriotissa** has a magnificent iconostasis. Near the village is a lighthouse from where the view toward two enormous white rocks (**Megali** and **Mikri Myzithra**), which jut up from the sea like pyramids, is wonderful. You will also have wonderful impressions from a visit to and swim in the famous caves of Keri with their emerald waters which lie below the village. But this presumes an excursion by sea from Zakynthos or Laganas which will give you the opportunity to admire the **Kamares (Arches) of Marathia** (large and small) which the rocks have formed over the sea under which row-boats pass.

3. Zakynthos - Machairado - Ayios Leon - Anafonitria - Navagio (39 km.)

You take the road to the south-west.

10 km. Machairado. A large village with two magnificent churches from the 14th century. The one is **Ayia Mavra** which survived the earthquake and the other **Ypapandi** which has been rebuilt. The interior decoration of Ayia Mavra is perhaps the most impressive in Zakynthos. The bell tower is also noteworthy, particularly its bells said to be the most melodic in Greece.

Going southwest from Machairado you ascend the mountain.

17 km. Kiliomeno (Ayios Nikolaos). A village at an altitude of 480 m. with the church of Ayios Nikolaos and its tall bell tower. You go right toward Ayios Leon.

25 km. Ayios Leon. A mountain village with a church of the same name from the 14th century. From here, left from your main route are some high, sheer cliffs which form

fantastic coves with emerald waters. Unfortunately, only a few are accessible from land, such as **Stenitis** and **Porto Vromi**. From Ayios Leon, you go left.

28 km. Kambi. A small village in the environs of which Mycenean tombs were found. At its end are two fearsome cliffs, 400 m. high. The cliff of **Schizi** to the east and south the cliff of **Fokas** at the base of which are marine caves.

32 km. Maries. You reach it after **Exo Chora**. It is a mountain village which surveys the Ionian Sea from on high. Its church is dedicated to Mary Magdalene.

36 km. Anafonitria. A village that took its name from the Monastery of **Panayia Anafonitria** which lies a short distance away and where Ayios Dionysios was a monk. It is an important monastery on the island and attracts many pilgrims.

There is a half-ruined tower within its enclosure, besides the church which is a triple-aisled basilica from the 15th century with wall paintings. From this village a dirt road heading south leads after 7 km. to the picturesque enclosed bay of **Porto Vromi**.

38 km. Monastery of Ayios Georgios Krimnon. An old monastery that was rebuilt high up and at some distance from the sea.

Brilliant decoration in the interior of Ayia Mavra.

39 Navagio. To enjoy what is perhaps the most beautiful landscape on Zakynthos you should leave your car on the flat area and walk toward the cliff. You can go to Navagio by sea taking part in one of the excursions which are organized in Zakynthos or Laganas.

4. Zakynthos - Alykes - Galazia Spilia (47 km.)

You set off from St. Mark's Square and head toward Bochali.
1 km. The road right leads to the hill of Stranis and then to **Akrotiri** and left to Bochali and Kastro. You go straight ahead to Tsilivi.
4 km. Tsilivi (Planos). One of the most beautiful beaches on Zakynthos with a big sand beach.

You return to the main road to Alykes.
20 km. Junction. A turn-off 2 km. right takes you to another beautiful beach at **Alikanas**.
21 km. Alykes. The extensive sand beach and the shallow, clean water is the reason it has been developed.
22 km. Katastari. Main village in the area at the foot of the mountain nestled in greenery with a view of the Bay of **Alykes**.

Near the village is the Monastery of **Ayios Ioannis Prodromos** built at the beginning of the 17th century.
31 km. A road right leads after 1 km. to the village of Orthonies.
33 km. A road left leads after 2 km. to Anafonitria. You go right.
38 km. A large village consisting of two settlements, **Kato** and **Ano Volimes**, renowned for its weaving and embroidery. Among the sights of the villages is the church of **Ayia Paraskevi** from the 17th century with a superb carved wooden and gilt iconostasis.
47 km. Ayios Nikolaos. A small harbour with a calm sea and an islet opposite. There is a con-nec-

Above: Navagio.
Middle: Beach at Tsilivi.
Below: Alykes.

Right: Captivating caves at Keri.

tion to Cephalonia from here. There is also where small boats leave from to visit **Galazia Spilia** (Blue Cave).

The sea excursion takes about an hour. The boat goes to the northernmost tip of the island, **Cape Chinari**, below the lighthouse.

As you move along the rocky coast you can see small and large caves at the entrance to which the sea is extremely blue.

The crowning point is at the end of the route when the boat passes under three large, stone arches to at last reach this large cave. There the colours alternate from deep blue to light blue and from light green to emerald. The spectacle is even more beautiful when the cave is lighted by the rays of morning sunlight.

Strofades

From the deep waters of the Mediterranean protrude the Strofadia, two strange little islands, 25 miles south of Zakynthos and 28 miles west of Messenia.

The Strofadia are known primarily for the **Monastery of the Metamorfosis** which was founded on the largest of them by the empress of Byzantium, Irene, in 1241 and which along with its massive imposing tower is still standing despite the merciless attacks of enemies and the wear and tear of time. Once it had 100 monks. Ayios Dionysios also spent time there. Though he died in Zakynthos in the 17th century, he was buried there in accordance with his wishes. Later his relic was transferred to Zakynthos.

Kythera

One asks oneself why Greek mythology chose Kythera, an island unknown to many, as the birthplace for Aphrodite, the goddess of love. No matter what your answer is, one thing is clear: Kythera is not only addressed to those in love but also to all those who are seeking a quiet shore to relax on. Today's approximately 3,000 inhabitants live off of animal husbandry, the cultivation of vegetables and a few olive trees. But remittances from Australia are also an important source of income.

Isolated from the rest of the Ionian Islands, Kythera is only 10 nautical miles from the southeastern tip of the Peloponnese, Cape Maleas, and 105 nautical miles from Piraeus to which it belongs administratively. It has an area of 278 sq. km., and a coastline of 52 km. The island is covered with low mountains, the highest of which, Mermygaris, does not exceed 500 m. Between the mountains are small valleys on which wheat and vegetables are cultivated.

You can go to Kythera from Athens by plane or from Piraeus by ferry boat or the speedy hydrofoils. You can also go overland down to Gytheio or Neapoli in the Peloponnese and then by ferry boat. From Kythera you can visit Monemvasia, Elafonisi, Antikythera and Crete.

HISTORY

According to mythology Kythera is the island of Aphrodite. The goddess of beauty and love was born on the foam of the sea; she first came ashore on Kythera and then went to Cyprus.

Kythera, which is also mentioned in antiquity by the name of Porphyrousa, was a naval base for the Minoans at the beginning of the 2nd millenium B.C. Porphyry, which there was an abundance of on the island, was the reason the Phoenicians came there, involving themselves with the processing of and the trade in this good, valuable during that period.

The Phoenicians were succeeded by the Myceneans. Their presence on the island is confirmed by the Mycenean tools which were found in Palaiopoli, near Avlaimonas. Later, during the period of the Peloponnesian Wars, Kythera, which was an ally of Sparta, was occupied by the Athenians for a brief period of time.

The centuries that rolled by were characterized by repeated pirate raids on the island which often led to its desertion. After a series of such events the Venetian occupation finally began in Kythera in 1207 with the Venetian Marco Venieri proclaiming himself "Marquis of Kythera". The Venetians gave a new name to the island, Cerigo, which is still used by the locals today with only a slight change: Tsirigo.

The pirate raids abated for a long time but in 1537 Kythera would experience a great calamity when Barbarossa attacked it.

After the dissolution of the Serene Republic by Napoleon, the Venetian occupation of the island came to an end and the French took over in 1797.

Reoccupation by the Russians and the Turks intervened until finally in 1809 Kythera passed under British rule. In 1864, Kythera, with the rest of the Ionian islands, was at last united with Greece.

Getting to know the island

Chora and Kapsali

Chora with its Venetian castle at the peak of a steep cliff, 300 m. above the sea and the picturesque Kapsali below with its two coves, the one next to the other, is one of the most beautiful landscapes in Greece.

Kythera or **Chora**, as it is called by the islanders, is the capital of the island with its traditional houses and 40 old churches built just below the **castle**. The settlement with the churches makes up the so-called **Mesa Bourgo**. Within the castle still survive the Catholic Cathedral to the Virgin, formerly Catholic, the one to Ayios Panteleimon with rare wall paintings, and Ayia Triada the oldest on Kastro; there is also a part of the palace of the High Commissioner, in which the historical archives are today housed, gunpowder magazines and two well-wrought aqueducts. At the **Archaeological Museum**, which contains important finds from the island, a special place is held by the marble lion which was placed above the main gate of the castle and which is not Venetian, as was originally thought, but ancient Greek.

Kapsali is the second port on the island, 2 km. from Chora. It has a leeward sand beach and in the summer a good deal of tourist activity. High up the cliff, above Kapsali, is the small white church of Ayios Ioannis Theologos and the cave in which it is said the saint intended to write Revelations. But the continual pirate raids forced him to leave the island and go to Patmos where he did write Revelations.

Chora - Ayia Pelagia (26 km.)

4 km. Livadi. From here a road left splits off after 1.5 km. Following the right branch you arrive after 7 km. at the Monastery of **Panayia Myrtidiotissa**, the religious center of the island. The monastery was built in the 19th century to house the old icon of the Virgin (Panayia) that was stored in the castle at Chora.

2 km. from the sandy shores of Kastri is the picturesque **Avlaimonas**, a small harbour with a Venetian fortress.

12 km. Dokana. From this village a turn-off left leads to **Mylopotamos**, a village of traditional architecture.

West of it is the renowned **Cave of Ayia Sophia**. It has stalactites, stalagmites, a small lake in the interior and a chapel with wall paintings at its entrance.

15 km. Aroniadika. The road right leads to the airport (5 km.), to the monastery of **Ayia Moni** (11 km.) and the coastal settlement of **Diakofti** (16 km.).

19 km. Potamos. The largest settlement on Kythera after the capital. From here a road leads left, after 7 km., to the beautiful village of Kavaras with abundant greenery and 3.5 km. later the beach at Plateia Ammos.

26 km. Ayia Pelagia. It is the main harbour of the island and is only 12 nautical miles from Neapoli in the Peloponnese, to which it is connected by ferry boat.

7 km. Karvounades. A large village practically in the middle of the island. From the village of **Fratsia**, which is 3 km. NE, a turn-off east leads after 10.5 km. to **Kastri** at the site of which was the ancient town of **Skandeia**, the port of Palaiopoli. Before Kastri the road passes below Palaiokastro, the hill on which the **Temple of Aphrodite** was located. A chapel to Ayios Kosmas nearby was built with stones of the ancient temple.

Chora with its imposing castle. Above, beach at Kapsali.

Antikythera

Lying between Kythera and Crete, this rocky little island has its own history. During the classical period it was called Aiglia and there was an ancient town there with a wall and a temple to Aigileos Apollon. Its ruins were found at **Potamos** the capital and the harbour of the island where most of its more than 100 inhabitants live, all of Cretan extraction from Sfakia.

Around 1900, an ancient shipwreck was found near the surrounding rocks and produced

Head of the Ephebe of Antikythera.

among other things the famous bronze statue know as the Ephebe of Antikythera, which is now in the Archaeological Museum in Athens.

Antikythera, which has an area of approximately 20 sq. km. is connected by ship to Piraeus, Kythera and Kastelli in Crete. The distance from the latter two is 27 and 35 nautical miles respectively.

Elafonissos

This is a small island full of pure white sand beaches and forests of small cedar trees. It does not belong to the Ionian Islands but is mentioned here because it is close to Kythera. It is at the southeast end of the Peloponnese, only 500 m. from the coast of Lakonia, to which it belongs administratively. It has an area of 18 sq. km. and a coastline of 25 km. It has one pretty fishing harbour where the 600 residents of the island are gathered, most of them sailors or fishermen.

The shores of the Peloponnese opposite are 11 km. from Neapoli, away and is connected by bus. It is also connected by ferry boat to Piraeus, Kythera and Kastelli in Crete.

The islets of Messinia

They belong to the Prefecture of Messinia in the Peloponnese, not the Ionian Islands, but they are mentioned here because of their geographical position.

Proti. An islet opposite the harbour of Marathopoli, port of Gargalianoi.

Sfaktiria. Historic islet which blocks the entrance to the Gulf of Navarino, facing the Ionian Sea. On its rocky soil is the tomb of the Russian soldiers who were killed in 1827 at the **Battle of Navarino**, of decisive importance for the Greek War of Independence against the Turks. On the shores of the island is the tomb of the Italian Philhellene **Santarozza**.

Sapientza. One of three little islands which make up the **Messenian Oinouses**, approxi-mately 1 mile south of Methoni. It is lush and good for hunting.

Schiza. Another islet of the Messenian Oinousses, 2 nautical miles SE of Sapientza. The third is **Ayia Margiani** which lies between the other two. It has a safe harbour in its southern section and a large cave on its northern side.

Venetika. A verdant little islet about a mile south of Cape Akritas, the southernmost part of Messinia. It has magnesite and rocky deposits suitable for whetstones. The sea is good for fishing.

THE IONIAN ISLANDS AND ISLETS

CORFU

Vlacherna	S Kanoni
Pontikonisi	S Kanoni
Vidos	N town of Corfu
Lazaretto	E Gouvies
Gravia	SW Arillas
Sykia	SW Arillas
Ortholithi	SW Ayios Gordis
Lagoudia	E Ay. Georgios Argyradon
Diapontia Nisia	NW Corfu
Ereikousa	NW Corfu
Mathraki	NW Corfu
Diapolo	NW Corfu
Othonoi	NW Corfu
Prasoudi	W Igoumenitsa
Syvota	S Igoumenitsa
Ayios Nikolaos	S Igoumenitsa
Cheironisi	S Igoumenitsa
Ayionisi	W Igoumenitsa
Xeradi	NW Igoumenitsa

PAXI

Mongonisi	SE Paxi
Kalsionisi	SE Paxi
Panayia	NE Gaios
Ayios Nikolaos	E Gaios
Antipaxoi	SE Paxi
Daskalia	S Antipaxi

LEFKADA

Cheloni	E Nydri
Madouri, Sparti	E Nydri
Skorpios, Skorpidi	SE Nydri

Lake of Ioannina (Pamvotida) and the lovely island.

Meganisi. .... *SE Nydri.*
Thilia. .... *W Meganisi.*
Petalou, Kythros. .... *S Meganisi.*
Kalamos. .... *E Meganisi.*
Kastos. .... *SE Kalamos.*
Provati. .... *N Kastos.*
Formikoula. .... *SW Kalamos.*
Ayios Nikolaos. .... *E Nikiana.*
Arkoudi. .... *S Lefkada.*
Sesoula. .... *W Chortata.*

CEPHALONIA
Vardiani. .... *W Platy Yialos.*
Dias. .... *SE Airport.*

ITHACA
Lazaretto. .... *Harbour Vathy.*
Atokos. .... *NE Ithaca.*
Drakonera, Provati. .... *E Ithaca.*
Petalas, Vromonas. .... *E Ithaca.*
Makri, Oxeia. .... *E Ithaca.*
Skrofa. .... *E Ithaca.*

ZAKYNTHOS
Pelouzo. .... *Bay of Laganas.*
Marathonisi. .... *NE Keri.*
Ayios Sostis. .... *S Laganas.*
Megalos Myzithras. .... *S Keri.*
Mikros Myzithras. .... *S Keri.*
Kentinaria. .... *E Keri.*
Korakonisi. .... *SE Ayios Nikolaos.*
Ayios Ioannis. .... *Bay of Vromi.*
Ayios Nikolaos. ..... *S Galazia Spilia.*
Vodi. .... *W Tsilivi.*
Strofades. .... *S Zakynthos.*

KYTHERA
Chytra. .... *S Kapsali.*

Gourounia. .... *E Chora.*
Karavonisi. .... *SW Myrtidiotissa.*
Strongyli. .... *SW Myrtidiotissa.*
Nisi tis Panayias. . *SW Myrtidiotissa.*
Gaidouronisia. ...... *NW Myrtidiotissa.*
Exo Nisi. .... *W Mylopotamos.*
Mesa Nisi. .... *N Mylopotamos.*
Nisakia. .... *N Mylopotamos.*
Armenopetra. .... *NW Potamos.*
Monopetra. .... *N end Kythera.*
Karavougia. .... *N end Kythera.*
Makrykythera. .... *NE Diakofti.*
Feidonisi. .... *E Diakofti.*
Dragonares. .... *E Avlemonas.*
Kornaroi. .... *SE end Kythera.*

ANTIKYTHERA
Thermones. .... *NE Potamos.*
Kofinidia. .... *W Potamos.*
Pori. .... *N Antikythera.*

ELAFONISOS

THE ISLETS OF MESSINIA
Proti. .... *W Gargalianoi.*
Sfaktiria. .... *Bay of Navarino.*
Pylos. .... *Bay of Navarino.*
Sapientza. .... *S Methoni.*
Ayia Mariani, Schiza. ... *SE Methoni.*
Venetiko. .... *SW Koroni.*

GULF OF CORINTH
Trizonia. *A small island with 180 inhabitants on the coast opposite Aigion.*
Ayios Georgios. .... *Gulf of Itea.*
Ayios Dimitrios. .... *Gulf of Itea.*
Ayios Konstantinos. .... *Gulf of Itea.*
Ayios Athanasios. .... *Gulf of Itea.*

Tsarouchi. .... *Bay of Antikyra.*
Daskaleio. .... *Bay of Antikyra.*
Kasidis. .... *Bay of Antikyra.*
Ambelos. .... *Bay of Antikyra.*
Katakavo. .... *SE Bay of Antikyra.*
Alatonisi, Vroma. . *S Bay of Sarantis.*
Tambourlo. .... *S Bay of Sarantis.*
Kouveli, Fonias. .... *S Domvrena.*
Groboloula. .... *S Domvrena.*
Makronissos. .... *S Domvrena.*
Alkyonides Nisoi. .... *N Schinos.*
   Zoodochos Pigi. ...... *N Schinos.*
   Glaronisi. .... *N Schinos.*
   Daskalio. .... *N Schinos.*
   Prasonisi. .... *N Schinos.*

ISLETS OF THE AMVRAKIKOS
Korakonisa. .... *Amvrakikos Gulf.*
Kefalos. .... *N Vonitsa.*

OTHER IONIAN ISLANDS
Panayia. .... *W Parga.*

SALT LAKE MESOLONGI
Prokopanistos. .... *W Mesolongi.*
Kotsikas, Komma. ..... *W Mesolongi.*

ISLETS INTO THE LAKES
Ayios Achilleios: *It is on Mikri Prespa Lake in Macedonia. It has a small settlement and the ruins of one of the largest basilicas in Greece, Ayios Achilleios.*

Yannina Island: *It is located in Lake Pamvotida with a length of 800 m. and a width of 500 m. A verdant island it has a settlement with 800 inhabitants and many monasteries, several of which are Byzantine, from the 13th century.*

Millions of years ago Aegeis, the dry land that joined Greece to Asia Minor, sank into the Mediterranean Sea and only the peaks of its mountains were left above the surface. These events gave birth to Crete, that large island with its high mountains and rare beauty. Its famed gorges, sheer coasts and strange plateaus, which seem like dry lakes, and its large, dazzling white sand beaches are the remains of this awesome cosmogony which created the island, but are also the magnet which attracts visitors all these years later.

It is not only its natural beauties that are of interest. There are also the antiquities of Crete. Ancient Minoan civilization with its palaces. The civilization that arose 4,000 years ago and lasted for over a thousand years on the island. It is even the Cretan Soul, unruly and courageous, that so much has been said about. You become so attached to these people, so proud and so hospitable, that you want to go back again and again from your very first visit as if Crete were your second home.

Crete is the largest island in Greece and the fifth largest in the Mediterranean. It has an area of 8,300 sq. km, a coastline of 1,040 km. and a population of 500,000. Administratively the island is divided into four prefectures: Chania with its capital at Chania, Rethymno with its capital at Rethymno, Herakleiou with its capital at Herakleion and Lasithi with its capital at Ayios Nikolaos. The southernmost part of Greece, Crete lies at the crossroads of three continents. Its crucial, strategic position has been the cause of many wars on the island. But the wars and the long years of slavery did not make it yield and the Cretans have proudly kept all the manners and customs they have had for centuries. One sees this if one happens to attend a traditional Cretan wedding or some other celebration. One can enjoy the Cretan lyra and the stalwart dances and

admire the dashing young men and slender young women in their traditional costumes. Wars and occupations were not able to prevent the intellectual and artistic flowering of the island. We are not speaking of the marvellous achievements of Minoan civilization here for they occurred during a time of peace. We are speaking of many years later. When the Byzantine churches on Crete were built and their wonderful icons painted (14th century). About the period when painting flourished and particularly the hagiography of the famous Cretan School (16th century) followed by the appearance of the great Cretan painter Domenicos Theotokopoulos, known as El Greco. Then when the works of Georgios Chortatzis and Vitcenzios Kornaros were played in the theaters (17th century). We are even speaking of the recent past, of that great

◹ **Caves**

Ц **Ravines**

◯ **Plateaus**

Cretan writer Nikos Kazantzakis. As in the past, so today, the Cretans continue to be employed at farming and animal husbandry. The main products of the island are olive oil, wine, the famous raki (tsikoudia), grapes, citrus fruit and cheese and the equally large output of early fruits and vegetables. Among its other products mention should be made of folk arts and crafts especially the weavings, embroideries, portable icons, ceramics and silver and gold accessories.

You can go to Crete by plane from Athens, Mykonos, Santorini, Rhodes, Karpathos, Kasos and Thessaloniki and by ferry boat from Piraeus, the Cyclades, the Dodecanese and Gytheio in the Peloponnese.

There are a large number of islets and rocky outcroppings around Crete, over 700 of them. We describe (or simply fix the location of) a total of 45 islands and islets of which 4 are inhabited.

Castle

Monastery

Archaeological site

Pánormos   Bali   Agia Pelagia

NO   Pérama   IRAKLIO   Akr. Hersoniaos   Akr. Ag. Ioannis   Sideros

M. Arkadiou   Anógia   KNOSSÓS   Málla   Eloúnda

Spili   Idéo Andro   Akr. Vamvakia   Váï

Amári   Móchlos   Sitia

LASSITHI   Kritsá   AGIOS NIKOLAOS

Zarós   DIKI   Zákros

Agia Galini   Viános   M. Kapsá

Festós

Mátala   Ierápetra   Akr. Goudoura

Akr. Lithinon   Léntas

Neolithic Period. Human beings appeared for the first time on Crete during the Neolithic period, the beginning of which is placed between 6000 and 5000 B.C. and the end around 2600 B.C.

Minoan Period. The beginning of the Minoan period coincides with the beginning of the Bronze Age.

The new civilization which would develop on and would come to dominate the island for 1,200 years was brought to Crete around 2600 B.C. by a people out of Asia Minor. Perhaps other people also came there from Egypt and Libya but they did not, however, have any relationship to the races of the Egyptians and the Semites. It is probable that all these newly arrived people belonged to the Indo-European race. Unfortunately, we do not know what language they spoke, just as we know very little about the history of Minoan Crete in general.

The lack of knowledge, however, in regard to its history has been partially obviated by the great wealth of finds the archaeological pick has brought to light. Due to these finds we have a fairly good idea of the achievements of Minoan civilization in art, social development and economic organization.

From these rich finds we can separate the Minoan period into smaller periods and sub-periods.

According to Evans the division was as follows:

Early Minoan Period
(2600-2100 B.C.)
Middle Minoan Period
(2100-1600 B.C.)
Late Minoan Period
(1600-1100 B.C.)

Later Professor N. Platon introduced a new dating system with new names for the periods:

The Prepalatial Period
(2600-2000 B.C.)
The Old Palace Period
(2000-1700 B.C.)
The New Palace Period
(1700-1400 B.C.)
The Postpalatial Period
(1400-1100 B.C.)

The latter chronological divisions also take into the account the following important dates for the evolution of Minoan civilization.

2600 B.C. The arrival of new people on Crete who brought with them a knowledge of how to work copper.

2000 B.C. The erection of the first large Minoan palaces.

1700 B.C. Their destruction by a terrible earthquake and their rebuilding a few years later, even more luxurious than before.

1400 B.C. The destruction of the second palaces, probably as a result of the explosion of the volcano on Santorini which signaled the end of the Minoan world (the Achaeans appeared immediately afterward).

1100 B.C. The conquest of Crete by the Dorians.

From the **Dorian Period to the Romans**. Practically from the beginning of the period (1100 B.C.) an important change was noted in art. The designs on pottery changed and iron appeared as a metal used in metallurgy for the first time.

Later, in the **Geometric period** (900-725 B.C.), art flourished, especially pottery.

Finally, during the **Archaic period** (650-500 B.C.) a new style, called the Dedalic, made its presence strongly felt in pottery.

Roman Period. The Romans under Metellus occupied Crete in 68 B.C. after bitter battles. Crete became a Roman province to which Cyrenaica was also subject, with its capital at Gortyn.

This Cretan town as well as Kissamos (Kastelli) flourished during that period.

Christianity appeared on Crete with the arrival of the Apostle Paul (63-66 A.D.).

First Byzantine Period. This period began in 396 A.D. when the emperor of Byzantium was Theodosius the Great. Peace prevailed on the island for many years until the first Arab attacks began in 650.

Arab Occupation. The Arabs, benefitting from the internal crisis in Byzantium, occupied Crete in 824. They made Herakleion their capital which they fortified by digging a large, deep trench all around it. That is when the town was called Chandax for the first time ("Khandak" in Arabic means moat).

The Arab occupation brought terrible hardships to the population of Crete. The Christians were slaughtered or Islamicized, the women and young people were herded in to the slave market at Herakleion to be sold and sent as slaves to the East.

Second Byzantine Period. The Arab occupation of Crete was a thorn in Byzantium's side and they often tried to retake it, without success.

The unsuccessful campaigns came to end in 961 when the Byzantine General Nikephoros Fokas captured Crete after fierce battles.

Venetian Occupation. The Venetians, after a war with the Genoans, prevailed and became the masters of the island in 1212.

The Venetian period, which would last for over 400 years, held new tribulations in store for the Cretan people who would react by revolting against their conquerors.

In the end, however, these struggles would not prevent a Renaissance from occuring on the island.

Turkish Occupation. This was the worst period for the Cretans. The Turks first occupied Chania in 1645 and then moved east destroying and burning whatever lay in their path. The great obstacle for them was the fortress at Chandax. It took a seige of 23 years to capture it. But after that they ruled the island alone and the Cretans would henceforth live in abject slavery. Their churches would be transformed into mosques, their property would be confiscated, their women dishonored and their children would be taken away to be made into Janissaries.

The Cretans reacted violently to all this and there were frequent uprisings and revolts the most important ones in 1770 (Daskaloyiannis), 1821, 1866 (the holocaust at Arkadi) and 1897.

Liberation and Union with Greece. The holocaust at Arkadi and the bravery of the Cretans stirred public opinion throughout the world. Four of the Great Powers of the time (Great Britain, France, Russia and Italy) intervened, the Turks were driven from the island and a "High Commissioner" was appointed, Prince George of Greece, who arrived in the island at the end of 1898 to administer the "Cretan Republic" as the now independent state was called. Another revolt would be needed to achieve union with Greece. That would be the one instigated by Eleftherios Venizelos in 1905 at Therissos. Union would become a reality eight years later in 1913 when Venizelos had already become Prime Minister of Greece.

The Battle of Crete (1941) - The German Occupation. Another brilliant page was to be added to the history of Crete. This was the great battle the allies of Greece along with the population of Crete waged against Hitler's paratroopers in May 1941. This was to be a part of the Cretan people's fierce resistance during the German occupation.

The reprisals the Cretans would suffer at the hands of their conquerors were harsh. Whole villages were levelled and their male inhabitants executed en masse. But the Cretan soul did not falter because it was well-versed in struggle and sacrifice after so many years.

the prefecture of Chania

It is the westernmost prefecture of Crete and has the imposing White Mountains which cover its largest extent. This majestic mountain range soars upward, lush and green, only a few kilometers from the north coast of the island to reach a height of 2,543 m., and then to descend, barren and sheer, to the Libyan Sea. Through the bowels of the earth that the Samaria Gorge passes through. Northeast of the prefecture is Souda Bay, the largest natural harbour in Greece, the bay of Chania, and further west the Bay of Kissamos, both with huge sand beaches.

Chania

It is the second most populous town in Crete and the capital of the Prefecture of Chania. Untouched by the development of tourism, it is still strangely reminiscent of the days when it was the administrative capital of Crete. The sights of Chania are concentrated mainly in the Old Town which is centered around the pretty **Venetian harbour**. At the entrance is the old Venetian lighthouse, opposite the historic **Firka Fortress** and the Naval Museum. Other sights are the Venetian neighbourhood of **Topanas**, the large walls of the Venetian fortress, built in 1540, **Kastelli**, the neighbourhood of **Splantia** with the churches of Ayios Rokkos, Ayios Nikolaos and Ayioi Anargyrioi. The **Archaeological Museum** is housed in the basilica of St. Francis, a Venetian church from the 14th century. Further south is the Cathedral. At the boundary with the New Town is the **Public Market** with its own characteristic colour and in the New Town itself the beautiful **Public Gardens**. Nearby are the **Historical Archives of Crete** which are the second largest in Greece in size and volume of documents. East of Chania is the aristocratic suburb of **Chalepa** and the home of Eleftherios Venizelos.

Chania is connected by plane to Athens and by ship (from Souda) to Piraeus.

Excursions from Chania

1. Akrotiri

6 km. The tomb of the Venizelos family. An exceptional view of the town of Chania.

9 km. Junction which leads to the beach of Kalathas and the alluring sand beach at Stavros.

14 km. The road right leads to the airport.

16.5 km. The Monastery of Ayia Triada Zangarolon. The church of the monastery, built in 1634, has a cruciform shape with a dome and an impressive facade. The monastery has a worthwhile museum.

20.5 km. The Monastery of Our Lady of the Angels or **Gouvernetou**. It is one of the oldest monasteries on Crete. It was most probably founded in the 11th century when the old main church was abandoned.

2. Therissos (16 km.)

You follow the road that goes east and at 1.3 km your turn right.

After passing through the Therissos Ravine you arrive at Therissos, the village where in 1905 Eleftherios Venizelos set up his headquarters for the revolt. There is a marble plaque on the house where his headquarters were located.

3. Omalos - Samaria Gorge (43 km.)

You follow the road to Omalos.

14.5 Fournes. Verdant village with many orange trees.

39 km. Omalos. A plateau at an altitude of 1,050 m., famed for its struggles for the liberation of Crete.

41 km. Left after 5 km. to the Kallergis refuge in the White Mountains from where the ascent to the highest peak Mt. Pachnes (2,453 m.) is made in about 7 hours.

43 km. Xyloskalos. From here you descend the celebrated **Samaria Gorge**, the most stupendous gorge in Europe, to the Libyan Sea. The gorge has running water, ponds and plane trees. 18 km. long, it requires about 6 hours for the walk through it which ends at Ayia Roumeli.

From here you can go on a ship of the line to Chora Sfakion. From Sfakia you will return to Chania. You can make this excursion from May 1 to October 31.

Beautiful town of Chania. Venetian harbour in the middle.

4. Chrysoskalitissa Monastery-Elafonissi (78 km.)

37 km. Kaloudiana. Turn left.
46 km. Topolia. A large village with the Byzantine churches of Ayios Ioannis, Ayia Paraskevi and Timios Stavros. A few kilometers beyond the village the **Topolia Ravine** begins. The road passes through a tunnel and arrives at the cave of **Ayia Sophia**. The chapel of Ayia Sophia is at its entrance.
57 km. Elos. The most beautiful of the villages in the area which are full of plane trees and chestnut trees (The "Chestnut Villages"). In October there is a **Chestnut Festival.**
61 km. Kefali. Village with a breathtaking view. Next to the school is the church of Ayios Athanasios, with wall paintings from 1393. Go past the right branch which leads to Sfinari and go left.
73 km. Chrysoskalitissa Monastery. Down on the south-west extremity of Crete is a bay with enormous black rocks. On the highest one of them is perched the most beloved but also the most remote monastery.
78 km. Elafonissi. A small island brimming with tranquility, colour and light. It has a lace-like coastline and dazzling sand dunes with small cedar trees and lilies.

5. Alikianos - Sougia (70 km.)

You follow the road to Omalos.
13 km. You leave the road to Omalos and go right.
14 km. Alikianos. In this village there are the ruins of the tower of the Venetian lord Damolino as well as the notable church of Ayios Georgios with wall paintings from the 14th century.
70 km. Sougia. A tranquil little harbour with a lovely sand beach. In the village church is a mosaic with depictions of peacocks and deer.

6. Kandanos - Palaiochora (74 km.)

On the road to Kastelli you turn left at the 19th km. at Tavronitis.
27 km. Voukolies. A village with Byzantine churches which have wall paintings from the 15th century.
57 km. Kandanos. The capital of the Province of Selino. It was destroyed by the Germans because of its participation in the resistance. There are many eminent Byzantine churches in the surrounding villages, full of wall paintings.
74 km. Palaiochora. A market town with a spectacular sand beach and a warm sea. It is even suitable for swimming in winter.

Left: "Portes" ("Gates") at Samaria Ravine.
Above: Chrysoskalitissa Monastery and passage to Elafonisi. Below: Palaiochora.

8. Vrysses - Chora Sfakion - Anopoli (84 km.)

32 km. Vryses. The main village in the area, with plentiful water.

48 km. Askyfou. A historic village at the beginning of a small but picturesque plateau of the same name. The large Imbros ravine begins after the village of Imbros. The landscape with its wild cypress trees is stunning.

68 km. A turn-off right leads after 12 km. to **Frangokastello** with a huge sand beach and a fortress built by the Venetians in 1371.

70 km. Chora Sfakion. Isolated on the difficult to reach coast of the Libyan sea, it was the center for the revolts to liberate the island. The old houses with the folk architecture resemble Aegean architcture and are built amphitheatrically around the harbour.

From Sfakia you can take excursions on a small boat to **Loutro, Ayia Roumeli, Sougia, Palaiochora** and the islet of **Gavdos**.

82 km. Anopoli. The village is built near the ancient town on a plateau 600 m. high. **Ioannis Daskaloyiannis**, who was from here, raised the flag of the Cretan revolution in March 1770 on the church of Ayios Georgios. Next to the town is the striking gorge of Aradaina and opposite it a plateau. Iron bridges join the two plateaus.

9. Lake Kourna - Rethymno (61 km.)

6.5 km. Souda. This is the harbour that serves Chania. It is one of the biggest harbours in the Mediterranean and is at the same time a naval base. At the entrance to the bay is an islet of the same name on which the Venetians built a powerful fortress.

14.5 km. A turn-off left leads to the coastal settlements of **Kalami, Kalyves, Almyrida** and **Plaka** with lovely sand beaches.

38 km. A turn-off from the main route left leads to **Georgioupoli** and right to the only lake in Crete, **Lake Kourna**.

61 km. Rethymno.

7. Kastelli Kissamos - Falasarna (59 km.)

5.5 km. Galatas. Seaside village with a pristine sand beach. From May 20-25 various activities are held there connected with the Battle of Crete.

8 km. Ayia Marina. An extensive sand beach opposite the islet of **Ayioi Theodoroi**.

11 km. Platanias. Village with a sand beach beside a verdant hill.

17 km. Maleme. The area around the airport is known for the heroism of the Battle of Crete in 1941. There is also a German military cemetery here.

24 km. Right is **Kolymbari** on the edge of the Chania with a beach. One kilometre north is the fortified **Gonia Monastery** or **Hodegitria** which today is the seat of the Orthodox Academy of Crete.

42 km. Kastelli Kissamos. It is built on the site of ancient Kissamos, the port of the ancient town of Polyrrenia.

Later, when it was occupied by the Romans, a new theater and Roman villas were built on top of the old town.

The town then passed to the Arabs and later the Venetians who built a small castle (Kastelli) from which it took its new name.

Kastelli is the capital of the Province of Kissamos, known for its superb wine. It has a harbour and is connected by ferry boat to Gytheio.

53 km. Platanos. There is a road to this village which leads after 8 km. to the village of Sfinari with a splendid sand beach.

59 km. Falasarna. One of the most ravishing sand beaches on the Crete with emerald waters. It is impressive for its extent and charm.

At the end of the sand beach is a steep and rocky hill on the top of which is the acropolis of ancient Falasarna.

the prefecture of Rethymno

It borders to the west on the Prefecture of Chania and to the east on the Prefecture of Herakleion. The main mass of Mt. Psiloreitis (2,456 m.), the highest mountain in Crete, commands the prefecture to the east. There is the Idaean Andron, the cave where, according to mythology, Zeus was raised.

The entire north coast of the prefecture is one vast sand beach, on the west end of which sits the pretty town of Rethymno. Near Rethymno is Arkadi, the historic monastery and on the south coast is another important monastery, Preveli. Next to it is the Kourtaliotiko Ravine with water running through it amid palm trees, one of the most beautiful landscapes in Crete.

Rethymno

The capital of the Prefecture of Rethymno, it is a town that has retained its traditional look.

You can confirm this as you stroll through its old, narrow lanes with the wooden balconies, the tall minarets and the Venetian mansions.

The old town is built on a headland at the end of which is the small, but well-preserved, Venetian fortress of **Fortetza**.

At the entrance to it is the **Archaeological Museum**. East of the fortress is the picturesque little **Venetian harbour** and the commercial harbour.

Near this little harbour is the Rimondi fountain and the Venetian Loggia.

Further south is the church of St. Francis, the Turkish School, and the Great Gate, the central gate to the Venetian fortifications.

The harbour of Rethymno is connected to Piraeus by steamship.

Old town of Rethymno with Fortetza and the beginning of the large beach.

Excursions from Rehtymno

1. Plakias (40 km.)

You follow the road that goes uphill toward the village of **Armenoi**.

19 km. Both roads lead to Plakias. The one straight ahead passes through the **Kourtaliotiko ravine** after 4 km.

21 km. Branch left leads to Spili and Ayia Galini.

29 km. Asomatos. A turn-off left leads after 4 km. to the **Lower Monastery of Preveli.** Another 3 km. and you arrive at the **Rear Monastery of Preveli** (St. John the Theologian) which is the main monastery. The monastery played an important role in the Cretan liberation struggles.

Two kilometers from the monastry the road ends at a path which leads to a **river with palm trees** which flows through the Kourtaliotiko ravine. It is worth the effort to go there and see at first hand the lake that has formed at its mouth.

36 km. From Asomatos you return to your main route to Plakias. At this point there is a branch which goes to Sfakia (42 km.) passing through the charming villages of **Myrthios, Selia, Kato** and **Ano Rodakino.**

40 km. Plakias. The ravishing sand beach and the beauty of the surrounding area have contributed to its spectacular development.

A short distance from Plakias are the celebrated sand beaches **Damoni** (2 km.) and **Ammoudi** (3 km.).

2. Spili - Ayia Galini

11 km. Armenoi (see excursion 1).

29 km. Spili. The lovely main village of the area at the foot of Mt. Kedros; it is the capital of the Province of Ayios Vasileios, renowned for its abundant water and dense flora. There, in the square with the plane trees, the water runs from the 19 mouths of stone lions.

55 km. Ayia Galini. A notable tourist center built on the slopes of a hill which is above the harbour.

3. Amari - Ayia Galini

You follow the road to Herakleion and at the 3rd km. turn right to Amari.

11 km. Prasses. A village with many Venetian houses, on the slopes of a verdant ravine.

29.5 km. Apostoloi. A village with old churches.

30 km. Ayia Foteini. A turn-off right leads after 4 km. to the village of **Merona** where there are noteworthy churches from the 14th and the 15th century with marvelous wall paintings and icons. At a distance of 7 km. from here is **Yerakari** at a height of 600 m. on the slopes of Mt. Kedros.

35 km. Asomatos Monastery. It lies in a gorgeous setting. There is an Agricultural School at the monastery.

40 km. Amari. The capital of the like-named province with dense flora and beautiful Byzantine churches in the surrounding area.

From Asomatos Monastery the road, after passing through the beautiful villages of Vizari, Fourfouras, Kouroutes and Apodoulou, meets the main road Rethymno - Ayia Galini - Herakleion.

Exit from Kourtaliotiko ravine below Prevelis.

4. Arkadi Monastery (22 km.)

It is one of the most glorious monasteries in Greece while in Crete it is revered for the holocaust that happened there. In this monastery, on November 8, 1866, about a thousand people (monks, warriors and women and childern) led by the Abbot **Gavriel** preferred to die by blowing up the powder magazine than to fall into the hands of the Turks.

The monastery was founded during the time of the Venetian occupation. Its high walls are reminiscent of a fortress and the church, which has a baroque facade, is considered to be one of the most beautiful in Crete. It is double-aisled and dedicated to the Transfiguration of the Savior and Ayios Konstantinos and Ayia Eleni.

There are many eminent relics in the monastery's museum.

To go to the monastery you follow the road to Herakleion and turn right at the 5th km.

5. Perama - Anoyeia - Idaean Andron (78 km.)

You follow the road to Herakleion and at the 11th km., at Stavromenos, you turn right.

24 km. Perama. The capital of the province of Mylopotamos. NE of Perama is the historic **Melidoni Cave** and S the village of **Margarites** with a pottery making tradition. Near the village are the ruins of the ancient town of **Eleftherna** which flourished from the Classical to the Roman period.

34 km. Mourtzana. Here you go right to the beautiful village of **Garazo**.

46 km. Axos. A picturesque village built below the ancient town of the same name. There are important Byzantine churches in Axos, such as Ayia Eirene from the 8th century and 12th century with incredible architecture and wall paintings and Ayios Ioannis from the 12th century.

Main church of Arkadi Monastery.

South of Axos is the village of **Zoziana** with one of the loveliest caves in Crete, **Sentoni** or **Sfentoni**.

55 km. Anogeia. A large, mountain village at a height of 740 m., which is a municipality and subject to the Province of Mylopotamos. It is near the border with the Prefecture of Herakleion. Anogeia is well-known for its fabulous weaving with brilliant colours and the traditional Cretan designs. Its central square and lanes are full of these woven articles, which are on display for sale, giving the village a flavor all its own. Anogeia, isolated on the north slopes of Mt Psiloreitis, was a center of revolutionary activities against the Turks. During World War II it was also distinguished as a focal point of the Greek resistance against the Germans.

Anogeia was horribly punished for these activities. The Germans razed it to the ground in August 1944.

It was rebuilt and today is a noted tourist center. During the summer, parties are organized in its tavernas at night, with Cretan dances.

76 km. Nida Plateau - Idaean Cave. At the end of the road and an altitude of 1,500 m. is the **Nida Plateau**. Next to the road is a tourist pavilion so you can rest and enjoy the view of the plain which seems like a huge dry lake, surrounded by high mountains.

A half a kilometer from the pavilion, on the rocky slopes of Psiloreitis, is the **Idaean Cave**. Magnificent, at the base of a gigantic rock, beneath the highest mountain on Crete; just the right place for a cave that mythology says was where Zeus, the father of all the gods, was raised.

From the Idaean Cave you can ascend to the highest peak of Mt. Idi, **Timios Stavros** (2,456 km.) in around 5 hours.

6. Rethymno - Herakleion

3 km. Perivolia. A splendid sand beach which has been touristically developed. A junction right for the national highway. The old road runs parallel to the new one, next to incredible sand beaches. The main ones are at **Adele** (5 km.) and **Stavromenos** (11 km.).

From Stavromenos you follow the national road which goes through **Panormos** (22 km. and then to Herakleion.

33 km. A turn-off from the main route left, leads after 2 km. to **Bali** a small but very pretty bay with a sand beach which has grown into a tourist center.

51 km. You now enter the Prefecture of Herakleion. From here a turn-off from the main route right leads after 3 km. to **Fodele** the village where the great painter **Domenicos Theotokopoulos (El Greco)** was born. The ruins of what is thought to have been his home are located near a beautiful Byzantine chapel. The village is thick with orange groves.

58 km. A turn-off left leads after 3 km. to the Bay of **Ayia Pelagia**, a modern tourist resort with a wonderful sand beach with crystalline water.

65 km. A turn-off left to **Ammoudara**, an extensive beach, west of Herakleion.

75 km. Herakleion.

the prefecture of Heracleion

Here is Heracleion and the famous Minoan palaces of Knossos and Phaistos. In the southwest corner of the prefecture is the plain of Mesara, the largest and most fertile on the island. There, according to mythology, is where Zeus and Europa, the beautiful princess, settled after he abducted her from the court of King Phoenix. Minos was born from the union of Zeus and Europa.

The prefecture of Heracleion is the largest Prefecture in Crete and is where the administration of the island is centered, at the same time having most of the important sights.

North of Heracleion is the islet of **Dia** which is used as a sanctuary for the wild goat.

Heracleion

Heracleion is the largest town in Crete, the capital of the prefecture of Heracleion and the administrative capital of the entire island. All this was certainly contributed to by its geographical position. It lies in almost the middle of the north coast, just outside Knossos, has one of the most important museums in the world, and is close to the most interesting archaeological areas: Phaistos, Ayia Triada, Gortyn and Malia.

The large artifical lake and the international airport of the town cover its communication needs which, however, are continually growing.

The town of Heracleion is surrounded by the famous Venetian wall and one can only enter through certain gates in it. The town's center is the square with the lovely Venetian **fountain of Morosini**. Near there is the **Basilica of Ayios Markos**, built in 1239, the **Loggia** (both Venetian buildings) and the church of **Ayios Titos** which most pobably was built after the arrival of Nikephoros Fokas (961).

Heracleion: Chania Gate and Morozini fountain.

Kastro or Koules on the harbour.

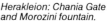

2. Knossos (5.5 km.)

The most important archaeological site on Crete. It contains the ruins of the largest and most luxurious Minoan palace, built in the middle of a large town. The first palace was built around 2000 B.C. and destroyed around 1700 B.C. The second one was built immediately afterward, more magnificent than the first. This was also destroyed, around 1450 B.C., most likely by the terrible eruption of the volcano on Santorini. The excavations were carried out in 1900 by the English archaeologist Arthur Evans who then reconstructed certain sections of the ruins.

The visit to the Palace, which has an area of 22,000 sq. m., begins at the West Court. You will enter the palace through the West Propylaia and proceed down the Corridor of the Procession. You turn left through the South Propylaia and climb up the monumental staircase to the upper floor (Piano Nobile) of the West Wing. You proceed first to the Tri-columnar Hall and then to the large hall and the sacred hall. You descend the small staircase to the corridor to the West Storerooms. You go to the Central Court to see in the South Corridor a copy of the wall painting of the "Prince with the Lilies". The original is in the Herakleion Museum. You visit the Tripartite Shine which faces the Central Court and then the Lobby of the Stone Seat, the Pillar Crypts and the Temple Repositories in which the snake goddesses were found.

From the Central Court you will then enter the Antechamber and the Throne Room with the famous throne of Minos, 4,000 years old, made of gypsum. Passing through the corridor of the North Entrance you arrive at the North Gate of the palace and the Hypostyle Hall or "Custom's House".

"The Adoration of the Magi" by Michalis Damaskinos (16th cent.)
One of the most representative works of the Cretan School on exhibit in the Museum of Ayia Aikaterini. Its illustration is completely different from the Byzantine tradition but it manages to mix the two styles, the Italian and the Greek, harmoniously and to render the artistic genius of the painter in all its grandeur.

The **Archaeological Museum** is one of the most outstanding museums in the world. It contains finds from all over Crete, focused primarily on prehistoric Minoan civilization, a civilization that ruled the island for over 1,200 years. The museum has two floors with a total of 20 rooms and is found on Eleftheria Square. Other sights in Herakleion are the **Venetian harbour** and the **castle** with the winged lions in relief above the gate. There is the imposing **Cathedral of Ayios Minas** with the old Ayios Minas next to it. There are also **Ayia Aikaterini of Sinai**, which operates as a museum, where the paintings of the famous painter Michael Damaskinos are kept, the **tomb of Nikos Kazantzakis** on the Mertinengo Bastion of the walls and the **Historical** and **Ethnological Museum**.

Excursions from Herakleion

1. Tylissos - Anogeia

Tylissos is known for the ruins of three Minoan villas (1700-1500 B.C.) which are located on the eastern side of the village next to a small grove of pine trees.
22 km. Sklavokambos. Ruins of a Minoan megaron.
36 km. Anogeia. (see p. 255).
57 km. Idaean Cave. (see p. 255)

South Propylaia.

In the south-west end of the palace is the North Lustral Basin and outside the space, the Theater. To see the East Wing, you return to the corridor of the North Entrance and just before entering the Central Court turn left. You will be in the Corridor of the Draught-Board and the Magazines with the Giant Pithoi. Further south you will come upon the pottery workshop or the "School-room" and a stone-carver's workshop.

Going even further south you will arrive at the Royal Apartments. You descend the Grand Staircase and visit the Hall of the Double Axes where the King's Megaron, the Megaron and bathroom of the Queen and the Repositories are, where the famous ivory "Bull-Leaper" was found. Finally, further south you will see the Shrine of the Double Axes, the Caravan Serai, the House of the High Priest, the Temple Tomb and the Royal Villa.

The Ladies in Blue wall painting from Knossos and Minos' Throne.

3. Zaros - Vrontisi Monastery - Kamares (55 km.)

You exit through the Chania Gate heading toward Phaistos.

29.5 km. Ayia Varvara. A lovely village at an altitude of 600 m. At the entrance, to the right, is a large stone outcropping with the church of Profitis Ilias on its summit, which is said to be the center of Crete.

From Ayia Varvara your turn right to **Zaros**.

39.5 km. Gergeri. A village built on a steep slope of Psiloreitis. Eighteen km. from here the marvelous **forest of Rouva** begins.

45.5 km. Zaros. A village with lush flora and abundant water. The old watermill still grinds wheat in the traditional manner. High up at the site Votomos, is a lovely artifical lake, at the entrance to a ravine.

50.5 km. A turn-off right leads after 1 km. to the **Vrontisi Monastery**, one of the most notable on Crete. It was built around 1400 and in the beginning was a monastic estate of the neighbouring Varsamonero Monastery. Wall paintings can be found in the church. The monastery's fountain from the 15th century is fabulous, with wonderful sculptures depicting Adam and Eve in Paradise.

The monastery began to flourish in 1500, when it appears the other one at Varsamonero was abandoned. It was a spiritual center and it is even said the great painter Michael Damaskinos lived and painted there.

52.5 km. Voriza. Below left is the **Varsamonero Monastery** (1330-1426), one of the oldest monasteries in Crete and perhaps the most important in terms of the number and the quality of its wall paintings.

55 km. Kamares. A mountain village on the slopes of Psiloreitis at a height of 600 m. It is the starting point for the climb up to the **Cave of Kamares** which was used as a place of worship during the Minoan period. The famous Kamares ware was found in this cave.

From Knossos a road meets, after 11 km., the road to Rethymno, Amari, Ayia Galini, and the plain of Mesara.

4. Phaistos - Matala

29.5 km. Ayia Varvara. After a few kilometers you will face, from the high up, the largest plain in Crete, **Mesara**.

45.5 km. Gortyn. For a length of 1 km. after **Ayioi Deka** there are the ruins of a large town scattered left and right of the road; during the Roman period this was the capital of Crete.

There was a small settlement on the site of Gortyn since the late Minoan period. But Gortyn became known later during the Archaic period and reached the high point of its glory in 69 B.C. when the Romans made it the capital of the Province of Crete and Cyrenaica and built many, majestic structures there, such as the **Praetorium** and the **Odeion**, next to which were found the famous **Law-Code of Gortyn** carved in stone blocks.

Opposite the ruins of the basilica of **Ayios Titos**, the road left leads after 33 km. to the coast at **Lendas**.

Ancient **Lebena** was on the site of modern Lendas; it was built at the beginning of the Minoan period and flourished much later during the Roman period when the inhabitants of Gortyn built a **Temple of Asklepios** there at the site of the therapeutic springs.

A gorgeous sand beach at Lendas is also suitable for winter swimming. Winter is so mild that it is said the swallows spend it there. From Lendas you can visit the remote **Monastery of Koudoumas** by caïque.

On your return you follow the coast road which goes west to the marvelous snad beach of **Kales Limenes** where the Apostle Paul landed.

53.5 km. Moires. A large transport, farming and commercial centre.

60.5 km. Left for Phaistos. The continuation of the road leads after 5 km. to **Tymbaki** and 3 km. more to **Kokkinos Pyrgos**, with a nice sand beach.

62 km. Phaistos. The second most important town in Minoan Crete with the luxurious palace of the mythical **Radamanthys**, the

Clay krater in Kamares style (Phaistos, 1800 B.C.).

brother of Minos. The palace was built twice. The first time around 1900 B.C. during the so-called Old Palace Period. This was destroyed by an earthquake and in 1700 B.C. a new and more luxurious one was built during the New Palace Period. The second one was also destroyed, around 1450 B.C., probably by the eruption of the volcano on Santorini.

The ruins of the second palace are what the visitor mainly sees today.

Unlike the Palace of Knossos, there have been no reconstructions or additions here. The ruins were uncovered and left untouched in the places they were found. The architecture here is like that of Knossos with the palace being built around a rectangular, oblong and flagged Central Court which is oriented from north to south. Around the palace was the large Minoan town of Phaistos.

Right: Dug-out caves and sand beach at Matala.

Just past Phaistos, a turn-off right leads after 3 km. to the ruins of a royal villa at **Ayia Triada** which was built in 1550 B.C. and was used as a summer palace.

Ayia Triada has given us a host of magnificent finds on display at the Herakleion Museum. Among them is the famous sacrophagus with the depictions of ceremonial libations.

68 km. Pitsida. Near the village are the well-known sand beaches of Komos and Kalamaki.
73 km. Matala. A fishing village which just a few years ago was known as a hippy center and today has developed into a tourist resort.

Matala was the port of Phaistos and later Gortyn. There are caves carved out of limestone cliffs on the sheer side of the north hill.

West of Matala in the open waters of the Gulf of Messara are two uninhabited islands, **Paximadia.**

5. Archanes -
Archaeological sites (16 km.)

You follow the road to Knossos. At the 11th km. you turn right.
16 km. Epano Archanes. A market town amid vineyards, which produces the fine **rozaki** grapes. In the environs of Archanes are the old churches of the Archangel Michael and Ayia Triada, from the 14th century.

Many of the areas near Archanes are of archaeological interest such as **Tourkoyeitonia, Fournoi, Anemospilia, the peak sanctuary** of **Jucktas** and **Vathypetro**.

6. Arkalochori - Ano Viannos - Arvi (84 km.)

At the 11th km. you go straight ahead.
33 km. Arkalochori. The main village in the area near which is a cave in which were discovered important Minoan finds. The old church of the Archangelo Michael is in the village.

39 km. Junction left for **Kastelli Pediadas** and right for **Avli**. Go straight to Panayia.
55 km. A branch right goes to the plain of Mesara.
60 km. A turn-off right leads after 3 km. to **Chondros** and after 9 km. to the coast of **Keratokambos** and further west **Tsoutsouros**.
66 km. Ano Viannos. A large village with dense flora, built high on the slopes of Mt. Dikte above a valley full of olive groves. It is the capital of the province of the same name and the homeland of **Yiannis Kondylakis**.

In Ano Viannos you can visit the churches Ayia Pelagia and Ayios Georgios.
70 km. Turn right to Arvi. The view of the Libyan Sea from high up is truly exceptional.
84 km. Arvi. A charming, seaside village which took its name from a monastery of that name which was built on the slopes of the mountain. It is a tropical landscape and the entire plain is covered with banana trees.

7. Herakleion - Ayios Nikolaos

From Eleftheria Square you follow the old road to Ayios Nikolaos up to Phoinika.

7.5 km. Karteros (ancient Amnissos). Here was the Minoan town of Amnissos, one of the three harbours of Knossos. Here is also the religious cave of Eileithyia, the patron goddess of child-birth.

13.5 km. Chani Kokkini. A dazzling coast of archaeological interest. Here are the ruins of the Minoan megaron of **Nirou Chani** from the New Palace Period.

15 km. Gournes. Seaside village.

20 km. Gouves (or Phoinikas). A tourist resort with a glorious sand beach. From here you will take the new national road.

29 km. Limenas Chersonisou. It is one of the largest tourist centres on Crete, owing to its fantastic sand beach and crystal-clear water. It flourished mainly during the Roman period.

34 km. Stalida. Another beautiful beach. From here a turn off right leads to the Lasithi Plateau (see page 267).

37 km. Malia. An area of spectacular development. This was contributed to by two factors: the former Minoan palace which is 2 km. further on and the dazzling sand beach.

39 km. The Palace of Malia. The third most important Minoan palace after Knossos and Phaistos. It has an area of 12,000 sq. m.

It was built like the other Minoan palaces, around 1900 B.C., destroyed around 1700 B.C. and then built again more brilliant than before only to be finally abandoned in 1450 B.C. after a new calamity.

40 km. A turn-off left leads after 3 km. to **Epano Sisi** from where you can go after 2 km. to **Sisi** with a nice sand beach.

From Epano Sisi, turning right, you arrive after 6 km. at the village of **Milatos** was a historic cave and 2 km., further the **shores of Milatos**.

51 km. A turn-off leads after 1 km. to **Neapoli**. A market town, it once was the capital of the prefecture of Lasithi. It has an **Archaeological Museum**.

67 km. Ayios Nikolaos.

the prefecture of Lasithi

The easternmost prefecture of the island is centered on the colourful town of Ayios Nikolaos. It is flanked by sand beaches, both on the north and south coast of the prefecture.

On the Lasithi Plateau the spectacle of 10,000 windmills is unique. Here is the renowned Diktaean Cave, the cave where, according to mythology, Zeus was born.

On the north east end of the prefecture is Vaï, the fabulous sand beach embraced by date palms.

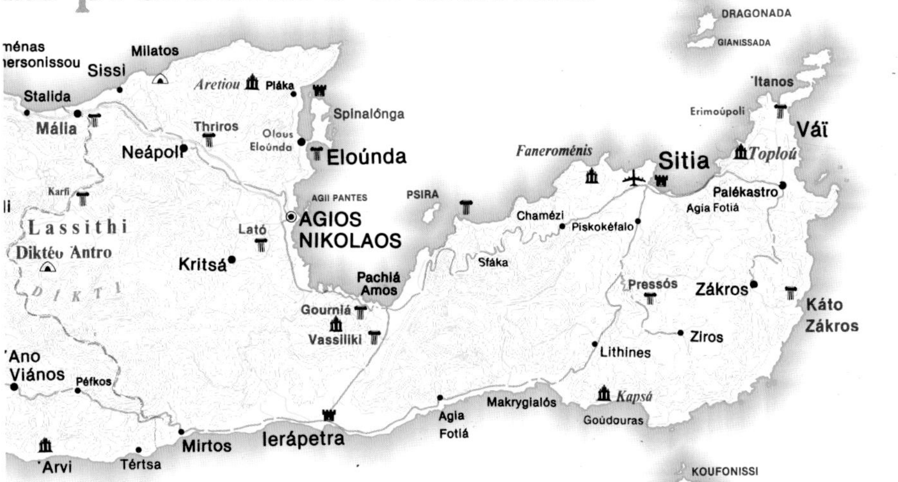

Map labels: PAXIMADA, DRAGONADA, GIANISSADA, ménas, ersonissou, Sissi, Milatos, Stalida, Aretiou, Pláka, Spinalónga, Itanos, Erimoúpoli, Váï, Mália, Thriros, Olous, Eloúnda, Eloúnda, Faneroménis, Sitia, Toploú, Neápoli, Karfi, AGII PANTES, PSIRA, Palékastro, Agia Fotiá, Lassithi, Lató, AGIOS NIKOLAOS, Chamézi, Piskokéfalo, Diktéu Antro, Kritsá, Sfáka, DIKTI, Pachlá Amos, Pressós, Zákros, Gourniá, Káto Zákros, Vassiliki, Ziros, Lithines, Ano Viános, Péfkos, Makrygialós, Kapsá, Goúdouras, Arvi, Tértsa, Mirtos, Ierápetra, Agia Fotiá, KOUFONISSI

Ayios Nikolaos

On the beautiful Gulf of Merabello is Ayios Nikolaos, the capital of the prefecture of Lasithi the leading tourist center in Crete. The picturesque harbour with the countless row-boats lined up next to each other and the houses built around it lend it a special beauty. Furthermore, the harbour and the sea with its gorgeous shores are and features which impress the visitor. Ayios Nikolaos is 67 km. from Herakleion and is connected by steamship with the Cyclades, Piraeus and the Dodecanese.

Mention should also be made of the **Archaeological Museum** which contains finds, mainly Minoan, from eastern Crete.

Ayios Nikolaos. The cosmopolitan capital of the Prefecture of Lasithi. The Bay of Elounda on the following page.

Excursions from Ayios Nikolaos

1. Elounda - Spinalonga - Plaka (15.5 km.)

9 km. At the neck of the peninsula of Spinalonga is ancient **Olous** (2nd cent. B.C. - 2nd cent. A.D.) whose ruins are today in the sea because the area subsided.

10 km. Elounda. A large tourist center. From here boats depart for a visit to the islet of **Spinalonga** with its Venetian fortress, the isle of tears at it has been dubbed because for 50 years this was the place of exile for lepers. You can also visit Spinalonga from Ayios Nikolaos.

15.5 km. Plaka. A seaside settlement with a lovely strand which has fine pebbles and crystalline water.

Above: The island of Spinalonga with its impregnable fortress.

Below: The enchanting Bay of Elounda. Spinalonga island appears in the background.

Right page, above: Panayia Kera and below the Lasithi plateau with its 10,000 windmills.

2. Kritsa - Ancient Lato

You follow the road to Ierapetra and then right at 1.5 km.

11 km. Panayia Kera. One of the pre-eminent churches in Crete, both for its architecture and its marvelous wall paintings. It is triple-aisled and dedicated to Ayios Antonios, the Assumption and Ayia Anna.

11.5 km. Kritsa. One of the largest traditional villages on Crete with heightened tourist activity, known for its embroideries, knitwear and woven articles. In August there is a re-enactment of the famed **Cretan wedding**. From Kritsa **ancient Lato** is 3,5 km. away. **Lato e Etera**, as it is called to distinguish it from **Lato pros Kamara**, which was on the site of Ayios Nikolaos, was once a powerful town, built around the 7th century B.C.

3. Lasithi Plateau - Diktaean Andron (49.5 km.)

17 km. You go past the right branch that goes to Vryses - Neapoli and go left.

40 km. Mesa Lasithi. It is a lovely village on the plateau which you can reach at an altitude of 870 m.

From Mesa Lasithi a turn-off right leads to the **Kroustallenios Monastery** which was founded in 1540. At a distance of 3 km. from the monastery is **Tzermiado**, the largest village in the Province of Lasithiou and its capital. Near the village are two notable archaeological sites. These are the **Trapeza Cave** and **Kastellos** hill. Both of them have furnished finds from the Neolithic, Early Minoan and Middle Minoan periods.

North of Tzermiado, there was a Late Minoan settlement at the rocky height **Karfi** (1,100 m.).

48 km. Psychro. A village with increased tourist activity because of the nearby Diktaean Cave.

49.5 km. Diktaean Andron (Cave). The road ends below the entrance to the cave. According to mythology, the cave is the place where Rhea gave birth to Zeus. The cave was a place of worship from the end of the Middle Minoan to the end of the Late Minoan period.

4. Ayios Nikolaos - Vasiliki - Ierapetra - Myrtos (51 km.)

12 km. **Bay of Voulisma** (area of the shores of **Kalo Chorio** and **Istros**) Golden sands and clear waters.

19 km. Gournia. On the right side of the road, on the slopes of a hill, are the ruins of a Minoan town.

The American archaeologist Boyd Hawes, who conducted the excavation, uncovered the foundations of an entire provincial Minoan town which flourished during the Late Minoan period (1600-1400 B.C.).

20 km. **Pacheia Ammos**. A tourist center and at the same time a communications hub. 22 km. after Pacheia Ammos you turn right to Ierapetra.

25 km. A short turn-off right leads to the village of **Vasiliki**. Near there, in Early and Middle Minoan ruins, was found the famous pottery in the Vasiliki style with the long neck which bends at the end, making it look like a tea-pot.

36 km. Ierapetra. The southernmost town in Greece with a ravishing beach on the Libyan Sea. Its name is derived from the ancient **Ierapytna** which in the 2nd century B.C. was one of the most important towns in Crete. It then subdued **Praisos** and practically the entire district of Siteia.

Like nearly all the large towns of Crete Ierapetra has a **Venetian castle**.

Ierapetra is an active tourist center. It is only 14 km. from the north coast and 36 km. from Ayios Nikolaos. The area has a reputation for its resplendent sand beaches, its mild climate, and unhampered sunshine for its early fruits and vegetables. It also has a small **Archaeological Museum** which contains finds from the Early Minoan to the Roman period.

51 km. Myrtos. A beautiful coastal village on a sandy beach. Near the village, the archaeological pick brought to light three **Minoan settlements**.

5. Ayios Nikolaos - Siteia

20 km. Pacheia Ammos.

44 km. Sfaka. From this village a turn-off right leads after 7 km. to the coast at Mochlos.

63 km. Chamezi. A village at an altitude of 380 m. Here at the end of September is a festival called "Kazanemata", the name given the traditional method of producing the renowned Cretan raki (**tsikoudia**).

73 km. Siteia. An attractive town with a harbour and a large sand beach. The capital of the easternmost province of Crete, it is built near the site of ancient Itea. The only ruins in the area are those of a **Venetian castle** to the east of the town. But the Province of Siteia is also one of the oldest centers of Minoan civilization as is shown by the finds at Mochlos, and the islets of **Pseira** and **Ayios Nikolaos**. You should not miss the **Archaeological Museum** and the small **Folk Museum**.

6. Siteia - Kapsas Monastery - Ierapetra (59 km.)

From Siteia you follow the road to Pisokefalo.

13 km. Four km. left is **Nea Praisos**. Ancient Praisos was an autonomous town which was inhabited from the Stone Age to the Venetian period.

32.5 km. A turn-off left to the **Monastery of Kapsas** next to the **Pervolakia** ravine, in front of a sandy shore. The monastery was probably built in the 15th century.

You return to the main route. Before it returns to Ierapetra the road passes along the endless sand beaches on the Libyan Sea with lovely settlements such as **Analipsi** (34 km.), **Makrys Yialos, Koutsouras, Achlia, Ayia Fotia** and **Ayioi Saranta** (55 km.)

59 km. Ierapetra.

Town of Ierapetra and its castle.

7. Siteia - Vaï - Kato Zakros (58 km.)

4 km. Ayia Fotia. A splendid sand beach that has been developed.

15 km. Toplou Monastery. It is a historic monastery on the northeast end of Crete, known for the struggle it waged against pirates and Turks. It was built in the 15th century, most probably on the ruins of an older monastery. It was a true fortress and even had a cannon. It has notable relics and wonderful icons.

23 km. A turn-off left leads after 1 km. to **Erimoupoli** (ancient Itanos).

24 km. Vaï. The renowned palm forest with a great sand beach. It is a tropical landscape which is an exception in Greece. It receives a large number of visitors who come to see the rare landscape and enjoy its marvelous sea.

25 km. Return to Palaikastro.

33 km. Palaikastro. Large village with a wonderful sand beach.

South of Palaikastro are the ruins of a Minoan town and southeast the Minoan peak sanctuary of Petsofas which has yielded important finds.

50 km. Zakros. A verdant village with alluring lanes. From here the road descends to the sea passing alongside the Ravine of the Dead.

58 km. Kato Zakros. A coastal settlement on a bay with pebbles and a crystal-clear sea.

This area became known for the famous Minoan palace which was discovered here by Professor N. Platon in 1961.

The **Palace of Zakros**, the fourth of the great Minoan palaces is very similar to the other three.

The difference is that the Palace of Zakros lay before a harbour which played an important role in the commercial exchanges with Egypt and other countries in the East.

The palace was destroyed the same year as the other large palaces, that is around 1450 B.C.

Above: Historic Toplou monastery.

Center: Sand beach at Vai.

Below: The beautiful town of Siteia.

ISLETS AROUND CRETE

THE PREFECTURE OF CHANIA
GRAMVOUSA. This islet, on the northwest side of Chanion with its sheer coastline, has a famous Venetian castle. You can visit it by renting a motor boat at Kastelli. NW of Gramvousa is **Agria Gramvousa** and SW of this **Pontikonisi.**

GAVDOS. This is the island of Calypso or so many believe and at the same time the southernmost settlement in Europe. It is 28 miles from Crete and around 150 miles from the coast of Africa. Its few inhabitants are scattered among its four villages. There is a superb sand beach at Sarakiniko, 30′ on foot from the harbour. You can go to Gavdos by caïque from Palaiochora or Chora Sfakion. South of Gavdos is **Gavdopoula.**

Thodorou.....................................*N Ayia Marina.*
Souda, Palaiosouda.....................*Souda Bay.*
Elafonisi.......................................*NW of Crete.*
Artemis.....................................*SE of Elafoniso.*
Koursaroi, Prasonisi..................*S Falasarna.*
Petalida.......................................*E Falasarna.*
Lazaretto....*E Chania.*
Schistonisi..................................*S Palaiochora.*

THE PREFECTURE OF RETHYMNO
Diapori....*E Bali.*
Prasonisi, Paximadia..............*SW Ayia Galini.*

THE PREFECTURE OF HERAKLEION
Dia, Paximadia...........................*N Herakleion.*
Glaronisi...*NW Dia.*
Megalonisi, Mikronisi...............*S Kali Limeni.*
Thetis.......................................*E Treis Ekklisies.*

THE PREFECTURE OF LASITHI
CHRYSI. It is also called **Gaidouronisi.** It is an islet with dazzling white sand beaches and forests of small cedars. It lies opposite Ierapetra and is about one hour by caïque. East of it is **Mikronisi.**

Spinalonga......................................*N Elounda.*
Kolokythia...*E Elounda.*
Ayioi Pantes......................*NE Ayios Nikolaos.*
Konida.................................*N Pacheia Ammos.*
Pseira....*W Mochlos.*
Ayios Nikolaos..............................*N Mochlos.*

DIONYSIADES:
   Yianysada......................................*NE Siteia.*
   Dragonada.....................................*NE Siteia.*
   Paximada.......................................*NE Siteia.*
Keramidi...*NE Siteia.*
Elasa...*E Vaï.*
Grandes.....................................*E Palaiokastro.*
Koufonisi.......................................*SE Crete.*
Strongylo, Makroulo...................*N Koufonisi.*
Trachilos.......................................*S Koufonisi.*
Prasonisi, Kimi, Kavaloi..................*SE Crete.*

Format: 17 × 24 cm, Pages: 176
Photographs: 180

GREEK
MYTHOLOGY
THE CREATION OF THE GODS - THE GODS -
THE HEROES - THE TROJAN WAR -
THE ODYSSEY

EDITIONS
TOUBI'S
ΕΚΔΟΣΕΙΣ
180 colour photographs and drawings - Complete index of names

GREEK
MYTHOLOGY

This special edition has been designed to present the main Greek myths. A work of considerable scope, written in a simple and expressive language, it is accompanied by 180 photographs and excerpts from ancient Greek literature.